# YOU MUST ONLY TO LOVE THEM

## LESSONS LEARNED IN TURKEY

# You must only to love them

## Lessons learned in Turkey

*Enjoy the journey —*

*Ann Marie Mershon*

*A memoir by*
*Ann Marie Mershon*

YOU MUST ONLY TO LOVE THEM
Lessons learned in Turkey

By Ann Marie Mershon

Also by Ann Marie Mershon:
*Britta's Journey ~ An Emigration Saga*
*Istanbul's Bazaar Quarter, Backstreet Walking tours.*
(with Edda Renker Weissenbacher)

Printed in the United States of America

First Printing, 2016

ISBN 978-1530678709

Maple Hill Publications
28 Romans Road
Grand Marais, MN 55604

annmariemershon.com

This book is dedicated to

# JOHN CHANDLER

…who realized before I did
that Istanbul and I would be a good fit.

# FOREWORD

In these difficult times of clashing cultures, we need to reach across national boundaries to fully understand that people are much the same the world over. We share similar needs for safety, sustenance, and love. We work hard, raise families, and seek time to play. Whether or not we express our spirituality in conventional ways, our desire to understand the world and its origins is universal.

My years in Turkey helped me view the world through a new lens. I discovered that America isn't the center of the universe, nor are we faultless in our dealings with other countries. I appreciated that people accepted me even when they weren't happy with my country.

I dream that these snapshots of my experiences in Turkey will broaden your understanding of the Muslim culture and the warmth of its people. Perhaps you'll even be motivated to visit the country that has stolen my heart.

*I've posted photos from these adventures on the web:*
*annmariemershon.com/memoir-photos*

# SKETCHY MAP OF ISTANBUL

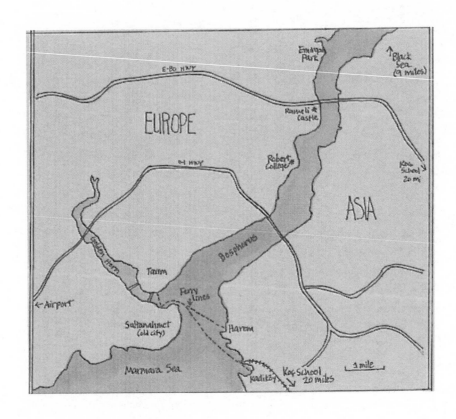

# PREFACE — NOT ME

Who would have thought I'd live in Turkey? It evoked an image of mustachioed Bedouins galumphing out of the desert on camels, and I could barely find it on a map.

No, thank you.

I yearned for adventure, an escape from a world that was imploding on me. A painful divorce had left me on the perimeter of social gatherings, keenly aware of my image as a divorcee. Not really a pariah, I felt like one.

After a few years alone I succumbed to a whirlwind romance, a stomach-churning, heart-fluttering relationship that survived a mere four months. This bleeding-heart liberal was no match for the wealthy conservative I'd fallen in love with. We'd have been a disaster together, so I was lucky it ended early. Devastated, but lucky.

But I digress. Travel had always intrigued me, and I wanted to spend a year or two in Europe. I fantasized strolling to a coffee bar in my Paris neighborhood, meandering through the Musee d'Orsay with time to admire each bronze ballet dancer, or climbing a mountain path to an alpine meadow above Salzburg. I fed my travel bug by sponsoring student tours overseas, and one afternoon I found myself chatting with a chirpy British woman on a beach in southern Spain.

"How do you like the Mediterranean?" she asked.

"Oh, it's gorgeous. Do you come here often?"

"I live here, dear. Well, part of the time. I rent an apartment just a few blocks from the beach, my sunshine get-away from the dreary London winters."

"Really?" I said. "Is it expensive?"

"Oh, it's nothing compared to London rents. My husband and I aren't wealthy, but this is my priority. It's my sanity, you might say. Anyone could do it. What brought you here?"

"I'm on tour with students. I enjoy their enthusiasm, and we're loving it here."

"I'm sure," she said as she set up her beach chair. "The sun always shines, and there's plenty of action."

As I meandered down the beach I pondered renting a studio apartment in Europe. Could I manage it?

Not a chance. As a divorced woman sitting on $25,000 of debt there was no foreign apartment in my stars, at least not without employment.

But then...

My mind started churning. My English degree could be my ticket overseas, and I also held degrees in theater and counseling. Why not? I was single and my sons were grown. The world was my oyster.

I started the wheels in motion, setting my sights on Paris (I speak French) and Salzburg (my favorite city in the world).

# 1 HOOKED

That spring I found a session on international teaching at an education convention—HOORAY! Teachers Bob and Patty Strandquist tantalized us with adventures teaching in England and Norway, lured us on with details for finding a position, and hooked me right in. As soon as I got home I posted my resume online and scoured listings of international openings. An open drama position at a chateau school in the Alps drove my pulse to dangerous levels, but I hesitated before clicking the link to apply. Conscience is a burden, and I forced myself to swallow my excitement. I was on contract and needed to finish the year. I soon learned that hiring conventions are held in February and March for the following year, so I'd have to commit to yet another year in Grand Marais. Lucky I still enjoyed teaching.

The next fall I received an e-mail from John Chandler, director of the Koç School (pronounced "coach") in Istanbul, encouraging me to consider a position there. Koç sounded weird, Istanbul too exotic. What if I had to wear a scarf? The school's website displayed glittering classrooms, a park-like campus—and no scarves. In fact, the students looked western: beautiful, dark-haired teens, unlike my fair-haired Minnesota students.

Mr. Chandler courted me online, responding instantly to each of my queries. I pored through his information, unsure about giving up my dream of teaching amid Paris's sidewalk cafes or beneath Salzburg's snowy Alps. Mr. Chandler insisted I was perfect for his school, and I read his interest as genuine and heartfelt. The school apartments were beautiful and the pay scale generous. Unfortunately, Turkey bordered Iraq, where we were at war. Istanbul was outside my comfort zone.

February of 2005 found me flying through a blizzard to the University of Northern Iowa's International Recruiting Fair. Waterloo is anything but picturesque, especially in a February freeze, but the conference was amazing. I felt like a gawky actress plunked in the wrong movie as I joined 600 teachers and 160 school directors swarming the convention center. I perused reams of school descriptions and sifted through the latest openings, my mind racing. What did I want? Would I even get an offer? Was I ready? I felt eager, yet alone as I meandered through the arena to sign up for interviews.

A tall, distinguished man stood beside the Koç School table. "Welcome. I'm John Chandler. How can I help you?" His handshake was powerful.

"Hello, I'm Ann Marie Mershon, pleased to finally meet you. I'm sorry, but I'm here to cancel my interview."

Mr. Chandler nodded with a knowing smile. "May I ask why?"

"It's the rote learning," I said. "I'm a hands-on teacher and believe in active learning and inquiry." (No point mentioning the scarf thing.)

"That's exactly why we're interested in you. You must have misunderstood. Rote learning was a reference to typical Turkish schools. Koç is a progressive school dedicated to stimulating and involving our students, preparing them for American and English universities. I think you'd fit well with our English team. Would you at least look at our video?"

I did, and I liked what I saw. Paris wasn't represented at the fair, and the Salzburg position was filled before my interview. Offered a position at Koç as well as three other schools, I was in a quandary.

I questioned experienced teachers about my choices: Istanbul, London, Warsaw, and Monterey, Mexico. "You can't pass up an opportunity to teach in Istanbul," one said.

"It's a cultural mecca," said another.

"If I could get a job in Istanbul, I'd go yesterday," said a third..

Still uncertain, I called my friend Luana, who'd toured both Europe and Asia. When I shared my options, she responded unequivocally. "Istanbul. No question."

Everyone had pointed the way, and I'd be a fool not to follow. Turkey it would be.

*I've posted photos from these adventures on the web:*
*annmariemershon.com/memoir-photos*

## 2 BREAKING FREE

So much to do! I had five months to pack, find renters, sell my car, and bid    friends and family farewell. My already busy life grew chaotic.

Each day I made a list of tasks for myself, and each day the mayhem increased. Treasures and collections of memorabilia got shuffled to the next box, the next room, the next day. Piles materialized everywhere: stacks of clothes and nicknacks for the thrift store, mountains of books for the library sale, and bags of detritus deserving only of the dump.

Packing up a life is a daunting task. I'd lived in my new house two years, yet everywhere I turned I discovered more things to sort, throw, organize, and pack. What would I need? What could I spare? I was appalled at the mass of things I couldn't part with: a table loom that hadn't seen the light of day in twenty years, notes from graduate school (how many years ago?), and boxes of photos rejected from albums, yet too dear to toss.

It was time to be ruthless. To pare down the chattels of my life. Scores of boxes still found their way to my garage attic.

The greatest impediments to my progress, though, were family and friends. Given a choice between packing and people, I always chose people.

As soon as school was out, I flew south to see my sons, who'd fled the frigid Minnesota winters for college in Florida then settled there. I seldom saw them, so my days hanging out with them in the sun were precious. We all shed tears when I left, and I promised I'd fly them to Istanbul.

From there I spent a week with my sister Laura and her family in Minneapolis. Laura and I are joined at the hip, and Erin and Matthew are like grandchildren to their Auntie Ann. Missing two years of their childhood would be the greatest trial of my move, so I devoted that week to them, teaching 8-year-old Erin to embroider and running through their antique duck sprinkler with little Matt. Halcyon days.

I arrived home in time for our monthly full moon bonfire on the beach. What can compare with watching a moon rise over Lake Superior with my dearest friends?

The next evening offered another tough choice: pack boxes or kayak with Annie. Easy. How else would I have gotten within spitting distance of a loon with a baby on her back and a second fuzzy chick paddling alongside?

Clean carpets or drive to the Park Point Art Fair with Susie? Another no-brainer. Morning walks with Thelma and my neighbors were a must, then there was the trip with my sister to Chicago, the trek with Susie to visit friends in Toronto, kayaking through the Apostle Islands, two canoe trips, and the list goes on. What a summer!

I wondered if I'd ever finish packing. I finally stashed the last box and moved into my father's house for the last few weeks, enveloped in the warmth of Dad and Eileen. My whole family drove up to celebrate Dad's 80th birthday with a boat trip to Isle Royale, followed by yet another round of farewell tears and hugs.

I had only one more detail plaguing me—my work visa.

It still hadn't arrived when I moved in with Dad, so I called Koç. Ayşe, the school's government liaison, got approval from Ankara just in time for me to pick up my visa in Chicago. For some reason this had to be done in person. I arrived at the hotel at midnight bedraggled, looking more like a backpacker than an international teacher. After looking me up and down, the desk clerk informed me there was only one room left—an executive suite. Poor me. The six-foot tub, plush bathrobe and embroidered slippers were the only silver lining in this ill-fated trip.

I arrived at the Turkish Consulate when it opened at 9:00. I'd booked a 1:00 flight back to Minnesota,  assuming they would check my photo against my face, sign a few papers, and send me off. I didn't have enough experience with Red Tape, especially Turkish Red Tape. The receptionist  seated me in a waiting room overlooking the Chicago River, where I waited. And waited. And waited. I'd worked myself into a sweat by the time the director called me into his office. "I'm very busy. I don't know when I can get this done. Come back this afternoon," he said, dismissing me with a wave.

I was furious but managed to keep from screaming at him—or worse yet, crying. I didn't need this man angry with me days before my flight to Istanbul. I took a deep breath and said, "I've left NUMEROUS phone messages telling you I had a 1:00 flight and asking you to let me know if I needed to book a later one."

He glared at me and growled, "Come back at 11:00 and see if it's ready." I'd never make it back to the airport on time, but what could I do? I calmed myself with a walk along the river and returned at 10:45. As I waited, the director chatted amiably with a few Turkish people in the lobby, unconcerned about my plight. At exactly 11:00 he strolled to his office and called me in. My work visa was ready. I paid the fees, thanked him, and raced out the door. I ran eight blocks to the train stop, where I waited 20 minutes for the next train, heart pounding. I arrived at the airport at 12:30, scrambled to find the right check-in, swiped my card through the electronic machine, and found the security line. My heart fell. There were a hundred people ahead of me, and the line wasn't moving. It was 12:45, my flight was boarding, and I wouldn't make it.

Luck was on my side. The flight was delayed an hour, and I reached the gate just as they were closing the doors. I collapsed into my seat, sweaty, exhausted, and grateful. I finally had my visa, and I'd be able to leave on Tuesday. Of course, Libby's vet papers hadn't come yet.

They arrived the day before we left. Whew!

# 3 HOME, SWEET HOME?

Eyes bleary with exhaustion, I couldn't sleep as our 18-seat Mercedes van motored us home. Home? After a year fraught with the details of seeking a new life, I was in Turkey. What would it be like? Would it change me? Lightheaded after the 36-hour trek from Grand Marais, I held my little black terrier/poodle to the window as we crossed a suspension bridge, the Bosphorus below us glittering in the afternoon sun. A medieval fortress blinked up from its stony ramparts at this bridge that spanned two continents—and more centuries. Contrasts abounded in Istanbul, contrasts that would challenge me.

On the far side a yellow sign announced WELCOME TO ASIA in bold black letters (along with a lot of Turkish words). My stomach lurched. "Oh, Jana—we're here. We're actually in Istanbul!" My young friend had traveled from Berlin to meet me, and I was relieved to have her share my first weeks in this strange country.

Instead of the arid, desert-like landscape I'd envisioned, Istanbul was a modern city sprawled on rolling hills, its lush trees and buildings climbing the steep ascents. Myriads of concrete apartment buildings flew by, punctuated by an occasional domed mosque, minarets spiking heavenward. Many of the buildings were streaked with gray, and garbage littered the roadside.

"Why are the buildings so dirty?" I asked Cyrus, the lanky Canadian who'd met us at the airport. His engaging smile had put me at ease as we'd navigated the sea of people in every kind of clothing from modern dress to full black hijab.

"Pollution. This city has between 15 and 20 million people, and many heat with coal. The buildings get covered with gray soot, then the rain splotches it even more."

Cyrus was interrupted by a melodic cadence echoing from a hundred minarets, the Call to Prayer. He paused, not in reverence, but at the noisy competition. The exotic strains gave me goosebumps. No one kneeled in the streets as I'd seen in Morocco. "The vast majority of

Turks are Muslim, about 97 percent, but many aren't religious," Cyrus explained. "In smaller towns you'll see people going to the mosque, but the call to prayer is generally viewed as a reminder of their faith. Turkey is secular, and most of Istanbul is quite modern."

It took an hour and a half to drive 40 miles along congested freeways. Traffic was a modern problem, one I never would have expected in Turkey. Little did I know.

We finally turned in and stopped at a brick guardhouse with mounted cameras, a barrier arm and a sliding iron gate. "Security is huge here," Cyrus explained. "Koç is an exclusive school with foreign teachers and very wealthy students, so we have two teams of security guards on duty 24/7. This is the only entrance to the campus, and there's another guard post in the housing complex. You'll get to know the güvenlik in time. They added the sliding gate a few years ago after the British Embassy bombing."

Oh, my GOD! A bombing? No one had mentioned danger. What was I getting myself into? I wanted adventure, but not bombs.

My fears dissipated as we followed a serene, tree-lined boulevard into the school's vast campus. Hibiscus and roses bloomed around a sprawling lawn that surrounded a white four-story building. The high school resembled a modern office complex with a wide marble stairway and pillared entrance. As we rode on I spotted a huge glass pyramid behind the front building and second huge building beyond.

"What's that glass enclosure?"

"That's the student commons. Impressive, isn't it?"

"Aren't there only a thousand students?"

"That's right. Why?"

"Well, the school is so huge!"

"It is. You'll be amazed at the facility. It's a fabulous place to teach."

I'd taught the past 21 years in a one-story rural high school with 240 students and 16 classrooms. I'd never find my way around that massive structure.

Down the road was an equally impressive elementary complex, where we turned up the hill into a housing compound of paved streets and two-story stucco buildings. It was so deserted it reminded me of a

Twilight Zone episode. We headed up to where a sheep meadow beyond the fence lent a rural look (and smell). No great fan of cities, I preferred to be in the country.

Cyrus and the driver helped drag my luggage up the marble stairs to a modern apartment decorated in cool blues and grays. "This *lojman* (employer-provided housing) will be your home for the next two years —and we hope longer. Make yourselves comfortable. The basket of goodies on the table is from Ileyn (Elaine), our liaison for foreign hires. There's also a settling-in allowance for you—money for groceries and a few household goods. Is there anything else I can do for you, Ann Marie?"

"Thanks, Cyrus. This is lovely." I followed him to the door and shook his hand, nervously avoiding the peck on each cheek that I knew was the typical Turkish farewell. I just wasn't ready.

Jana's clear gray eyes probed mine. "Ann Marie?"

"That's what's on my passport. It feels weird, though—maybe I should just stick with Ann."

"No, you shouldn't. You deserve a new beginning after all you've been through. Give it a try...Ann Marie." She was right. I did want a new start, but would a different name provide it?

"I'll give it a few weeks," I conceded. This was my new life, and I was going to make the most of it.

"Your apartment is gorgeous!" Jana said, surveying the contemporary furniture. Bay windows overlooked the campus and the distant hills of Istanbul. She wandered into the master bedroom. "A whole wall of closets—and two dressers. Wow!"

Libby was sniffing busily as I followed Jana into the second bedroom. It had a single bed, a dresser, and a computer desk with high bookshelves. The white walls felt stark, but I'd hang pictures soon. Even posters would be an improvement. Jana dropped her backpack on the bed, pushed a shock of hair off her high forehead and grinned. "I'll sleep in here."

We stepped out onto a marble-tiled balcony and surveyed Istanbul's distant purple hills enveloped in a rosy haze.

"I'm so glad you came, Jana. It's easier with a buddy."

"My pleasure," she said, wrapping an arm around my shoulders. I liked being with someone nearly as tall as me. "Maybe I should just move in."

"I wish," I sighed. As much as I'd have loved it, I'd be going this one alone.

# 4 BUS OR TAXI?

After exploring Istanbul for a few days, Jana and I flew down to visit Ephesus, Turkey's most famous ruin—a maze of crumbling marble. (Remember Paul's Letter to the Ephesians?) Our airfare was half the cost of a car rental and MUCH faster. (Subsidized airlines?) At the Izmir airport Jana spurned pushy cabbies and led me to a public bus into the ancient city once known as Smyrna. After a confusing ten-block hike through dark, muggy streets, we found our hotel, which the Lonely Planet had dubbed "charming and friendly." Garbage littered the street outside, a rude desk person spoke only a smidgeon of English, and a dead cockroach welcomed us on our filthy carpet. The room was stifling, the windows didn't open, and the air conditioner was worthless. Not an encouraging beginning for our week on the Aegean. I did my best to rise above the oppression I felt, but it wasn't easy.

The next morning I hailed a taxi to the bus station.

"Where is the bus to Selçuk?" I asked, hoping the driver spoke English.

"You go Selçuk? I drive you."

"No, we'll take the bus. Bus station, please."

"I drive you cheap. Only $75." I was surprised he said dollars.

"No—too much. Bus station."

"OK, $50 to Selçuk. Business not good."

A sleepless night had left me frazzled. It was hot, we had Libby, and we were already crammed into the taxi. "OK. $50 to Selçuk." The driver grinned back at us. Fearing I'd been duped, I tried to look on the bright side. Maybe the fare would cover the cost of replacing his absent front tooth. The countryside was flat and brown, and when we stopped the third time for directions to Selçuk, I wondered if our driver knew what he was doing.

It took an hour, but he finally found the Nilya B&B. Heavy doors stood in a tall stone wall, framed by trees and plants. A young woman opened the door to welcome us with a gentle smile. Her hair was tucked into a lace-edged scarf, and she wore loose, calico skirt-like pants. Explaining that it was too early to check in, she led us to a courtyard shaded by fruit trees and hanging plants. White-cushioned chairs and fringed hammocks beckoned, the perfume of roses heavy in the air. Quiet murmurs from the breakfast area melded with the warble of birds and a gurgling marble fountain. I finally relaxed.

When Jana pulled a bag of figs from her pack, my mouth watered (I'd first discovered their succulent sweetness the day before.) A shaggy spaniel ambled over to snarl at Libby, who cowered under my chair. An hour later we were guided to to our room. A carved door opened to a spacious room with white chenille spreads. A myriad of embroidered pillows, bright weavings, Turkish rugs, and hand-painted ceramics tastefully accented the white. Jana went straight for the air conditioner and engaged the turbo setting, which we nicknamed "The Blizzard"—noisy but effective. The decor was different from anything we'd known, and we were charmed, collapsing happily onto our beds.

I was touched by small things in this village—the cobbled streets, a stooped woman sweeping away flower petals with a short broom, and flowers cascading from rusty olive oil cans. We explored mornings and evenings and escaped the searing afternoon sun by reading in the Nilya's breezy courtyard. I hadn't felt so relaxed in months—maybe years. Would Istanbul offer me this kind of peace? A former Koç teacher had said he'd stood by the fence to watch the sun rise each morning. That sounded lovely after my hectic life.

It was a joy to have the leisure to read. Each afternoon I lost myself in Orhan Pamuk's *Snow*, recommended to help me understand Turkey's culture. Since scarves aren't allowed in public buildings in Turkey, the girls had to choose between the scarf and education. I admired the fervor of those who wouldn't remove their scarves to attend school. However, I couldn't help believing that scarves subjugated them. I scolded myself for judging their culture through my Western lens, but I couldn't help it. When cultures clash, is either one right?

# 5  POINTED SHOES

Every time we left the Nilya, Jana and I were hounded by a greasy-haired rug merchant with black shoes tapered to a pencil point. Jana ignored him, but I made excuses each time we saw him. I'd been taught not to ignore anyone but my bullying brother.

We spent our second morning at Ephesus, hoping to explore it before the afternoon heat. Kemal, our diminutive, white-haired guide, regaled us with stories as he skirted clusters of tourists. He got special permission for Libby to join us on our tour, which warmed my heart. I could see my dog might inhibit my travels.

Ephesus had been a major trading center in Roman times, with over a quarter of a million people. This ruin is best known from St. Paul's diatribe against its corruption. It was famous, too, for the Temple of Artemis, one of the seven wonders of the ancient world. Once four times the size of Athens' Parthenon, only one of its columns remains. Ephesus also appeared in Revelations, cited as one of the Seven Churches of Asia. Why had I never learned about it in school? Of course, I may not have been listening. I'd abhorred social studies, but experiencing history firsthand triggered a new fascination. Kemal explained that we'd known this area as Asia Minor in historical accounts; Turkey wasn't an independent nation until 1923.

We chuckled at the community outhouse, its thirty keyhole-shaped toilets cut side-by-side into long marble benches lining three sides of the room. "These public toilets were devised to keep citizens under control," Kemal explained. "Each morning the servants would arrive at sun-up to warm the seats for their masters, who would arrive later and sit for hours discussing the issues of the day. Someone was always posted as a spy to report the latest gossip to the ruling families."

I was awed by the facade of the library, a two-story colonnaded building that had been reconstructed with the original marble. Kemal whispered conspiratorially about the library's secret entrance to a brothel across the street.

As we finished our tour, he explained, "Ephesus died as the waters of the Aegean receded, cutting it off from commerce. Without trade, the city had nothing, and they had no means to dredge the harbor." We were amazed that the city now lies five kilometers from the sea.

That afternoon Jana, Libby, and I squeezed into a blue mini-bus and headed for a nearby beach. With forty people sandwiched into a bus built for 18, the ride was stuffy and sweaty—but thankfully short. Though many riders avoided Libby, one woman and her son couldn't stop petting her.

At the beach I was astonished to see women sitting in the shallow water fully dressed. Some wore scarves and long dresses while others had full-body bathing garments of lightweight printed fabric, like hooded running suits. Their husbands stood beside them in modern swim trunks.

"Can you believe that, Jana? The men are nearly nude while the women have to stay covered? Come on!"

"It's usually the husband's decision," Jana noted. "I hate the whole idea."

"I'm trying to come to terms with it, but I don't believe these women have a choice."

"Well, those women do," Jana said, pointing up the beach to a bevy of bikini-clad women stretched out on beach chairs. "I'll bet they're mostly Germans, though," she added.

I hoped not. I wanted them to be Turks.

We found a beach cabana, changed into our suits and dove into the tepid Aegean, sheer bliss after the sweaty bus ride. Libby scolded us from shore, where I'd tied her to a wicker beach umbrella.

On our trek back to the Nilya, who should we meet but our old friend, Mehmet, the carpet dealer. Exhausted, I promised to stop by his shop before leaving Selçuk. Anything to get him off our backs.

On our last day we bussed to Şirince (Sheer-EEN-jay), a charming mountain village famed for its fruit wines. Whitewashed buildings with ceramic tile roofs charged up the steep hills, one above the other, rock paths and stone stairways dividing them. Şirince was first inhabited by Christians but resettled by Muslims after Ataturk's 1923 forced population exchange between Turkey and Greece. The village's two Christian churches were crumbling from disuse.

Jana and I ambled along the main street sampling peach, blackberry, and apple wines in quaint wine shops. Feeling a bit light-headed, we left that pursuit to wander up the village's steep lanes passing chickens, goats, and the occasional donkey. Each new scent stopped Libby in her tracks, and I finally picked her up so we could make progress. Neatly-paired sets of shoes waited beside each doorway, and I yearned to step inside and see what their homes were like. "Look up there!" Jana exclaimed, pointing at an open-air teahouse perched above us. How could we resist?

"Check out this view! It's like a photo from National Geographic!" I exclaimed as we gazed out over the patchwork of peach and plum orchards blanketing the mountainside. Heavily-laden grape vines hung from the teahouse eaves, and I resisted the temptation to pop a grape into my mouth. A stooped woman in a scarf and *şalvar* (calico skirt-like pants) left her chore of rolling dough at a low round table to greet us. "*Merhaba. Hoş geldiniz,*" she said. (Hello. Welcome.)

"*Ayran, lütfen,*" I said. We'd discovered *ayran* in Selçuk and found the salted yogurt drink refreshing. She set our glasses down with a broad smile, and I wondered if her crooked teeth were brown from tea or poor dental care. Probably both. Though I hated my annual dental visits, I was glad not to be in her shoes. She fussed over Libby and shuffled off, returning with a bowl of water.

Later we discovered a small thatched-roof niche where a leathery, wrinkled man sat cross-legged whittling spoons from cedar limbs. A display of carefully finished spoons lay on a hand-hewn table, and he beamed at us when we spoke, his toothless grin attesting to many decades. Communicating with signals, we each bought a few. They weren't cheap, but could he possibly support himself carving spoons? I later learned from our Nilya hosts that he walked five miles up that mountain every day from Selçuk. Amazing.

We took the mini-bus back down to Selçuk, and as we climbed the dark hill home, light gleamed from Mehmet's carpet shop.

"We really should go in," I sighed. "I did promise."

"But I'm so tired, and he hasn't seen us."

"It'll only take a minute, Jana. One cup of tea and we'll leave."

Mehmet brought tea in tiny tulip-shaped glasses as we perused his shop. The worn wooden floor was surrounded by stacks of folded and rolled carpets, much like other shops we'd passed.

"What can I show you?" Mehmet asked.

"I'm sorry, but I really can't buy a rug. We'd love to see what you have, though."

Explaining as he went, Mehmet showed us kilims (woven), carpets (knotted), and sumacs (woven and embroidered), piling one on another as he pulled them from his collection. I was drawn to the silk carpets, brilliant-hued masterpieces with a rich sheen. Mehmet picked up a tree-of-life carpet in soft shades of green with maroon and red, then flipped it around. The pale colors transformed to deep, rich hues when the nap faced us. The intricate designs of the silk stole my breath.

"How do you like this one?" Mehmet asked, pulling out a narrow silk carpet with three pink and white medallions on a field of light blue, framed with intricate floral patterns and long twisted fringe. When he saw my smile he offered me his "teacher price" of 400—was it dollars or lira? (A dollar was about 1.3 lira at the time.)

"I'm sorry, Mehmet. I really need to wait until I learn more about carpets."

"Ah, but you will never find better price than this, and I can see you love this carpet. It is beautiful, no?" I had no idea whether his price was fair.

"Yes, it's lovely, but I haven't been paid yet. I have no money."

"Do you have a credit card?"

"I never charge anything unless I can cover it."

"It's gorgeous," Jana interjected. Thanks a lot.

Mehmet eyed me carefully. "I will make special offer only for you. You must take this rug home then look at other rugs in Istanbul. I know you will not find so fine carpet for such good price. Later you send me money or return carpet. You are teacher, so I trust you. In Turkey we love teachers too much."

I was uncomfortable. It felt shady to take this rug with no down payment, yet Mehmet seemed sincere. Why was he doing this?

Jana convinced me that I couldn't lose, and I finally succumbed. Mehmet wrote my name in a spiral tablet with a note that I taught at the Koç School in Istanbul, and I took his business card. I expected he'd charge something on my credit card, but he didn't even ask for it. He rolled the carpet in brown paper and put it in a black nylon duffle.

"I have important warning to you," he said as he handed me the package. "You as American woman must be very careful for Turkish men who try to take advantage of you."

Right.

# 6 AND WE DO NOT ALLOW DOGS

I was thrilled to arrive in Sultanahmet after our early morning flight. This historical center of Istanbul had buildings over a thousand years old. The sun was already blistering as sidewalk shops came to life, and the Halı Hotel's dark lobby welcomed us with a relief of cool air and the rich scent of coffee. Mahogany paneling displayed deep red carpets and lavish weavings adorned with cowrie shells and bright tassels. The word *halı* means 'carpet,' and this hotel had them everywhere.

"I have a reservation for Mershon," I said, dropping my backpack near the desk.

"I must apologize, but rates are double this weekend because of the Formula One races," the young clerk informed me in carefully-enunciated English. He paused, eyebrows up. "And we do not allow dogs."

This whippersnapper didn't know who he was up against. I assumed my snooty-English-teacher attitude. "I was informed that the rates would be double, but I was also assured that I could bring my dog. (A goodie-two-shoes, I never lie—but this was an emergency.) She's well behaved and has been traveling with us for a week." (At least that part was true.)

"No dogs," he said firmly. My heart pounded. We'd never find another hotel room on the Friday of Istanbul's first Formula One races. "I made this reservation including my dog. She's in her case and won't make a sound, I promise. If she barks, you can kick us out." He scowled, nodded, and took my 300 lira for two nights (about $230). I wondered if he'd given in because I was a foreigner. I didn't yet understand the influence of using the Koç name; their family is the second-wealthiest in Turkey.

Heaving a sigh of relief, we squeezed into the wood-paneled elevator and lurched to the third floor. A woven runner led the way between walls flanked by framed antique carpets. The decor lived up to the hotel's name.

Our room was small but clean, decorated with kilims and carpets. I was shocked at the low, cot-like twin beds, but the furniture was lovely—an antique desk, a dark wood armoire, and a Lilliputian bench and table. The highlight of the room was our view of the Blue Mosque and the Haghia Sophia. Libby explored, sniffing the corners, then hopped on my bed, circled a few times, and curled up on the pillow.

Jana and I changed into light dresses. My sleeveless shift hung nearly to the floor, and I was jealous of Jana's short skirt. Though shorts weren't acceptable in Turkey, knee-length skirts were. I made a mental note to shorten all my long dresses. Poor Libby was stuck with her black fur coat. I carried her through the lobby smiling at the desk clerk, who nodded without a smile.

Noses in our guidebooks, we found our way through the maze of streets to the Grand Bazaar's 35-foot entrance. The main entrance was topped with intricate spikes above a gilded coat of arms carved on a field of green, symbolic of the powerful Ottoman sultans. Sidewalk-to-roof displays of rugs, purses, and multi-colored hanging glass lamps flanked both sides of the entrance. We were two of billions of shoppers who'd stepped through this archway in the past 500 years (250,00 to 400,000 a day).

We entered between massive iron doors to an indoor street, and no one objected to Libby. Our eyes were drawn to a high, golden-arched ceiling decorated in bands of intricate blue and red geometrics—hence the name *Kapalı Çarşı*, Turkish for 'covered bazaar.' Storefront windows flanked both sides, with gleaming displays of gold and jewelry. We were entering a 75-acre labyrinth of over 4,000 shops, many less than ten feet wide.

The covered street teemed with people from all over the world, chatting, gawking, and snapping photos. Most were dressed in Western clothing, but we spotted saris, caftans, and even burkas as we pushed our way through the crowded street.

A dashing fellow with bright teeth and bedroom eyes fell into step beside Jana. "Where are you from? How long have you been here? How do you like Istanbul?" The usual. "Can I show you to a wonderful carpet shop?"

I looked at Jana. "Why not? It'll be air-conditioned, and this place is stifling." Our young guide grinned and led us through the maze of streets, chatting as we walked. I worried that we'd never find our way back out. I tried to memorize our route as displays evolved from jewelry to scarves to leather and souvenirs, with a bright cacophony of merchandise hanging higher than we could reach. As we delved further into the bazaar, the crowd thinned. Soon he waved us into a carpet shop.

"Welcome," chirped a beaming young man as he jumped from his seat. "My name is Selçuk (Sell-CHOOCK). Where are you from?" I was already tired of this come-on, but what could I do? He reached to turn on the air-conditioner. Relief! I doubted my northern blood would ever adapt to Istanbul's heat.

"I'm from Minnesota, and my friend Jana is from Berlin."

He shook our hands and waved us to a cushioned bench piled with embroidered pillows. "Can I offer you tea or Turkish coffee? Or maybe some cool water—plain or bubbly?" We ordered water and collapsed on the bench. How different this was from shopping in America where the most one could expect was a "May I help you?" Here we were welcomed as though entering someone's home.

Selçuk was relaxed and pleasant, far more companionable than Mehmet had been. I found his little-boy demeanor appealingly honest as he showed us his treasures, chatting amiably without pushing. When I asked about silk, he pulled out an intricate placemat-sized piece in soft shades of green and gold, its fine detail begging a magnifying glass. Selçuk beamed.

"It's a work of art!" I exclaimed. "How much?"

"This is a prize," he said. "It costs over one thousand dollars." My eyes widened. Maybe Mehmet was on the level after all. If I were a wealthy woman I'd have bought that little gem right then. But I wasn't.

We bid Selçuk farewell, and when I asked for directions back out of the bazaar, he found someone to guide us to an exit. I was charmed by his kindness. Once outside we grabbed a late lunch of *döner*, delicately spiced lamb cooked on a rotating skewer, thinly sliced and piled into crusty bread (for under $2). Turkish fast food, it satisfied our hunger as we continued along the bustling street. There were just as many stores outside the bazaar as inside, but at least we could see the sky.

At the top of the next hill we spotted a Starbucks. WHAT???? I couldn't resist an iced latte, a taste of home, and another chance to cool off. Coffee had been a great disappointment thus far—Turkish coffee is a thick, sweetened espresso-like drink with the sludge of powdered grounds filling a third of the tiny cup. Delicious, but not the cup of coffee I yearn for. I made a note on my map so I could find my way to Starbuck's the next time I was in the city.

I refused to give up good coffee completely.

# 7 A CISTERN AND A MOSQUE

Libby barked when someone entered a neighboring room in the wee hours. I bolted up and clamped her muzzle, heart pounding. Istanbul was going to be a challenge with a dog. No one knocked at our door, but I held Libby under the sheet beside me for the rest of the night.

The next morning we headed for a 'must-see,' the Basilica Cistern. The ticket lady didn't spot Libby at my feet. Whew! As we descended a broad, concrete stairway we were enveloped by cool, damp air resounding with Gregorian chants. Thirty-foot columns stretched in endless rows over a vast underground pool. Water dripped from the brick-domed ceiling as we followed a wooden walkway through the maze of columns, each softly lit from below. My neck prickled at the ethereal atmosphere.

A plaque informed us that the cistern's 336 marble columns had been "recycled" from nearby Roman ruins and placed underground over 500 years earlier. Aqueducts carried water to Constantinople from a forest 19 kilometers away, and this cistern supplied water for the palace and nearby buildings. Midway down the long cavern we discovered a unique column carved with teardrops like the eyes of peacock feathers, stained green except for a clean white circle around a small hole. The uniformed guard showed us how to make a wish by putting a thumb into the hole and circling around it with the rest of our fingers. We complied, amused. I wished for a romance, already fearful of the loneliness looming ahead.

At the far end of the cistern we discovered two marble Medusa heads that had been pilfered centuries ago from other parts of the city. Green with algae, the heads supported huge columns—one snake-haired head resting upside down while the other lay on her side. No one knows why.

"The cistern was my absolute favorite thing," Jana announced as we emerged into the blinding Saturday heat. "I think in the whole country." I had to agree. Each new site seemed to outdo the others.

We needed to find a rest room, and all we could find were public floor toilets near the Blue Mosque. We paid a half lira, took a few squares of toilet paper, and faced the challenge. Actually, it was a lot like peeing in the woods. I stood over a flattened porcelain toilet in the floor with ceramic tiles around it, stooped, and peed into the very clean basin. It's actually sanitary, as you touch nothing. This one had a flusher chain that ran water through the receptacle and down the drain, and it also had a spigot low on the wall with a little plastic pitcher for further cleansing.

After exploring some gift shops and grabbing a light lunch, we headed over to the Blue Mosque, an awe-inspiring edifice with six minarets. But it wasn't blue. We found the tourist entrance, surreptitiously snapping photos of men washing their heads and feet at ornate gold faucets outside—required ablutions before prayer. I was fascinated by this unfamiliar behavior. Did they realize we were there? We put our shoes in plastic bags then covered our hair with scarves. A guard blocked my way, pointed at Libby and shook his head. Humph. Istanbul wasn't dog friendly, though it harbored many well-fed strays. Libby and I waited outside while Jana went in, then I took my turn.

The mosque was hushed as soft light filtered through stained glass windows. Columns ten feet thick were cloaked in brilliant blue-and-white ceramic tiles, drawing my gaze up to massive painted domes reaching heavenward from the elephantine pillars. This was where the "blue" came from—the stunning blue tiles. The floor's deep red carpet was divided into hundreds of individual prayer spaces. A few men bowed, kneeled, and genuflected while scores of whispering tourists crowded behind a wooden railing at the back. I was irritated to see that some women were bare-headed. I may not agree with the scarf, but I respect the culture of covering in a mosque.

How different this was from my staid Lutheran upbringing. The most demonstrative we'd ever been was bowing our heads for prayer (sometimes, anyway). I noticed a wood lattice screen behind us—a separate area for women. I peered inside to find more women at prayer than the few men scattered in the vast sanctuary. Once again I was rankled to see women treated as second-class citizens. I wanted to understand but was hard-pressed to do so. Would I ever find peace with this culture?

As we left the mosque, the melodic chant of the call to prayer echoed from loudspeakers above us, then repeated from other minarets, almost in competition. We strolled through the park where spokes of bright pansies and verbena radiated from a central fountain. "That's the Haghia Sophia across the way. Want to see that, too?"

"I'm pretty mosqued out," Jana replied. "Let's grab a cup of tea. I need to use the facilities." The cleanest rest rooms were often in restaurants, and a cup of tea bought respite for weary legs.

We treated ourselves to a quiet dinner at the Blue House Hotel. Because it was early, they allowed us to have Libby on the roof, and the view overlooking Sultanahmet was awe-inspiring. I had to pinch myself to believe that this was indeed my new home. The air finally cooled, and as we finished our lamb shish-kabobs, a light show danced across the Blue Mosque's façade, a dramatic finish to our day. And to our week together. Jana was flying home.

# 8 NAVIGATING BLIND

Tears flowed as Jana woke me to say goodbye early Sunday morning. Mine were about parting with this dear friend but also about navigating an alien world alone. At least I had Libby.

After a quiet breakfast on the upstairs balcony, I donned my backpack, popped Libby into her case, and headed for campus. Directions in hand, my confidence faltered. Could I do this alone where so few speak English? I stopped to review Ileyn's instructions: "Take the tram down to Eminönü (I could manage that), then take the Kadiköy ferry across to the Asian side." I'd do that much then look at the next step—no point in overwhelming myself. Public transport only cost a lira, but I had only ten left.

I managed the tram and followed the underpass to the ferry landing. So far, so good. My heart pounded as I scanned the stations along the pier, already buzzing with people. I stopped a gray-haired ticket-seller in a captain's hat to ask for the Kadiköy ferry.

"Where are you going?" he asked.

"I'm going to the Koç School." I showed him my instructions.

"There is much easier way. You must believe me. I am knowing Koç School. You do not have to take so many transport. Take this ferry to Harem, then ask for bus to Koç School. There are too many buses at Harem *iskele*; someone will help you find Koç bus." What a relief! Why hadn't Ileyn know this?

"Oh, thank you!"

"Good luck, beautiful lady!" He kissed my hand before continuing down the pier, calling "Ferry ride along Bosphorus! Leaving ten minutes!"

I muscled Libby's case through the turnstile and climbed the ramp onto the quickly-crowding ferry. People filled the outside wooden benches first, while others filed inside to settle on upholstered wooden benches. I hefted Libby's case upstairs for the better view. I lifted her out and she sat at my feet, quiet but content—so trusting. A stooped man in a vest and fez came around selling tea, which was tempting, but I passed. No idea when I'd find a rest room. As we chugged away from Eminönü I was moved by the majesty of Topkapı Palace and the mosques of Sultanahmet. Enormous Turkish flags flapped above the rooftops, their white stars and crescents impressive on a field of red. I was feeling better.

At Harem my stomach lurched as I scanned the scene: hundreds of busses –green, blue, long, short. How would I ever find the one to Koç? I approached a man in a chauffeur's cap. "Do you speak English?"

"*Hayir, ama giteceğim,*" he answered, then disappeared. Did he want me to wait? I gave it an optimistic try. Soon he returned with a bushy-browed man in a plaid shirt. "How can I help you, Lady?"

Ah, hope! "I need to find the bus to the Koç School."

"The Koç University?" he asked.

"No, the high school. Near Pendik."

"There is no bus to Pendik here," he said. "You must take ferry to Eminönü, then take Kadiköy ferry and train."

My heart sank. The man at Eminönü must have thought I meant Koç University. I didn't even know there was one! It would take all day to get home if I had to backtrack. And I wouldn't have enough lira! Frantic tears filled my eyes.

"Maybe I can help. One minute, please." Once more I waited, heart pounding. My hair was sizzling, my blouse glued to my back. I'd never felt so alone. Libby cowered beside me in the midst of bus-station chaos as I prayed this man would find me a way home. He returned smiling. "I found bus driver who knows Koç Lisesi. He will help you. Come."

He led me through a sea of busses to a blue mini-bus similar to those I'd used with Jana. I settled  behind the driver with my purple backpack on the floor and Libby's case in my lap. It was tight, but I felt safe. The driver nodded at me knowingly. "Do you speak English?" I asked. He shook his head. "Koç Lisesi," he said.

"*Yvet,*" I answered. Yes.

It took fifteen minutes for the bus to fill, and we were finally off. We drove and we drove and we drove. Body odor permeated the bus as it filled and emptied numerous times, mostly with men. A few smiled at me, while most avoided my gaze. I wasn't alone, just caught in the isolation of the wrong language. We drove forever. "Don't worry, Libby," I whispered. "We'll get home." I hoped so, anyway.

An hour later the driver pulled over under a bridge and signaled me to get out. He wasn't going to abandon me there, was he? He said something to the other passengers, then motioned me to follow him up a stairway to the overpass. He crossed the bridge, jay-walked through traffic, and led me to a crowded bus stop. When he paused to light a cigarette, I said, *"Teşekkür ederim,"* (Thank you) and handed him five of my remaining lira. He pushed my hand away, indicating that I should wait. I shook my head and pointed to his bus. He looked back at his stranded passengers and nodded, then strode over to some men standing nearby. I heard "Koç Lisesi" and "Tepeören" (a town near the school). He returned and indicated that I should follow these men; he would go back to his bus. I tried again to tip him, but he shook his head resolutely.

A grizzled man with a crocheted scull cap strode over and asked me something in Turkish. *"Anlamadım,"* I said. I don't understand. He repeated himself, more loudly this time. *"Anlamadım!"* I repeated. He tried a third time, even louder. *"Anlamadım!!!"* I boomed. Was he deaf? He nodded, nonplussed, then stood silently beside me, my aged protector.

The men chatted among themselves, occasionally nodding toward me. Each time a bus came they shook their hands at me. After twenty minutes another bus pulled up and they all nodded. Two men spoke to me, one gently guiding me onto the bus and explaining my plight to the driver, who nodded as I climbed aboard with Libby, now back in her case. Though ferries were dog-friendly, I wasn't so sure about busses.

After an hour of driving and stopping, the last passengers got off. I was the only one left, and the driver scolded me in Turkish. Apparently the trip was over, but we weren't at Koç. I was confused—and devastated.

I climbed off the bus and spotted two boys in red school vests. "Koç

School?" I asked. They smiled and nodded, indicating that I should stand with them. They were fascinated with Libby, first teasing then petting her. When a blue mini-bus finally came, one insisted on holding Libby's case as the other helped me on the bus. They sat in front of me, asking me questions in Turkish. *"Anlamadım,"* I repeated, wishing I could speak their language. I'd spent months with *Teach Yourself Turkish* but still knew only a few phrases. I vowed to work harder.

Before long I spotted the school gate. Relief! I couldn't remember the words for getting a bus to stop, but the boys took care of it for me. I disembarked, four hours after leaving the hotel. *"Teşekkür ederim!"* I called as the bus pulled away, the boys waving through the back window.

I was finally home, and I'd had my first taste of Turkish hospitality.

With a sigh of relief I lifted Libby from her case, showed my ID at the gate, and hiked across the deserted campus to my *lojman*. I rummaged for my key and opened the door to a silent, stark apartment. No Jana to talk to. Just me. I dragged a chair out onto the balcony, propped my feet on the rail, and sipped a Nescafe as I gazed out over the hills and pondered the years ahead—two years far from home, away from my friends. The Turks had already wormed their way into my heart, but I'd never be one of them.

Would I build solid friendships at school? Could I be happy here? Loneliness settled hard in my gut, and that night my sleep was wracked with nightmares of being lost, once in a forest and later in a strange city. I tossed and turned, yearning for an Excedrin P.M.—and a fan.

I finally caught a few hours of blessed sleep.

# 9  GROCERIES: NO EASY BUSINESS

The next morning's sun brightened my mood. My cupboards were bare, and my first order of business would be groceries, then I'd find out whether Polly had arrived. We'd met a month ago over lunch in Minneapolis with Jim, a former Koç teacher.

"The kids are pretty wild," he'd warned. "They're always running in the halls, hitting each other, and screaming at the top of their lungs. Once a whole group of boys jumped on each other in the hall between classes and piled into a tangled mess. My wife quit after her first year because she couldn't stand the kids, but I enjoyed their energy."

Polly had called after the meeting to reassure me. She'd taught with Jim's wife, who tended to exaggerate. "Don't worry—we'll be fine."

Still concerned about this "exuberance," I'd consulted Uygar, a tall, angular young Turk who worked as a business intern at a local resort. When he learned I was moving to Turkey, he'd called to meet for coffee. I was touched. "Koç is the Harvard of high schools in Istanbul," he'd explained as we sipped lattes on the beach, sun glinting off Lake Superior to silhouette sailboats moored in the harbor. "It is a prep school for American colleges. You are very lucky to teaching there." His dark eyes glowed with enthusiasm, and I found his grammar missteps endearing.

"I'm glad to know that, but I need some advice. I understand Turkish students are hard to control. Should I be strict?" Discipline wasn't my forte; I tend to be more understanding than firm. "If I'm harsh, will they hate me? Say nasty things about me in Turkish? Can I trust them?"

"Turkish students can be very loud sometimes and happy—also very sad if things are going wrongly. You must only to love them. Then they will respect to you. It is mistake to being harsh."

Funny how all these memories were flooding back. I wondered how I'd do with my students. Time would tell. Right now I needed food.

Ileyn had suggested Snowy's, and I knew better than to bring Libby.

"Be a good girl while I'm gone," was my code for "You're not coming." She dropped her tail and moped to her bed.

I pulled cash from the school's ATM and posted myself outside the security gate to wait for the mini bus. After the half-hour ride I wandered up and down the street hunting for Snowy's, finally discovering it nestled in the basement of a three-story building. I descended a wide marble stairway to a market with displays of toasters, irons and fans piled high in the entry—all with labels I couldn't read. I considered buying a fan but couldn't imagine lugging it home on the mini-bus.

I wandered through narrow aisles of unrecognizable cans and packages, thankful for those with pictures of their contents.

I tried to use my little electronic translator, but it didn't really help, except to identify the contents of containers I thought were something I wanted--but weren't.   I'd have do my best today and write out a grocery list in Turkish for my next trip.

A can that looked like it might be beans was actually okra. Not my favorite. I stuck with things I could see in glass jars, cans with pictures on them, and fresh produce. The only bread I found was white bread in Italian-sized long loaves. Crusty white bread is standard in Turkey.

The dairy case was mostly yogurt (almost the same word, *yoğurt*)—scores of different brands ranging from small tubs to gallon pails. A staple in the Turkish diet, yogurt replaced milk as their source of calcium. And where was the milk? I knew the word, *süt*, but didn't see any in the dairy case. I finally discovered a display of small rectangular cartons on a shelf. Irradiated milk needs no refrigeration.

Half the store was fresh produce. Nuts, grains, vegetables and fruits filled barrels and slanted wood bins. Some mystified me: golf ball-sized green  fruits and spotted yellow fruits that resembled miniature peppers. In no mood to experiment, I stuck with grapes, peaches and the luscious fresh figs.

I followed the lead of other shoppers, bagging my produce and handing it to the clerk, who weighed it and slapped on a label. I paid about two cents each for home-grown tomatoes, a dime apiece for juicy, sweet peaches, and 25 cents for a healthy cluster of green grapes. A loaf of bread was 15 cents. I marveled at the low prices.

I hunted in vain for beer and wine. Alcohol might be a thing of the past. I'd miss my evening glass of wine but was thrilled to find ground coffee tucked at the end of a vast aisle of teas. I had no idea there could be so many kinds. I had my press pot and would gladly abandon my jar of Nescafe.

The clerk spoke to me as I checked out. *"Anlamadım,"* I said, the word that had become my primary conversation of late. He shrugged and checked me through, then selected the necessary amount from the handful of cash I proffered. I knew Turkish numbers, but he talked so FAST!

I'd brought my backpack, planning to catch the mini-bus back to campus, but I'd bought too much. I crammed five bags into my backpack and still had two bags and a melon left. I sighed and headed off to hail a taxi, but a sunny girl in a red vest stopped me. "We have a service bus to take you home, Madam. You can wait for it right here." She spoke perfect English, thank goodness.

"I live at the Koç School. Will they go that far?"

"Of course. Just tell the driver," she said with a smile, then handed me a cup of sweet-tart cherry juice. Grocery stores in Turkey provided transport for their customers, as less than a quarter of Turks owned cars. Snowy's was the only one that ever offered me a beverage, though. I tried to tip the driver when he dropped me at my door, but he shook his head. A mere *"Teşekkür ederim"* seemed little payment for this kind service, but I said it with a grateful smile.

# 10 POLLY, TERRI, AND…

After stashing the groceries, I pulled out my Koç directory and looked up Polly's unit number. I wandered the streets hunting for number 28, where a pink hollyhock greeted me beside the stairway. When she opened the door, Polly's blazing hair and bright smile lifted my spirits. "Hey, Ann Marie! Come on in! How are you?"

A sweaty, tousled man with thinning brown hair rose from the couch. "Marc, this is my friend Ann Marie. Ann Marie, my boyfriend Marc will be here for another week. We just got back from Şile (she-LAY), a beach city up on the Black Sea. When did you arrive?"

"I've been here over a week—traveling on the Aegean with a friend."

"Wow. I'm jealous. Şile was a disappointment of crowds and dirty beaches, but, well—here we are in Istanbul!!! Can you believe it? How about a glass of wine?"

"Wonderful!" I said. Who cared that it was 2:00? "Where did you get it? I couldn't find any at the grocery store."

"Don't worry—I'll show you. They have beer, too."

Thus began my first friendship. Polly lived up to the freckled redhead stereotype: fun-loving, outgoing, interesting and eager for adventure. As we chatted, she confided that her school district had only granted her a one-year leave. Bummer. I'd signed a two-year contract, but I could always back out if I wasn't happy after a year.

We decided to throw a dinner together and include Terri, a new teacher from Washington whom I'd met online. She offered her new patio table, and we gathered on her tiny lawn to share cheese, bread, olives, and fruit as well as copious amounts of wine, toasting repeatedly to a bright future at Koç. We'd all landed, done some traveling, and now we had friends.

Terri was a bundle of smiles and energy, gray-blonde hair framing her pert face in a halo of frenetic curls. With teary eyes she described the end of a seven-year relationship with a young Mexican who'd been the love of her life. "I couldn't have children for him, and I needed to set him free to build a family," she said. My heart went out to her, though I was a little jealous. Both she and Polly had lovers, and where was I? Divorced three years, I'd had only one romance—a failed one.

Workshop would begin the next day, hangovers or no. We'd be teaching at different levels, but the three of us could spend evenings and weekends together exploring Istanbul.

The next week was a whirlwind, a workshop for the twenty new teachers, so many because the Turkish system had just added the twelfth grade.

I was eager to start planning yet frustrated that our offices had been dismantled for remodeling. How would I prepare? Where were our desks, files, and materials? What about computers? Starting the year unprepared was a nightmare come true. My thirty years of experience might help me wing it, but I needed materials at least. Just when things were going smoothly, they caved in.

Our consolation was the parties. So different from home. Tony and Marnie Paulus, the new director and his wife, hosted a backyard reception for new hires during workshop. "Check this out!" Terri exclaimed as we strolled toward their lawn, which was set with tall, linen-draped cocktail tables. Black-vested waiters circulated with trays of hors d'oeuvres and wine. The buffet dinner was delicious, and it was fun to socialize with the rest of the new staff. What a contrast to Grand Marais, where my district treated teachers to pancakes on the first day of workshop.

I was astonished to learn that our housing complex had a social center with a bartender on duty five nights a week—just for teachers!

Our third day of workshop was a city tour of Istanbul's most famous sites, finishing at the Grand Bazaar. A group of us strolled down the gold-laden jewelry street, where a handsome young Turk approached me. "Hello!" he said. "How have you been?" Did I look like an idiot? I'd had enough Turkish come-ons to last me a lifetime. When I ignored him, he blurted, "Don't you remember me?"

"No, I don't."

"You were here a few weeks ago with a little black dog and a

German lady. I brought you to a carpet shop. Don't you remember?" I blushed. Thousands of people came through the Grand Bazaar every day, and this young man remembered me. "Oh, my goodness! Selçuk Carpets?"

"Yes, that's right," he beamed. "I'm at your service. Can I help you find anything?"

Amazing—Turkish hospitality.

Polly, Terri and I ventured forth that Sunday, taking the mini bus, train, and ferry out to the Princes Islands, a group of islands in the Marmara near Istanbul. We toured Heybiliada in a horse cart, as no cars are allowed on the islands. Who knew there was this haven of quiet so close to the bustling city? It was a delight.

During our first weeks I grew closer to Polly, who was interested in everyone and everything, fascinated and fascinating. She had an impish, elfish look to her, maybe because she was. It just made her all the more fun to be with. Terri needed more quiet time, while Polly and I were eager for connections and adventures. I'd found my bosom buddy, and I was happy.

The rest of the faculty joined us for the second week of workshop, and workers miraculously pulled our offices together. Carpets were laid, desks carried in by uniformed female staff (we called them 'worker bees'), and offices assigned. The Turkish work ethic is phenomenal, and things get done. We spent the whole weekend in our offices scrambling to prepare.

Maybe we'd make it.

# 11  RAISE YOUR HAND IF YOU UNDERSTAND

I didn't have to teach the first day—thank goodness. An all-school assembly began with the entire student body standing in silent tribute to Ataturk, Turkey's revered founder. On command everyone snapped to attention and sang the national anthem. I was astounded, especially when I compared it to the lackluster way my American students said the pledge or sang "The Star Spangled Banner"—if they knew the words. I'd had students refuse to say the pledge because of the reference to God, so different from this unquestioning loyalty.

Students spent the rest of the morning in homerooms going over schedules and filling out forms, after which we were all treated to a catered lunch on the lawn—with a thousand uninvited bees.

I faced my first class of ninth graders the next morning. Standing before them in a simple cotton skirt and blouse, I was mortified as perspiration soaked through—less from the heat than the stress of this two-year commitment. What had I been thinking? An aging Scandinavian blonde, I loomed ghostlike in this arena of olive-skinned, dark-browed beauties.

Three rows of paired desks held teens in uniform, and they weren't sweating. The girls wore crisp white blouses and gray Glen plaid skirts with white stockings and black shoes. Their long black hair ranged from wild curls to sleek tresses, except for one redhead. The neatly-barbered boys (no long hair at the elite Koç School) wore white shirts with red and black striped ties, dark pants, and black shoes.

It was all so new to me—so different!

The bell rang and they quieted.

"I need to know whether you understand what I'm saying," I began. "My name is Ms. Mershon, and I come from a tiny tourist town in northern Minnesota where I lived in the woods... bla bla bla bla bla..."

They eyed me intently, a few smiling.

"Raise your hand if you understood everything I said." About two thirds of them raised a hand, some tentatively. Relief. "Here's what we'll do. If I'm going too fast for you, please raise a finger, and I'll slow down." Silent nods. Maybe this wouldn't be so bad after all. If these kids were an exuberant breed, they behaved far better than my American students. I'd been misinformed.

My eleventh graders were heaven, a group of eager, interested, and attentive young scholars. There were sixteen girls and five boys, and though I hate to be sexist, thirty years of experience have taught me that classes with more girls are easier. I had no class list yet, so I passed around an empty seating chart and asked them to enter their names. Big mistake. Between strange names, different Turkish letters, and illegible handwriting, my list was a mess. But the kids were darlings.

So far so good, I thought at the end of the day. My students had been eager, quiet, and respectful—easy to love. Each class had quieted when the bell rang, waiting silently for me to begin. They seemed to understand me, though I struggled to unravel their strong accents. Mini-lessons and practice would fix their grammatical errors, and I would develop drills to minimize their accents. I must "only to love them," and it would be easy.

# 12 EZGİ, KADIR, EREN, GÖZDE...

I'd promised my students I'd learn their names in two weeks, but they were all gibberish to me: *Ezgi, Kadir, Eren, Gözde, Selim Can,* and so on. The only one even remotely familiar was *Ahmet.* Oh—and *Can,* which is pronounced 'John.' (The Turkish 'c' is pronounced as our 'j'.)

I decided to bring my camera, take a photo of each student and download them into my computer. The next day I entertained my classes with a slide show of their classmates, and they helped me label each photo, often sharing what the names meant. Most Turkish names are a common word. *Ezgi* means "melody," *Kadir* means "worth," *Eren* is "saint," *Selim* means "healthy," *Gözde* means "favorite," and *Can* means "soul or heart." A common endearment, in fact is *Canem*—"my heart, my dear, or my soul." I found that fascinating. I managed to master their names in a few weeks, but it took hours.

By the end of the first week things were falling apart. The ninth graders charged into the room chattering so loudly they couldn't hear the bell. I had to raise my voice to quiet them, something I've always hated doing. Each day it took longer, and once I got their attention they were easily distracted—an airplane flying overhead, a bee in the classroom, or even a hiccup would set them off. Heaven forbid that anyone should pass gas.

I turned to John Richardson, my brilliant Welsh mentor. John was a traditional Brit, a diminutive dynamo with a ready smile and a phenomenal memory of all things literate. He encouraged me to have the class stand at attention beside their desks when the bell rang, as he did.

"Good morning, Class."

"Good morning, Mr. Richardson. How are you today?"

"I'm fine, thank you. You may sit down." His routine wasn't my style, so  my ninth grade nirvana continued to deteriorate.

One afternoon a hornet flew through an open window, triggering a chorus of shrieks. My heart lurched when Kemal leapt onto the sill to attack it—I envisioned his plunge from our screenless third-story window. Oh, my God! They were totally out of control. How was I going to survive the year? I was an alien in their world, and I had no idea what to do. Were they testing me?

One boy, Başar (Bah-SHAR) was my greatest challenge. He resided in La-La Land, and each time I called him back to reality, he would smile and comply— until I turned my back. "Başar, look around the room. What is everyone else doing?"

"Huh?" He'd lift his head, look around then pull out his notebook.

"How about a pencil?" I'd prompt. He'd pull one out. It was sort of a game we played. Poor guy. Ironically, *başar* is the root of a verb meaning "to succeed."

Friday night I invited Polly over to celebrate our first week. Once we'd settled on the couch with a glass of wine, I said, "I'm exhausted, but I think I'm going to like it here."

"Lucky you," she answered glumly. "I've never been so frustrated in my entire life. It took me a half hour to get the second graders into a fricking CIRCLE! I don't think I can do this, Ann Marie."

"Oh, come on. You're probably just worn out. Give it a few weeks, Polly. You'll get used to it, and the kids will come around."

"There aren't any English picture books, there's no music, and I can't even get a tape player. They wanted me to teach 'The Little Red Hen,' for Crissake! It's not the kids, it's the system. It's totally antiquated! And I have two little boys who are so rammy they should have full-time aides. They're totally out of control, poor things. I talked to the counselor, and she just nodded her head and sipped her tea."

"I thought you liked it here." I was beginning to panic. Polly was my kindred spirit, and I was counting on her. She couldn't leave.

"I do love it here," she explained. "The city is awesome, my *lojman* is sweet, and the people are all great. I even love the guards. It's just that I can't teach in a system that goes against everything I believe as an educator. They hired me for my expertise teaching English as a second language, and I can't use any of my skills in this backwards system."

"I'm having some problems, too, Polly. My ninth graders are out of control. Let's give it a few more weeks. I'll bet you can change things for the better. If they hired you for your expertise, they should take advantage of it."

"I'll try, but I don't know, Ann Marie. I'm not optimistic."

At our ninth grade meeting the second week I discovered that everyone was struggling with behavior. Because of a change in the entrance exam, many students had low English skills, the classes were larger than usual, and the students were so rammy that one teacher nicknamed them our Newfies—Newfoundland puppies. In their defense, they were innocent and respectful, except for that doggoned "exuberance." Administration agreed to bring class sizes down by adding a section, and we laid plans to regain control. We'd nip those behaviors in the bud.

I decided on blatant behavior modification. Each ninth grader started the day with 5 behavior points and lost a point each time I caught them speaking Turkish or talking out of turn. I carried a class list on my clipboard, tallying infractions. "Was that mark for me, Ms. Mershon?" a student would ask, usually Eren, a handsome, callow boy who interrupted me with incessant questions and comments.

"If you talked out of turn, it's likely," I'd respond. (Oh, so clever.) "You're welcome to check the list after class." Discipline improved. In fact, it was miraculous. Turkish students are driven by grades, and I had them by the throats. Even Eren.

Although my system worked, I felt like the Wicked Witch of the West. My connection with the kids was deteriorating, which I knew could be fatal. I held a class discussion about discipline, writing their concerns on the board. We agreed to implement a reward system, which brought smiles all around. I printed little "Bonus Bucks" worth a point on any assignment and handed them to students who acted positively—getting straight to work, helping someone, erasing the blackboard, etc. My sullen students became little angels. Well, for the most part. They still had trouble staying quiet.

One morning Harun, a skinny curly-headed boy, had lost all five of his behavior points. After class he scurried up and stood fidgeting beside Yasemin, who was asking a long-winded question about her homework. Unable to wait another second, he peered up through his goggle eyeglasses and blurted, "Ms. Mershon, you are sexy."

I blinked. "What did you say?" I was 56 years old.

Wide-eyed, he added, "One Bonus Buck?"

Yasemin and I burst into laughter. I couldn't decide whether to scold him or give him 100 Bonus Bucks, but instead I gave him a hug. Not exactly what he was after, but he sure made my day.

In spite of their boundless Newfie energy, my students were respectful. Never once did a Turkish student smart off to me, a daily occurrence in America. Turks value teachers and respect their elders; I was both. Of course, my students often talked out of turn, worked on other homework in their laps, passed notes, and teased each other. They were teens, after all. I got that. How could I help but "to love them?"

One major difference between American and Turkish students was their work ethic. The first time I assigned an essay to my ninth graders, everyone turned it in on time—a first in my thirty years of teaching.

In contrast to my two ninth grade classes, my eleventh grade IB class (International Baccalaureate) was sheer joy—a teacher's dream. These were students who'd opted for the higher-level IB curriculum, a standardized program for international schools, so they were eager to work hard. Well, mostly. A few did as little as possible, but most blew me away with their work ethic. We started the semester with *Death of a Salesman*, a play I'd never loved—too depressing for my Pollyanna tastes. Nonetheless, I approached it earnestly. We started by reading the first scene aloud in class, and I encouraged them to slow down and focus on enunciation to minimize their accents.

At the end of the scene, I asked for reactions.

"In this scene Miller introduces the three major themes of denial, contradiction, and order versus disorder," Pelinsu offered. I was dumbfounded. How could she see this so easily?

Kadir raised his hand. "I think this scene establishes the conflicted relationship between Willy and Linda." Again, I was surprised.

After just a few more comments I realized something. Not only had they already read the play on their own, but they'd memorized the Cliff's Notes, something American students would never bother to do. These kids were eager to learn—and to impress me by parroting what they'd found online. Well, I wanted more. I'd need to find a way around this rote "discussion." Grasping at straws, I decided to try some theater— actually psychodrama, a strategy I'd learned in a graduate counseling course.

"Everyone push your desks back to make space in the middle of the room." They stared at me aghast, then reluctantly obeyed. "We're going to create a family sculpture," I explained. "Who'd like to be Willy Loman?" Selim Can raised his hand. "Now, how do you think Willy would stand?" I asked.

"I think he'd sit because he's worn out and beaten," Selim Can said, grabbing a chair and striking a pensive, downcast pose. They were with me now—over the shock of my strange approach.

"I think he should stand," Ezgi countered. "He's the head of the family."

"What do the rest of you think?" I asked, and soon everyone was engaged in analyzing the characters and their relationships as they sculpted the Loman family. Once all four characters were posed to the satisfaction of the class, I had them interact, followed by a more genuine discussion where students analyzed the characters interactions without parroting from Cliffs Notes. We all enjoyed ourselves, the 80-minute period flew by, and I was pleased to see everyone thinking for themselves. Creative teaching is a challenge I embrace, and never more than with these engaged and motivated Turks.

# 13 THANK YOU, SERVICE BUSSES

I intended to devour every flavor this exotic culture had to offer. Among the school-provided teacher transits was a Friday bus to the Kurtköy street market and an evening "movie bus." After our second week Polly and I signed up for both, eager for new adventures. I hoped Polly would fall so much in love with Istanbul that she wouldn't leave. I needed a buddy.

I'd heard street market produce was cheap and delicious; maybe the market could replace Snowy's. I'd rely on the school's Turkish lunches and supplement at home with fruits, vegetables, and cheese. I wasn't big on cooking.

We hopped off the bus and Polly yelled, "Run!" We raced across the street against the light, laughing as cars honked, then forged into an alley past odiferous fish stands, gawking at the friendly chaos and, of course, snapping photos. The market snaked through back streets about eight or ten blocks in every direction, shaded by makeshift tarpaulins strung high on poles.

Meticulously arranged produce stood in pyramids and stacks on every table, tomatoes, potatoes, cucumbers, and eggplants predominating—an endless cornucopia. We walked past displays of fresh fish, olives, cheeses, spices, nuts, bread, candies, clothing, shoes, yard goods, and housewares. It was a bouquet of bargains, each with an eager vendor calling in his own sing-song, an enthused cacophony of voices piling on one another. I imagined they were yelling something like "Peaches! Figs and lemons! Apricots!" and "Buy the tastiest tomatoes here!"

"*Bir milyon, bir milyon!*" Was the only thing I recognized, one million. Turkish currency had recently changed from Turkish Lira (one million lira = 70 American cents) to New Turkish Lira (one lira = 70 cents), but people still thought in millions. Shoppers milled and bargained everywhere, bustling from one table to the next as they dragged tall plaid bags on two-wheeled metal carts. Most of the women wore full-length trench coats and flowered scarves tied under their chins. They had to be sweltering, even in the shade.

Then there was us.

Polly's red hair and my white/blonde were beyond conspicuous in this throng of dark-haired shoppers. Vendors singled us out, calling *"Hoş Geldinez!"* (welcome) as we passed, a few even in English. "Where are you from?" followed us up and down the narrow passages, the only English many of them knew. Turkish culture pulsed on these streets, and I yearned to participate. I had to learn Turkish. Vendors posed for photos as soon as they saw my camera, but women shoppers turned their heads away. A group of little boys in bright blue school uniforms followed us through the crowd, hounding us to talk with them and take their photos. One planted himself in my path and demanded, "What is my name?"

I smiled. "MY name is Ann Marie." Then I pointed to him. "What is YOUR name?"

He giggled. "Ahmet."

"MY name ees Kemal," another interrupted, throwing his arm around his friend's shoulder. Soon they were all shouting their names, their rowdy behavior a contrast to the prissy white embroidered collars they wore over blue school tunics. They were certainly boys, though, saluting and grinning as I snapped their photo then huddling to laugh at their images in my camera.

The lanes were soon packed, so Polly and I split up to finish our shopping. A round-faced woman in a pastel-flowered scarf helped as I purchased eggplants, gently guiding me to the best ones and negotiating a lower price for me. Did they charge more because I was a *yabanci* (foreigner)? I filled my backpack with twenty pounds of loot: eggplants, tomatoes, cucumbers, apples, oranges, garlic, onions, olives, pistachios, and household sundries—all for about $8. I couldn't believe it. I wouldn't have to go to Snowy's for weeks (thank goodness), but I wasn't sure I could eat it all. Polly and Terri would help.

I hurried off the bus on campus, stashed my groceries, scrubbed my face, and headed back out to catch the movie bus—again with Polly.

Terri had declined our invitation without an excuse. I hoped she was O.K.

"Bagdad Street. Where is that?" I asked Jacqueline, a French teacher from Canada.

"It's pronounced bah-DOT (Bağdat), Ann Marie. It's on the Asian side, a high-end shopping street. I think you'll like it. It has high-class stores, restaurants, and about a million taxis."

I'm not big on shopping, and the movie options were disappointing, so Polly and I decided to explore. We wandered up a wide, marble-tiled sidewalk along the bustling four-lane Bağdat Caddesi, stopping at a Starbucks for a cup of real coffee. When I saw bags of coffee beans, I grabbed two. Who cared if they cost $18 a pound? I could finally use my grinder and enjoy quality coffee at home.

"Hello, Ms. Mershon!" a voice called from back in the line. I was delighted to see two of my ninth graders, red-headed Su and her friend Selen striding up to greet us. "It so funny to see my teacher Starbucks!" Su beamed.

"How are you?" asked Selen.

"I'm great, and very happy to find a Starbucks. Do you come here often?"

"We see many friends here. Everyone love Bağdat Street. See? We buy notebooks for English class. See?"

"Good for you. That's wonderful." They stood grinning at me for a moment, unable to come up with more conversation.

"Nice to seeing you, Ms. Mershon. Have nice day."

I looked at Polly. "In a city of 15 million people, I run into two of my students. Amazing."

"Their English is terrible," Polly said. "Did you hear that?"

"I thought they did fine. They communicated."

"You've got a lot to learn, Ann Marie. You will, though. You will." I'd have to listen more carefully. I've always hesitated to correct spoken English, but maybe I'd have to change my ways. Polly was a second-language pro, and I was a mere lit and writing teacher.

We continued up Bağdat, coffees in hand, soaking up the atmosphere as sunlight filtered through lush boulevard trees and taxis honked their way along Bağdat's choked lanes. We found a T.G.I.F. Restaurant (seriously overpriced) wandered into a few exclusive dress shops (far beyond our budgets), and finally discovered a funky restaurant tucked behind some stores. We ordered hamburgers, fries, and beer, our first non-Turkish meal— delicious except for the runny ketchup.

"Oh, my God!" Polly exclaimed. "Look at the time! The bus leaves in twenty minutes!" How did the time go so fast? We were blocks from where we'd been dropped off—and not quite sure where it was.

We paid our tab and raced back down Bağdat Street, desperately trying to recognize landmarks along the way. "Boyners. I remember that," I said as we hurried past.

"Yup, and there's T.G.I.F."

We had no idea how far we'd come, so we ran down each side street, searching desperately for the theater marquis. Nothing. If we didn't catch the bus, a taxi would cost us 100 lira, about $70. We were frantic.

"Hey, you guys!" a voice called from behind.

"Patty! Oh, my goodness! There is a God." Patty was a Koç teacher, a perky pixie-haired woman with an enigmatic smile. She led us to the bus, another three blocks down Bağdat. "Once you have cell phones," she said, "you can call someone on the bus to wait for you."

"Cell phones tomorrow," I proclaimed. None too soon.

# 14  DON'T GO!

I focused on school all week, thankful for friendly office mates. Most of the younger teachers were single, while the majority of teachers my age were married couples who hung out with each other after hours. Once again, I was on the outside.

I'd had a best friend as long as I could remember. When I was small it was Joanne across the street, then when we moved to the suburbs, Lynda and Sally were constant companions. I slid through a few more friends in college, and for the past 25 years Annie had been my confidant, supporter, and adventure partner. She was positive, energetic, and empathetic—a perfect friend.

Polly was like that. She could dive into a heart-to-heart, break into a goofy little dance in the street, or commiserate with me to indulge in one more brew. Terri was our third middle-aged single teacher, and though she was an absolute sweetheart, she often opted out. I wondered if she was depressed. Whatever it was, she seldom joined us as we explored the nooks and crannies of Istanbul, watched football at John Clemens' *lojman*, or tipped a few at the social center. Polly was a good listener and a great storyteller—the perfect companion.

On our third week she dropped the bomb. "I'm going home at the end of September. I'll give the school time to find a replacement, because I won't be like those jerks who bailed in the middle of the night," she explained. No matter how I begged and cajoled, she stood firm. She absolutely refused to teach in that elementary environment. I was devastated.

Director Tony Paulus was upset over her decision, too. New to international schools, he seemed to take her decision personally, although it was clearly about the language program and not him. "Do you think it's because of her boyfriend?" he asked me confidentially, gray eyes intent.

"Absolutely not," I said. "She'd prefer to stay, but she's appalled at the archaic way English is taught in the elementary. She said they won't let her teach the way she knows is best, and she refuses to compromise her teaching ethics."

"Could it be that bad?" Tony didn't yet realize that the elementary program lagged far behind the States in second-language education.

"I guess it's pretty bad, Tony. I think I've landed the best gig here," I admitted. "In secondary English we have a forward-thinking department head, autonomy from the Turkish education rules, and we don't have to deal with the discipline issues they have in the elementary. I only have her word for it, but Polly calls the elementary counselors and deans the 'tea ladies'—if that gives you any idea."

"I still wonder," he said. Wonder away, Tony. She's leaving.

It would be a lonely year without Polly. I'd pinned my hopes on our friendship, and they were dashed. I planned a farewell dinner for her at a nearby restaurant, and fifteen of us attended. She made us all promise not to cry, but it wasn't fun. We were all too disappointed. Everyone loved Polly.

After she left I moved into her apartment, a brighter and breezier one than mine. Instead of cool blues and grays, it was furnished in warm rusts and greens, and the entry was level with a pasture. The bleating of sheep and the soft clanging of their bells sang through my new home—a small consolation for a lost friend.

I felt more alone than I had since I arrived. I'd never make it through the year if I didn't find a buddy. Terri and I got along well, but she was unhappy and couldn't offer the intimacy I craved. We were just too different. She meandered while I dashed. She attended church while I was a skeptic. She liked tequila, and I preferred beer. We liked each other, and I was one of few who understood that beneath her scattered demeanor was a brilliant mind. She knew more about history and literature than I'd forgotten. Sadly, she was still mourning her lost love.

"Maybe what I need is a man," I thought. When loneliness gripped me, I'd fantasize about meeting the perfect someone. Possibilities percolated. Could I love a Turk? There were certainly some gorgeous ones. I didn't mind being single but missed having someone to cuddle, to share morning coffee, to prepare meals for. My favorite Quaker quote said it best: "Thee knows it takes a mighty fine husband to be better than none." I didn't expect to find a husband, but a relationship was sounding good.

I'd intended to join eHarmony after I returned home from Turkey. I'd find the perfect match—someone who'd love me for who I was. In my previous marriage I'd never measured up, and it hurt. I yearned for someone positive and generous. But could I wait two years? I hoped a lover would assuage my loneliness. Maybe two.

The dreary October skies nearly drowned me, and one lonesome Friday evening I clicked on eHarmony—for future reference, of course. I worked into the wee hours completing an endless series of personality and interest inventories, developed a profile, downloaded a photo, and (who would have guessed?) entered my credit card data. Bleary-eyed, I crawled into bed for a few hours sleep.

E-harmony connections progress through numerous stages, and after a few dead ends I knew I'd wasted my money. What man wanted an overseas romance? I mean, really.

Enter Phil, an anesthesiologist from Michigan. We raced through e-Harmony's rudimentary steps of getting to know each other and quickly progressed to open-ended questions. Phil was frank, kind and understanding in his communications, and within a few weeks we were chatting on Skype. The skies may not have brightened, but my attitude sure did. Each morning I woke excited to read Phil's e-mails and eagerly anticipated our weekend chats. Oh, a budding romance! My heart was full and my loneliness dispelled.

November found me still at loose ends. I Skyped with Phil and my sister but still felt isolated. I watched from my window as parties of people gathered on the lawns below, laughing with their children. I lacked the enthusiasm to reach out. A lonely depression had set in, at least as much as it can for an inveterate Pollyanna.

With November break just weeks away, the silk carpet stashed under my bed started poking at my guilt button. I unwrapped it and laid it out on my bed, where its light blue background glowed against my maroon spread, the intricate medallions matching perfectly. I wanted to keep it, but I didn't want to be cheated. Selçuk at the Grand Bazaar was the only rug dealer I'd met in Istanbul, and I wasn't sure I could trust him; his price on that tiny silk rug was exorbitant. I decided to ask Jamilah, my office mate, for advice. She'd lived in Istanbul a few years and was known as a shopping pro.

"Can you recommend a carpet dealer, Jamilah? I have a silk rug that I'd like to have appraised before I pay for it."

"What? You have a carpet you haven't paid for? How did you manage that?" Jamilah was a striking woman from Singapore, and I loved her sophisticated British accent. She listened wide-eyed as I explained how Mehmet had entrusted me with a carpet.

"It might be mercerized cotton," she said. "Some dealers pass that off as silk because it's shiny and bright, and they get a silk price for cotton. I know two reputable dealers in Sultanahmet, and I'll introduce you to them this weekend, if you like." I jumped at the chance. Maybe Jamilah would be the buddy I craved.

Saturday morning I re-rolled my carpet and hopped on the service bus to the city. We took the ferry across to Eminönü then rode the tram to Sultanahmet. The entire trip took a few hours. Our first stop was Harem 49, where I met Hüseyin Palyoğlu and his assistant Cemil. After a long chat over the obligatory cup of tea, I pulled out my treasure. "This is a nice carpet," Cemil said, running his hand across the nap, "but the shape is not even, and it's not a common size. It's worth four or even five hundred lira, but it needs to be blocked and reshaped a bit."

We got the same reaction from Erol at Adnan & Hassan in the Grand Bazaar. Both dealers felt the shape of the rug detracted from its value, and that it was a bargain at 400 lira but not worth $400 (about 520 lira). I thanked them for their kindness, admired their sumptuous displays, and marveled at Jamilah's wrangling over an elaborate tribal piece. She vacillated between intense interest and apathy, eagerness and refusal, and though Erol lowered the price considerably, she walked away with a shrug. It was all part of the game, which I found fascinating. Jamilah bought it the next Saturday—for even less.

When I got home that night I rummaged through my collection of business cards for Mehmet's phone number and called him on my new Turkcell phone. "*Efendim* (revered one)," he answered. "*Mehmet ici* (Mehmet here)."

"Hello, Mehmet. This is Ann Marie, the teacher from the Koç School. Do you remember me?"

"Ah, Ann Marie—how are you? How do you like your beautiful silk carpet? I was just thinking of you."

"I'm fine, thank you. The rug is beautiful, Mehmet, but..."

"How do you like Istanbul? How do you like teaching at the Koç School? It is a wonderful school, I know."

He persisted with friendly chatter, but I finally managed to explain that the shape of the carpet was a problem. I offered him 400 lira.

"What??? Your carpet is worth far more than $400, Ann Marie. How can you insult me like this?"

"I'm so sorry, Mehmet. I love the carpet, and I have some friends coming down to Selçuk over Ramazan. They can bring you the money."

"How can I take only 400 lira for a silk carpet?"

"If you can't sell it to me for that, my friends will bring you the carpet."

"Ann Marie! 400 lira! I need at least 450 lira. I cannot sell that carpet for 400. We agreed on $400!"

I was determined to hold firm, especially after seeing Jamilah in action. "I'm sorry, Mehmet. I don't want to cheat you, but I will only give you 400 lira."

He bullied and cajoled me, to no avail. I thought I'd be returning my lovely carpet, but he finally gave in. I was happy, and he had a sale.

Jamilah opened my eyes to the world of Islam. An intelligent, liberated woman, she was the only Muslim I knew well. She'd done her master's thesis on "Western Constructions of Middle Eastern Women," and her stern elegance brightened as we discussed all things Islamic: scarf wearing, fasting, women's roles, divorce, and Ramazan. Turkey has Ramazan, while the rest of the world has Ramadan; the Turks like to do things their way.

Muslims believe that Allah revealed the first verses of the Qur'an, the holy book of Islam, during the month of Ramazan. Throughout the month chanters recite the entire Koran in local mosques, one of its thirty divisions each day. It's a month of fasting during daylight hours; about a fifth of our students fasted.

My first "taste" of Ramazan had been a visit to the local bakery near sundown. Men were lined up waiting for the *iftar* bread, a huge round flatbread that comes piping hot from the wood-fired oven directly into their hands, crusty on top and soft inside. They carry it home for the *iftar* meal, which breaks their fast at sunset.

Traditional Muslims let nothing pass their lips during the day—not even water, cigarettes, or medicine. Some won't even lick a stamp or swallow their own saliva. Imagine. One evening I was on the mini-bus at sunset when the driver was sharing his *iftar* loaf with a man in the seat beside him. He offered me some as well, but I didn't want to short them on their long-awaited treat.

Jamilah fasted, too, from October 5th to November 2nd that year, and she helped me arrange a Saturday *iftar* meal for a group of friends visiting from America. I decided to fast that weekend with Jamilah. We checked into the Side Hotel (See-DAY) Friday evening and headed to Sultanahmet for the Ramazan festival, a 30-day fair on the

Hippodrome, a long park beside the Blue Mosque. About four blocks long and a block wide, the area was ringed with bright-colored booths offering food, tea, and souvenirs for a crowd of Muslims from across Turkey. Most of the women were scarved, and many men wore crocheted *kufi*—skullcaps. The makeshift restaurants teemed with people sitting on wicker stools at low wooden tables, waiting to eat. Undulating flute and oud (Turkish lute) music filled the air as well as barbecue smoke and the tantalizing odors of *döner* (spiced, skewered lamb) and kabobs.

Everyone was poised for the evening meal laid out before them, some sitting on the open lawn. Jamilah and I had purchased a loaf of *iftar* bread which we held unwrapped, ready to devour. After waiting all day long, this was big. The sky darkened as the call to prayer resounded from competing minarets nearby. Chatter hushed as everyone launched into their meal.

"Most people gain weight over Ramazan," Jamilah explained. "We get up before dawn to eat a hearty breakfast, then starve ourselves all day. Most people are so famished they eat more than normal then go straight to bed so they can get up to eat again before sunrise."

"And when it falls in the summer?" I asked. With Islam's 354 day calendar, Ramazan is eleven days earlier each year.

"It's misery. You eat at 9:30 at night, and again at 4:00 in the morning. It's a long time without food, and we get tired and weak. But we do it. Every time we have a hunger pang, we focus on our love for Allah. Difficult is good." I was relieved to be a heathen. Christianity requires few sacrifices.

Jamilah arranged for the hotel to deliver sandwiches to our room before dawn, a common Ramazan service. We woke at 5:30 to eat, then went back to sleep. We continued our fast throughout the day in spite of constant offers of tea from shopkeepers. That evening we met my six Minnesota friends at their hotel and walked them down to the Bahara Restaurant for our *iftar* meal. Tables were pre-set with heaping plates of salad, bread, olives (my great weakness), and hot lentil soup, which tantalized us as we waited for the call to prayer, hands folded in our laps. The restaurant gradually filled with Turks, who craned their necks to see our group of American tourists. A scarved woman at the next table caught my eye, smiled and nodded—her warmth touched me.

The room gradually hushed as sunset drew near, and at the first notes of "Ah-LAHHHH..." everyone dove in. The delicately-spiced *mercimek* (lentil soup) was thick and buttery. In fact, every flavor was ambrosia, enhanced by the long wait: smokey grilled kabobs, crisp-fried anchovies, and sautéed rice pilaf. Chatter in the room increased as the famished diners relieved their hunger, and by the time desserts arrived, we were too stuffed to take another bite. We found room, though, for the traditional tulip glasses of tea.

Our first vacation finally came. Şeker Bayram was three days of celebration at the end of Ramazan—three days of feasting and sweets. (*Şeker* is sugar and *bayram* is holiday.) School was called off for the long weekend, and my boarding students happily flew home to their families, whom they hadn't seen in months. Jamilah invited me to join a group of teachers for a cheap flight to Antalya, a picturesque city on the Mediterranean

A beach weekend sounded idyllic; Antalya brags 300 days of sunshine each year. Once we settled into our hotel, I yearned for a glass of wine, but since Jamilah didn't drink we had tea. I missed Polly.

My heart fell when we woke to drizzle the next morning. Once the rain abated, we walked the shore to Antalya's ancient harbor with a young family that was also staying in our hotel. We meandered ancient stone streets, stepping into shops carved from the old city's centuries-old stone walls. I was amazed at how often shopkeepers and shoppers would stop us to admire little Naomi and Madison. Apparently the Turks are nuts about babies. We strolled along the harbor, marveling at the gleaming wooden *gülets* (sailboats) with touts promoting their Mediterranean tours. Suddenly the skies opened, and we raced for cover under the roof of an open-air restaurant. Wind slashed through the restaurant even after the rain abated, and just when we'd decided to find an enclosed restaurant for lunch, a handsome blue-eyed man in a tweed jacket appeared with a pile of woolen pashminas to warm us. "This is typical in Turkey," Jamilah explained. "Their kindness is a trademark." How could we leave?

When Christine folded her pashmina into the stroller over Naomi, the man removed his jacket and placed it over her shoulders.

Our waiter, who was probably the owner, brought a tray of raw fish and prawns for us to select for our meals, and while we waited for them to be grilled, little Madison entertained us by shaking her head to jingle the coins on her new belly dancer cap. Warmed by complimentary Turkish coffees, we left content. The sun emerged to embrace us as we continued our explorations.

Later that afternoon we ambled back to our hotel, stunned at the majesty of snow-capped mountains jutting straight from the water beyond the beach. Imagine a Florida beach skirting the Rocky Mountains. We stopped to watch a sailboat glide across the water as the evening sun painted the vista in pinks and lavenders.

We joined the other Koç teachers for a mid-day cruise featuring a sumptuous grilled fish lunch off Duden Falls, and that evening we sought a recommended restaurant before our flight. A smiling woman with bobbed hair held the door for us as wait staff in white shirts, bow ties, and black linen aprons rearranged tables to accommodate the double stroller. As soon as we'd settled, our waitress asked, "May I hold your baby? She is too sweet!"

Christine nodded. "Of course." The woman lifted Naomi, cuddled her close, then walked away from the table to show her off to the staff, who kissed and cooed at her. I was dumbfounded.

"Don't worry, Ann Marie. They do this everywhere. We're used to it."

"Really. They just take them?"

Almost on cue, our waitress returned. "My friend works across the street. May I take her to there?"

Christine nodded and smiled. Never in America—but this was Turkey.

# 16 WHAT'S AN EDDA TOUR?

"There's an Edda Tour of the hans next Saturday, and I thought you might want to join me," Jamilah announced. "The tour is inexpensive, but it's early so we'd have to stay overnight in a hotel."

"So what's an Edda Tour—and what's a han?"

"You'll find out, and I promise you won't be disappointed." Jamilah's enigmatic communication was exasperating, yet she'd never led me wrong. I agreed to join her. We were growing closer, and it felt good to have a friend. I missed Polly's carefree abandon, and I have to admit I missed sharing a glass of beer or wine, but Jamilah was opening the muslim world to me, and I was fascinated.

"Edda's Tours are amazing," she began as we squeezed into seats on the busy Friday afternoon ferry. "She takes us through the back streets around the Grand Bazaar, sharing its history and introducing local artisans." We floated past the Sultanahmet mosque silhouetted against a mauve sunset as I envisioned a tall, stately tour guide with an authoritative air.

A half hour later we filed off the ferry with a thousand Turks, pushing our way down the stairs and through an underground bazaar —a wide tunnel choked with people and lined with shops selling discounted shoes, clothing, watches, and trinkets. Though it challenged my claustrophobia, I found the atmosphere exhilarating. Once again we stayed at the Side, our favorite hotel/pension. It was a sweet place, and the rates were reasonable.

When we met Edda the next morning, she was the opposite of what I'd imagined. A tiny, sprightly woman in her 60's, Edda sported a brilliant blue scarf, a jaunty knit cap, and a winning smile. She began our tour with historical background about the Çemberlitaş (burnt) Column.

"At one time this column held a huge golden statue of an Appollo-like Constantine. It fell in 1106 during a storm and crushed several passers-by to death. Constantine had a small church built at the foot of the monument with relics of the three dominant religions: Pallas's wooden statue represented paganism; the Hatchet of Noah and the stone from which Moses made water flow was for Judaism; and the remains of a loaf and a basket from when Christ fed the multitudes, the gown of the Virgin, pieces of the True Cross, and the Crown of Thorns all represented Christianity." I found that hard to believe but held my tongue.

Ten obedient sheep, we followed Edda's brilliant knit glove held aloft on an antenna-like pointer through the crowds. She shepherded us through cobbled back streets and courtyards into the Grand Bazaar, where she transported us to its inception 500 years ago. Standing in the oldest part of the bazaar, she pointed up at the intricate brick-domed ceiling, then described the ancient cabinet-like shopfronts that had once lined each lane below it. Edda described sumptuous fabrics hanging from the pillars, and how an auctioneer would urge bidders to higher and higher prices. I envisioned wealthy women in gilt draped garments followed by attendants carrying their purchases. Next she guided us into the Antique Bazaar where she pointed out a small minaret constructed over the stalls, and later to another easily-missed pulpit high on the wall over some shops. We learned that the Grand Bazaar's 75 acres hold numerous prayer rooms and small mosques..

Edda guided us through the bazaar and past its minuscule financial exchange—a crowd of businessmen talking on cell phones. Beyond it was the Çuhacı Han (Chew-HA-jee), where artisans crafted jewelry in gold. "This building houses 300 postage-stamp ateliers (workshops) as well as nine gold-melting forges and scores of wholesale outlets."

We learned that hans were ancient inns, complete with stone stairways and corridors, secret passages, and hidden workshops. Often built around huge courtyards with arched arcades on two or three levels, they offered temporary housing for merchants and artisans who plied their trades in the bazaar. Few people live in them today, but the workshops and storefronts have teemed with trade for centuries. Each han houses a particular craft, and Edda had friends in all of them.

She led us up a narrow stairway worn by hundreds of years of use, around an open balcony overlooking the courtyard, down a dark passage, through a creaking metal door, and into Kaya Değirmenci's tiny jewelry workshop. Eight goldsmiths perched around a workbench setting gems into rings, tiaras, and necklaces. Edda demonstrated how each piece was embedded into a waxen handle to make it easy to hold. Each worker had a leather lap-apron attached to the workbench to catch fragments of gold or gems that dropped. "The metal grid on the floor is there to keep people from walking off with gems or gold bits stuck to their shoes," Edda explained. "Every week the grid is taken up, the floor is swept, and the treasures are sifted from the dust. Nothing is wasted—the gold and silver bits are collected and melted down, and of course the gems go right back up on the workbench." Though the working conditions seemed cramped, Edda pointed out that it was a great honor to work near the Grand Bazaar.

Edda brought us through a silver han, a textile han, and too many others to list. My legs were weary as she led us  behind the bazaar, encouraging us to look up as we wandered. The cluttered street level shops were eclipsed by the splendor of ancient facades above them. I continued to marvel at Edda's energy as she stopped to point out each ancient building, toppling minaret, or birdhouse built into a han's outside wall.

She finished our tour with a ramble through the ancient Büyük Valide Han, the largest in Istanbul. "This was once a busy textile han, where 54 massive looms wove scarves, blankets, and linens. The booming looms were so loud, though, that the government shut them down, and now most of the upper stories are deserted." We followed Edda along a well-worn stone passageway and waited as a stooped, elderly man in a worn wool sport coat unlocked a massive door. We climbed up a circle of crumbling steps to emerge onto the han's multi-domed rooftop. There we were met by the noon call to prayer echoing from scores of minarets, a cacophony of *muezzins* competing with one another as we gazed out over Istanbul, enchanted by our view of the Bosphorus, the Golden Horn, and the Sea of Marmara.

This was Istanbul in all its glory.

# 17 THE HORROR OF EXAMS

My weekdays were full. I graded papers constantly, thankful for a schedule that allotted half my time for prep and meetings. I felt well-prepared for my classes and was able to return assignments within a few days. I doubt I've ever taught as effectively as I did in Turkey, and I reveled in the give-and-take of ideas at weekly team meetings. Though I sometimes felt like a dunce (How could they know so much about literature?), I reassured myself that my strengths were creativity and positive enthusiasm. It was the most stress-free teaching I've ever done. Well... until exams.

Turkish students took exams six times a year, and they were stressful. At Koç, all the students in a grade took the same English exam at the same time in their homerooms. Students would perch tensely at their desks with pencils and erasers at the ready, and once they received their papers, they dove in, writing and erasing furiously to beat the clock (usually 80 minutes). We supervisors watched vigilantly (they call it "invigilating"), as the pressure to cheat was monumental.

I've never liked exams, but at Koç I abhorred them, and grade moderation was daunting at best. "Let me explain the moderation process for you new teachers," Koray, our assistant English chair, announced at our eleventh grade meeting. "I'm going to give each of you a copy of three exams, but without student names. I've labeled them A, B, and C. You'll grade each exam using the attached rubric (guidelines), then we'll meet to compare grades and discuss our differences. Our goal is to agree on exactly what we're looking for and how we'll assess their writing—an absolute requirement in Turkey. You'll get used to it. And thanks."

I headed back to my office to grade the three essays, carefully noting strengths and weaknesses. Each essay received a grade for content, another for organization, and a third for language. I was confident I'd been fair.

The next day we tallied all our grades on a blackboard chart, and Koray computed an average for each category. Mine were consistently high. One essay received grades ranging from two to nine on organization, and I'd given it an eight. How could that be? We analyzed each essay item by item, debating what was reasonable to expect from second-language students, how much insight they should exhibit, etc. The assumption at the end of the meeting was that we were all on the same wavelength. Right.

In grading my own students' exams I strove to be harsh, constantly referring to the three samples as benchmarks. I read each exam twice, grading it first in pencil, then comparing it to the others. I spent twelve hours on 21 exams.

At least five exams from each class had to be reviewed by other teachers, especially those with particularly high or low grades or on a borderline between grades. This meant each of us devoted another five or six hours to reading other teachers' exams. By the time we'd finished, my head was spinning. It broke my heart to lower a grade, and I was thrilled when the reviewer supported my original assessment. (No one ever suggested that I raise a grade.) And I still faced two sets of ninth grade exams. UGH!

I believe in having students demonstrate knowledge and understanding through projects and presentations, but while in Turkey, I did as the Turks do. Grade and moderate, grade and moderate, grade and moderate. I'd had no inkling that grades were so momentous in the Turkish culture, especially in the more elite schools. Turkish families often sue over grades, so when John Richardson discovered that I'd let a ninth grader take her exam home to show her parents, he exploded. I had to run around the school to find her and take it back so we wouldn't be sued. Who knew?

Every single exam was catalogued and filed away in a warehouse at the end of the year. Unbelievable.

# 18 THAT INFERNAL LANGUAGE

Turkish both fascinated and daunted me, but I was determined to learn it. I'd devoted many hours to a manual called *Teach Yourself Turkish* before I moved to Turkey, but my progress was slow. I'm convinced Turkish is one of the most difficult languages in the world. At least it is for me.

Koç offered Turkish class two afternoons a week in an elementary classroom, and though our young teacher was darling, I was frustrated by her focus on grammar. My students cheerfully helped when I was stumped with homework, tickled at my efforts. In spite of that, though, they laughed uproariously whenever I spoke Turkish. It must have been nuances in pronunciation—differences I couldn't hear.

The Turkish *r* is slightly rolled (which I thought I'd mastered), and the difference between the *i* sound (what we would call a long *e*) and their *e* sound (our long *a*) were always confusing. Then there were the four more impossible letters: *u, ü, o,* and *ö,* which involved various contortions of the lips and tongue. I did my best.

One day while my ninth graders were reading *Romeo and Juliet*, I called on Eren, one of my more gregarious boys, to explain a passage. Before answering he said, "Ms. Mershon, my name is pronounced A-RAIN."

"A-RAIN," I repeated.

"No, it's A-RAIN!" What was this? Why was he smiling? Of course, Eren was usually smiling.

"I know. That's what I said. A-RAIN." I heard a few stifled giggles.

"NO!!! A-RAIN," Eren urged. "Listen to me and watch my mouth, Ms. Mershon. A-RAIN."

"A-RAIN," I repeated slowly, exaggerating my enunciation. A few students laughed. Was my pronunciation wrong or was Eren playing games with me?

"Aren't I pronouncing it correctly?" I asked the class.

"No!" they chorused, grinning. Could the whole class be in on a joke, or was I really not hearing the difference?

"You say it, Irem," I urged. Irem would be honest.

"A-RAIN," she said, her long-lashed eyes wide with anticipation as she awaited my response.

"A-RAIN," I repeated. Irem shook her head. Everyone burst into laughter. What could I do but join them? Once they'd quieted, I shrugged my shoulders and pointed at Eren without saying his name. "Young man...(more laughter)...Could you tell us who Romeo was in love with at the beginning of the play?"

Eren beamed. "Wasn't her name Rosalind?"

"That's right, but don't roll the *r*," I corrected. "Try again."

One afternoon my ninth graders launched into the classroom after lunch, laughing hysterically. "Can!" they screeched. "Can!" Baffled, I asked Batuhan what was so funny. (Remember that 'Can' is pronounced 'John' in Turkish.)

"Oh, Miss. You must look to Erdem's phone. It is too funny. Did you see new bins for recycling soda cans? We put Can inside and Ahmet took a photo." Was this so hilarious? I walked over to Ahmet, and as I looked at the photo, the boys burst into gales of laughter. The picture showed Can standing in a bin with the English word 'CANS' lettered across the front. I guess you had to be there.

"Very PUNNY," I said, seizing the opportunity to explain puns, assuming that even between languages Can (John) and CAN might be considered a pun. Were those kids fun or what?

Turkish places all the grammatical information at the ends of words, with the most crucial information consolidated into a verb (often with multiple endings) at the end of the sentence. Consider the word *kullanmiyorum*, which means "I don't use." The root verb is *kullan*, and it has three added endings: *mi* is the negative, *iyor* is the gerund form (-ing), and *um* is the first person singular ending. It's like saying "Forks, knives, and spoons during picnics I don't use."

Even worse, Turkish is a harmonic language, so in addition to the usual six verb endings (1st, 2nd and 3rd person, singular and plural), each of those six endings has four possible forms, depending on what vowels appear in the word. In order to get vowel harmony along with the right tense, you need to choose from 24 possible endings—and that's for EACH of the multiple endings attached to the verb. For instance, the *miyorum* at the end of *kullaniyorum* becomes *müyörüm* when the base verb is *gör*, 'to see.' Oh, my goodness.

To add insult to injury, the Turkish alphabet is slightly different from ours. They have 29 letters (with no Q, W, or X), but the good news is that each letter always makes the same sound. No need for spelldowns in Turkish classrooms—if you can say it, you can spell it.

I took Turkish nearly every year but never developed more than a rudimentary knowledge of the language, probably because most of my social contacts were at school, where we spoke English. Turks were always pleased with my attempts to speak their language, and my visiting friends were impressed, thinking I was fluent. Not so much.

# 19  FEELING FETED

How different my life was in Istanbul. I awoke each morning to a faint call to prayer, then walked Libby around the 200-acre gated campus, guarded round the clock. Even in November it was warm enough to sip morning coffee on my balcony as sheep bells sang through the air. My students spoke a language I was only beginning to understand, and I was finally making friends and enjoying an online romance. Life was good—at last. It was about time.

Another major change was how I was treated. In Turkey teachers are revered, unlike in America where we were more apt to be criticized than lauded.

When Mustafa Kemal Ataturk assumed leadership of Turkey in 1923, he made education a priority. The literacy rate was under 10%, and he made school mandatory for both boys and girls. Eighty years later, Turkey had nearly 90% literacy, and teachers mattered. On Teachers' Day I discovered a bright red gift bag on my desk—a thermal stainless coffee mug with my name engraved on its side. At home our P.T.A. gave each teacher a candy bar for Teachers Week. Woo-woo.

At 9:00 classes were suspended for a Teachers Day assembly, where each teacher received a red carnation, and the entire 40-minute program was devoted to us. Students congratulated me all day, often with hugs, and I got another carnation at lunch.

I was deeply touched by an e-mail from Director Tony Paulus, who wrote, "It has been said that the life of a child can be completely transformed by the influence of a teacher. Today we formally honor and celebrate you, but we do so understanding the importance of what you do every day of the year, and we thank you from the bottom of our hearts." I'd heard things like this before, but Tony's message brought tears. Maybe because in Turkey I believed it.

Parents treated us to a vast buffet of Turkish delicacies in the teachers' lounge, and at an English meeting we feasted on a three-layer cake filled with pudding, pistachios, and dark chocolate. I was dumbfounded.

The big event, though, was an evening gala. I'd been told it was a dressy affair, so I'd purchased a glittery top and actually spent time fixing my hair. Never mind that it took two luxury coaches over two hours to deliver us to the Hilton (Istanbul traffic)—we were jazzed! A receiving line of school administrators welcomed us to a cocktail hour with wine and hors d'oeuvres served by tuxedo-vested waiters. A five-course dinner followed with live music, dancing, and door prizes (stereos, TV's and cruises). Dressed to the nines, we 400 teachers and staff ate until near bursting, then danced with abandon, mostly to western music. When the orchestra played Turkish songs, the Turkish teachers went wild, jumping on chairs and beaming as they danced and sang along. How could I not love them? Cinderellas all, when the clock chimed twelve we fled the ball to our busses—classes would begin in eight hours.

In all my life I've never felt so feted, so valued, so full.

# 20 IMPROVISATION 101

"It's time to plan our Thanksgiving dinner," Marnie announced at our weekly baked potato potluck, and the wheels started churning. Dinner plans grew like loaves and fishes. I signed up to bring my two Thanksgiving favorites, olives and cranberry relish. Little did I know.

Olives were no problem. At the street market I purchased a selection of green, garlic-stuffed, and succulent black olives—for a song. I'm nuts about olives, and I wasn't having Thanksgiving without them.

Cranberry relish, on the other hand, posed a problem. We'd all learned to improvise in Turkey, so I rose to the challenge. A few weeks earlier I'd spotted cranberries in the market, but when I went to find them, I learned they were actually small cherries, and their season had ended. I'd have to find a substitute. What was red and sour like cranberries? Pomegranates! My favorite relish recipe is raw cranberries crushed with whole oranges and sweetened with sugar. I'd substitute pomegranate seeds and no one would be the wiser.

I bought two huge pomegranates and broke one open to unleash a fountain of scarlet juice. This would never do. I struggled to free the seeds from their white membranes, but the skirmish grew to disastrous proportions. My white countertop and I looked like the front lines of the Civil War. I stapled a plastic shopping bag to my shirt and continued to coax seeds free. It didn't look like enough, so I stirred in some tart cherry jam. It tasted odd, so I added sugar and lemon juice. Close, but not quite. I enlisted my electric hand blender to smooth it up a bit, and it disintegrated to a seedy juice. DRAT!

Now what? I set the entire concoction on the stove, added more sugar, boiled it like mad and prayed. I got jam.

Pomegranates: 1, Ann Marie: 0.

I swallowed my pride and called Evelyn, who'd mentioned she had some cranberries in her freezer. When I went to pick them up, I was tantalized by the smell of turkey roasting in their *lojman*. Next year I'd bake a turkey.

Marnie faced a similar battle with pumpkin pie. She'd had a friend smuggle in a pre-baked pie shell, and she'd make the filling from scratch. Unfortunately, Turkish pumpkins are hard as rocks. After battling one for hours, Marnie confided in a Turkish teacher who explained that she could purchase pumpkin already peeled and cut at the market. For brown sugar, unavailable in Turkey, she softened granulated sugar with grape molasses for her dark brown pumpkin pie, but who cared? It was delicious.

Nearly everyone improvised as we endeavored to recreate the American holiday, and the results were impressive. The Social Center was bursting with over 100 appropriately thankful revelers from across the globe. In spite of being an ocean away from family and friends with no football games in sight, I had a lot to be thankful for. I lived in a community of warm, caring people who supported each other's precious traditions.

And I went home with leftover turkey.

## 21 CHRISTMAS? HERE?

Autumn's grays transformed to brilliant December skies. I was thrilled with the sunshine, yet apprehensive about Christmas in this snowless Muslim world, away from family and friends. I missed the joy of a first snowfall, cookie-baking, hanging needlepoint stockings and decorating the house—oh, and the music! I always wrapped gifts to the strains of Mario Lanza and Mahalia Jackson.

This year I'd wrapped gifts in August and left them behind, so there was no need. I listened to Christmas favorites on my Mac, sweet even with its tinny speakers. "I'm so sorry you'll be away from family for Christmas this year," Annie wrote in an e-mail. As tears welled, I reminded myself that I'd chosen to live overseas. I'd be just fine.

With less than 2% of the country Christian, Turkey escapes Christmas commercialism, though some stores indulge in displays of Santa and snowflakes for New Year's. In school my students and I discussed important holidays for each of our cultures, and I read O. Henry's short story, "The Gift of the Magi," which brought me to tears, as usual. They seemed touched by the story and pleased to have Christmas Day off (a concession to a staff that was half foreigners, mostly Christian).

Teachers again mobilized to create Christmas. First was the cookie exchange. I managed to concoct gingersnaps with butter (no shortening in Turkey), boysenberry syrup (better than molasses anyway), and whole cloves pulverized in my coffee grinder (which was never the same). Mollie made chocolate-covered peanut butter balls, intoxicating me with their rich, buttery sweetness. I've made them every year since. Our bartender Şakir Bey built a roaring fire and converted the pool table to a cookie buffet. ("Bey" is a title like "Mr." that comes after a person's first name in Turkey.) Şakir Bey had become a treasured friend for those of us who frequented the Social Center. Not only did he serve us drinks and make the best French fries on the planet, but he coached us in the Turkish language. Since he and

I were both in our 50's, we shared the fond nickname *"genç arkadaşım,"* my young friend. Everyone adored Şakir Bey. Someone fixed mulled wine, and we sat around the fire sharing Christmas memories.

Friday evening was the big event: a progressive dinner, brainchild of Marnie Paulus. I'd come to love this career woman who resisted the traditional role of "Wife of the Director," yet took on this event to help us feel more at home. She was easily the kindest person on campus.

The evening commenced in the Paulus's luxurious sunken living room with hors d'oeuvres, mulled wine, and an instrumental ensemble of teachers who entertained us with jazzy renditions of "Jingle Bells" and "Winter Wonderland." Dan and Lisa (Canadians) topped off the evening with a spine-tingling performance of "Baby, It's Cold Outside." My contribution was chatting, applauding, and tipping a cup of mulled wine.

Our group of 60-plus soon progressed to Ayşe Kaftan's *lojman* for a holiday spread of hors d'oeuvres. She'd prepared a selection of Turkish delicacies to knock our socks off, including an unforgettable spicy chestnut spread. Christmas decorations abounded, and she had sprayed her windows with snowflakes. My heart swelled at the efforts of our beaming, round-faced Ayşe.

Our next stop was the Social Center for the main meal. Şakir Bey hosted us once again with a blazing fire, and red-berried centerpieces graced each table. Teachers supplied turkey, dressing, vegetables, relish, and potatoes. Just like home, only with an international crowd.

We were well behind schedule when we finally moseyed to Jale's *lojman* for desserts, a gift exchange and dancing. We enjoyed a mad bout of stealing each others' gifts; the gift of the hour being a ham and a bottle of maple syrup, neither available in Turkey. After four months without pork I lusted for that ham.

The next evening Terri and I took a service bus to Taksim for Midnight Mass at the Catholic church. Taksim, the old European area of Istanbul, boasts night clubs and Christian churches along its famed İstiklal Caddesi (Independence Avenue). Ornate wrought-iron fences opened onto the church's wide courtyard. The cathedral's high vaulted ceilings and ornately carved statuary took my breath away. I wished the stained glass windows had sunlight streaming through and decided to return some Sunday morning. As we pushed our way through the crush of worshippers I heard Turkish, Polish, English, French, and languages I couldn't identify. We found a spot to one side of the sanctuary, but the service was in Turkish and Polish. I didn't think God would mind too much if I ducked out early to explore midnight Istanbul. Terri stayed. İstiklal was packed with people, most dressed for a usual night on the town. I wondered if many even knew it was Christmas Eve. High across the wide pedestrian street strings of huge, glittering snowflakes glowed and—believe it or not—red Coke bottles. Though I was disheartened by the commercialism, the energy of the crowd was intoxicating. It was Christmas Eve in Istanbul!

On Christmas Day I invited friends for eggs Benedict and was invited to two Christmas dinners, both with ham. Score!

It felt like Christmas for at least those few days. I'd grown to love my Koç friends, and I gave and received a few gifts, but it was more about sharing a treasured holiday together.

Christmas did happen in Turkey.

## 22 NEW YEAR'S A LA TURKA

My friend Deidre flew from Germany to celebrate the New Year in Termal, a mountain spa across the Marmara that had been recommended by a BBC correspondent I'd met in August. She told me never to write an article about it, fearing tourists would destroy its ambiance.

Deidre and I had rediscovered each other at our 35th high school reunion, trading tales of divorce, travel, and English students; we had a lot in common, and she was a blast. I'd visited her in Oldenburg a few times, but this was her first visit to Turkey. She was touched by the warmth of the Turks, starting with a ferryboat waiter, a bow-tied and vested fellow who served our Turkish coffee with a flourish, a wink, and a grin. "Germans are so grim!" she complained.

A stout, balding bellman met us with a crooked smile at the door of the Çamlık, a once-elegant hotel in Termal. He carried our backpacks to our room and returned later that evening to help us with the television, clearly a ploy to visit. Who wants to watch Turkish TV? We offered him a glass of wine, though, and much to our amusement he accepted it, though he never sat down. Heck, it was New Year's Eve!

After he left, Deidre perused the spa brochure. "Every word in this piece is English, but the similarity to the English language stops there," she laughed. "Listen to this: 'Human being at antiquity believes that there are some powers on the steam and hot water coming from underground.' "

"It sounds like an essay from my worst ninth grader."

"Here's another one: 'It is possible becoming slim of obese patients. When the stimulant affect of the cure is combined with the exercise.' "

"Most of their patrons are Turks, so I doubt many native English speakers see this."

"Well, at least two," Deidre grinned. "And I imagine the others enjoy this brochure as much as we do—sort of a community service on their part." Though someone had done their best, the translation was terrible. I offered to edit it for them, but the manager declined.

Their dining room had been transformed to senior prom proportions for New Year's Eve. Fabric-draped chairs bore huge golden bows, and an immense candelabra with garish floral arrangements dominated each table amid more glittery bows. The entryway and dance floor were festooned with balloons, bows, and more flowers. Deidre laughed. "Well, prom date, lezzies forever!"

"When in Rome..." I answered, as we posed for a photo. We were the only foreigners. Waiters appeared with individual *meze* plates, an artful presentation of my favorites: smoked, garlicky eggplant, vegetables swimming in delicately spiced olive oil, tongue-tingling *ezme* (red pepper paste), and various mayonnaise salads. *Mezes* are my favorite, so I was stuffed before the meal. Who cared?

Our wine glasses were filled constantly, and we danced between courses to work it off. The main course was an assortment of grilled lamb, chicken, and sausage, served with rice pilaf and long roasted peppers, typical Turkish fare. A tumult at the next table caught my eye as their centerpiece burst into flames.

"Oh, my GOD!" I screamed.

"It's a Roman candle!" Deidre exclaimed, eyes wide. She stood to open the window behind us while I looked for the nearest exit. No one seemed bothered by the ruckus but laughed hysterically as they dodged sparks. The room filled with smoke, windows were opened to clear the air, and the band continued. Deidre and I shook our heads and took to the dance floor, which was filling for the midnight countdown. I was pleased that I could count backwards in Turkish: *On, dokuz, sekiz, yedi, altı, beş, dort, üc, iki, bir—MUTLU YILLAR!* Other dancers gave us cheek-to-cheek New Year's kisses, even a few of the men. I felt embraced by the entire crowd, who'd included us warmly.

"Are you about ready to call it a night?" I asked. My lids were heavy—a little embarrassing when the Turks were just revving up.

"Are you kidding? There's still Baked Alaska on the menu. How about if we wait a little longer? It should come soon."

My mouth watered as our waiter presented us with an ambrosia rainbow. I eased a bite onto my fork and slid it into my mouth, eager to savor the mingling flavors of Neapolitan ice cream, cake, and meringue. Deidre and I looked at each other wide-eyed, then broke into hysterical laughter, nearly wetting ourselves.

"I should have known that Turkey and Baked Alaska just aren't compatible," I laughed. "Their ice cream sucks." Turkish ice cream is a gooey cross between taffy and marshmallow creme, and their cake is usually dry. Put those together with yesterday's meringue, and you've got gooey-ice-cream-and-zwieback surprise.

*Mutlu Yillar!*

# 23 A DIABOLICAL SYSTEM

I abhorred the Turkish grading system. The last three weeks of school before semester break were devoted to review and exams—and stress. Turkish students lived for grades, and every single one had computed the exact grade he or she needed on the semester final to get their "target grade" for the term.

"Ms. Mershon, I need an 89 on this exam. Make sure I get it, OK?"

"Come on, Cem. If you need an 89, you need to study hard. Your exam grade is in your hands, not mine." The pressure was palpable, and I blamed the  system.

Turkish grades ranged from 0 to 5:

    5 = 85-100 percent
    4 = 70-84 percent
    3 = 55-69 percent
    2 = 45-54 percent
    1 = 25-44 percent (failing)
    0 = 0-24  percent (failing)

The problem with this system was that a student who earned 85% in class received the same grade as the student who earned 100%. Consequently, students "aimed" for the low end of a grade range. Even worse, some targeted a 45, the lowest passing grade. All they wanted was the prestige of a Koç diploma. Grades don't affect college entrance in Turkey, but the prestige of a high school does.

Between high school exams and the ÖSS (the college entrance exam), school was a living hell for many students. Every year they took at least ten courses, each with six exams.

After a week of pounding review and another of exams, students were free to watch movies in the auditorium. Well, some of them. The rest hung out in the halls—sheer bedlam. Students agonized over impending grades as teachers slaved over grading and moderation.

Fortunately, parents weren't allowed to communicate with teachers after exams, and students were banned from our offices. We sat diligent at our desks for hours—grading, grading, grading. It had to be right, or we'd be appearing in court.

Once grades were posted, we headed down the hall for a final department meeting to review the semester—and celebrate with an array of multi-layered cakes adorned with whipping cream, custard, pistachios, fruits and chocolate.

"Let's take a minute to see what people are up to over break," our English Chair suggested. Roger was a soft-spoken Canadian, a tall, slender man with thinning light hair and warm, blue eyes. I was surprised, yet waited curiously as we tipped back in our swivel chairs around the long tables. I assumed some of us would be going overseas for break.

Lisa spoke first. "Dan and I are going to Switzerland. We've never skied the Alps."

"We're going to Syria," Roger offered. "Lorraine has some photography shoots planned."

"Wendy and I are going to Micronesia to dive," Robert announced.

I was amazed. How many countries had these teachers visited? Was everyone traveling?

"Corinne and I are visiting the Hague," said Michael, a driven teacher who never slept more than five hours.

Jerry was next. "I'm flying home to Ireland," he announced in his endearing brogue. His tight smile indicated discomfort with sharing— he was a private man, probably about my age, though he looked older.

The list of destinations continued. "I'm heading to Paris with a friend...Egypt for a Nile cruise...flying to Crete for a week, then driving around Turkey...meeting friends in Italy. First Rome, then on to Florence and Naples... Barcelona to visit a friend at the international school there...a safari in Tanzania...Dubai."

"I'm flying home to Singapore to be with my mother," Jamilah said apologetically. It may not have seemed exotic to her, but it certainly did to me.

I had big plans as well. "I'm going to Japan to visit my AFS daughter and meet her family for the first time," I said. I didn't mention that I would rendezvous with Phil after returning to Istanbul. I wasn't ready to reveal my tentative romance.

"I have a reservation at an ashram in India."

Not one of the eighteen English teachers was staying on campus, and only a few were traveling in Turkey. I'd assumed travel would be a perk of international teaching, but apparently it was compulsory.

## 24 THE DREADED PINK SLIP

When a pink form appeared in my mailbox, all in Turkish, I hurried to Canan, our school's bureaucracy expert. I assumed I was in trouble. Sue, an elementary teacher, stood by Canan's desk holding a similar one. "Bad news, Ann Marie. You have a package at customs."

Horror stories surrounded customs. Terri had spent eight hours and nearly $500 picking up her laptop in October. After that debacle, the school started providing a driver to guide teachers through the process. We were advised to tell friends to ship only packages small enough for our mail slots.

"If you don't go soon, they charge storage fees, and they sometimes return packages. How about tomorrow afternoon?" This worked well, as we didn't have class on Friday afternoons. Canan gave us each two copies of our passports and residence permits and reminded us to bring the originals—and the pink notice. My goodness. Talk about overkill.

Patti joined Sue and me on the service bus with our favorite driver, Mehmet. (So many Mehmets in this country!) That 18-passenger van seemed wasteful for just three of us, but what could I say? The traffic was slow, but the sun shone as we chatted about our upcoming break.

"We're going to the job fair in Bangkok," Sue said. "We're bringing the twins, and after the fair we're staying at a beach hotel. I can't wait. All I want to do is sleep. Carmen is just getting over pneumonia, and I'm exhausted. I really don't have time for customs; I still have to pack."

We drove over an hour, only to find the building closed for lunch. We waited in the shade as chocolaty aromas wafted from a nearby factory. The doors finally opened, and the gathering crowd formed a somewhat-orderly line down a dark corridor flanked by glass-windowed cubicles, each with a large number taped to the glass.

The first stop was window number—gosh, I don't remember, but not number one—where they took my pink slip and my passport and rifled through boxes of similar pink slips, then handed everything back along with another paper. Off to window eight, at the far end of the building. Not a computer in sight.

I handed my new Official Notice to a man who took it and disappeared. Should I wait? Should I leave? I decided to hover like those around me. Behind the barrier I could see four or five workers who called out names one by one, none too loudly. I heard "Koc School" and hustled over to another window, where I was given yet another Official Notice and told *"Bir."* One.

I wandered the corridor hunting for window one. Mehmet recognized my confusion and led me to the far end of the hallway where a high counter was marked with the number one. When I got to the front of that line a scowling man checked my passport and residence permit, stapled the photocopies of my passport and residence permit to the Official Document, and gave me a third Official Form, which he stamped. *"Dokuz,"* he said. Nine.

Window nine was just across the hall. There were actually two windows, but a line had formed at the left-hand one, so I joined it. When it was finally my turn, a man rifled through my pile of papers then stapled, stamped, stapled, and stamped. He had me print my name, sign my name, and write my phone number on the back of one of the sheets. He indicated that I should move to the next window, where another man took my sheets, stapled them again and had me sign my name on another one of the pages. For good measure, I guess, he also stamped everything a few more times and charged me two lira (about $1.40). *"Sekiz"* he said. What? Window eight was my fifth window, and I'd already been there! This was the height of pointless bureaucracy. Curious about what package might be worth all this effort, I did as I was told.

Back down the hall, all the way to the first window I'd visited—no, the second. Anyway, there I handed over my multiply-stamped-stapled-and-signed Official Documents and received a package from home. Whew!

Sue and Patti weren't so lucky. There were discrepancies between the names on the packages (Sue and Patti) and the names on their passports (Suzanne and Patricia). The customs officials got nasty with Sue, who dissolved into tears. (Come on! She had a sick kid and was stressed about packing.) She had to start all over.

Patti saw what happened to Sue, so she wrote both forms of her name on all the sheets and snapped at the customs officials. They didn't hassle her. Sue's tears continued in spite of Mehmet's warm ministrations. The official at window *dokuz* handed her a tissue and smiled warmly, a rarity in bureaucratic settings.

Once on the bus, we unwrapped our packages. Mine, a Christmas gift from my family, had been investigated. The hand-crafted wooden jewelry box was broken (repairable), and I enjoyed rifling through its contents: candies, a book, hand-crafted earrings, and a squeeze toy and treats for Libby. Patti had also received Christmas gifts, which she opened with shrieks of pleasure. Sue's package from her mother in Canada was a pile of used magazines and a pair of socks. Tears spent, she giggled at the irony, and soon we were all laughing hysterically. All that anguish for socks and old magazines.

# 25  TOKYO VIA MADRID

The cheapest fare to Tokyo was on Air Italia via Madrid, flying west to go east. Oh, well. I spent my six-hour layover perusing some museums but finally got to Japan.

My first culture shock was Tokyo's airport rest room. The toilet seat was heated (downright cozy), and I waved my hand over sensors to flush it, run the faucet, get a squirt of soap, and dry my hands. Mayu, waiting outside customs, did her little run-shuffle to me, arms outstretched. "MOM!!!! MOM!!! I'm so happy to see you!" My heart swelled to see my darling bundle of enthusiasm.

"Oh, Mayu. I've missed you so much! I can't believe I'm finally in Japan." After an endless, tearful hug, we stepped into an elevator that spoke to us in a friendly female voice. Who knew Japan was so automated? We disembarked at Starbucks, joy of joys! I'll never outgrow my lust for strong coffee.

Cups in hand, we hopped a high-speed train, right on time. In Japan a 6:43 train arrives at 6:43. Always. People line up in orderly queues, a welcome change from Istanbul's free-for-all. "Mayu, everyone's staring at me. I'm a head taller than anyone—and so pale!"

"Don't worry, Mom. They're all jealous," she said. I tried to ignore the stares as we chatted through the rolling countryside south of Tokyo.

Once in Shizuoka we walked six sunny blocks to the Suzuki home, not at all what I'd expected. It was a western-looking two-story house with a heavy wooden door. Rows of coat hooks and tidy paired shoes lined the entry hall. Mayu's porcelain-faced mother, Naoe, met me with a bow and a broad smile. She spoke no English, so Mayu translated as we sat at a western-style table for a snack of green tea and odd-flavored jelly sweets. On one end of the room was a couch and television, and at the other end was a kitchen with cupboards different from any I'd seen. Each shelf had its own glass-fronted door with a latch. "So nothing falls out in an earthquake," Mayu explained.

There was a two-burner stovetop, a double sink, and long counters polished to a shine. Naoe cooked with only the two burners and a crock pot, though their family is upper middle class.

Mayu showed me to the far end of the living area, where she opened sliding doors to a raised platform covered in woven rush mats. The only furniture was a low, square table at its center. "We'll eat dinner there," Mayu said. "This is our traditional Japanese table." Their home embraced both modern and traditional, upstairs as well as down. The girls slept on wooden beds, while across the hall their parents used futons on a woven rush floor. I slept in the girls' room, where the bed was comfortable but the hard buckwheat pillow was a challenge.

Mayu led me to the shower, yet another adventure. Inside a tiled room a deep, square stainless steel tub sat beside an open shower—no stall. Mayu showed me how to set the  temperature to 42 degrees (108.6 F.), and the temperature was perfect the minute I turned it on. An anteroom held a sink, mirror, towels, and a vanity. No toilet. The toilet was in its own room at the end of the entry hall. It had a heated seat, which Mayu said was necessary because they didn't have central heat. I loved it.

When we gathered for dinner, I was relieved to find an open cavity under the low table with a heater to warm our feet as we devoured a tantalizing meal of rice, stir-fried vegetables, and teriyaki beef. Naoe was an exceptional cook, and both Mayu and her sister translated for us through the meal.

After a week with her family, Mayu and I took a high-speed train to Kyoto. I never touched a door, a toilet seat, or a faucet on the train, my every need anticipated by automatic sensors. It was a relief to see human stewards come through with food and beverages, bowing as they entered and exited each car. I was charmed by Japan's clean, serene and respectful culture.

Our Kyoto hotel room was also fully automated. Everything electric worked from a bedside console, and the toilet had adjustable heat, a built-in bidet, and a temperature-adjustable dryer with an additional feature: a button that played a recording of a toilet flushing to mask anatomical orchestrations. (If I seem obsessive about the toilets, it was because they blew my mind.)

I was dumbfounded by the splendor of the temples and shrines of Kyoto. Each had its own personality, it's unique style of gold plating, brightly-painted ornamentation, and fantastical creatures sculpted into rooftop cornices. We saw golden Buddhas and many-limbed gilt maidens in every temple. The meticulously tended gardens, pools and lakes mesmerized me, but I was most awed by the Japanese reverence for aged trees, whose sagging branches leaned on massive wooden crutches.

When we returned to Shizuoka, Mayu's father arranged a farewell dinner at their favorite sushi restaurant. Mayu, Naoe and I were the first to arrive, so we settled into captain's chairs at the seaside bar. The white-coated bartender brought us clear glass bowls of raw snails— oversized slugs straight from a broccoli patch.

My stomach churned at the thought of chewing those slimy monsters. "I'm so sorry, Mayu, but I don't think I should eat these. I'm allergic to calamari, and I think I may also be allergic to snails."

"Are you sure you don't want to try just one, Mom?" Mayu said, popping a corpulent snail into her mouth.

"I'm really afraid to, Mayu. I'm so sorry. Here—you and your mother share mine." (So generous.) Mayu smiled as she tipped a few into her mother's cup and took the rest. They relished each bite, and I shuddered as I anticipated the next courses.

Mayu's father, aunt, uncle, and grandmother soon joined us. Her grandmother was the tiniest adult I'd ever met; her head came just above my waist. At 86, she'd given up her weekly mountain hikes but was still sharp and had a wide, embracing smile. I instantly understood why Mayu adored her. I did, too.

Our private dining room had a long, low table surrounded with fat cushions. I sat between Mayu and her grandmother, and Mayu interpreted. Tray after tray of artfully arranged raw sea creatures were passed around. Mayu explained what each was, and the only thing I passed up was calamari. I even tasted the eel, which had a hint of a smoky flavor. My favorite was Toro, tuna belly meat. It was all scrumptious.

On our way to the airport, Mayu grinned in eager anticipation as she asked, "What was your favorite thing in Japan, Mom?" Was it the shrines? The temples? Mount Fuji? The food? The technology?

"Oh, Mayu. Everything was wonderful, but my favorite is your family. They're warm, wonderful people, and I love them all—but especially you. I can't wait to show you Istanbul."

She'd be arriving in a week for a month-long tour of Turkey.

I was running late, and of course Murphy's Law prevailed. I shivered by the school gate twenty minutes waiting for the mini-bus, then another twenty for the train in Pendik. So much for my sunny winter. As I paced away another 25 minutes waiting for the ferry across the Bosphorus, my stomach churned. Was I out of my mind? Would Phil even be there? It was zero hour. I prayed that he'd found his way to the Halı Hotel, where I'd reserved two rooms.

Heart pounding, I checked in and instead of waiting for the elevator raced up the three stories to Phil's door. I paused, unsure. I was about to meet a man I knew intimately yet had never seen, never touched, never kissed. Butterflies flitted from stomach to throat as I reached to knock. The door was opened by a tall man in a dark turtleneck and navy sweat pants. His rosy, beaming face and warm blue eyes registered relief. "Oh! You're here! You actually CAME!"

At that moment I knew I could love this man. I caught my breath. "I'm so sorry I'm late! It took me four hours to get here— two more than I'd planned!"

"You have no idea how glad I am to see you," he said with a gentle smile. "You're even more beautiful than your pictures. Please, come in. I was just figuring out how I'd manage a week alone in Istanbul. There's plenty to see here, and now I have you to discover it with!" He placed a hand on my back to guide me into the room, prudently leaving the door ajar. I perched on the edge of the bed as he settled in a worn wicker chair, reaching for his tour book and a city map. Well-prepared, I thought. Good.

"Do you need to rest up first?" I asked.

"No, I won't waste precious time napping. What's the easiest thing to see before dinner?"

"The Blue Mosque is just a few blocks away, and I know a cozy restaurant nearby."

Phil beamed, the warmth in his face easing my anxieties. "That would be wonderful."

I dropped my pack in my room, and Phil held my hand in the crook of his arm as we headed out into the late afternoon chill. How long had it been since I'd walked arm-in-arm with a man? It felt glorious.

"I expected that the Blue Mosque would be blue," I chattered, "but the name is really about the hand-painted ceramic tiles that cover the walls and columns inside. Sadly, there are usually more tourists than worshippers."

"I read that it's the only mosque in Istanbul with six minarets. It was built 400 years ago by Sultan Ahmet," Phil informed me. "Do you know much about the sultans?"

"Not really. I know it's a relatively new mosque, especially compared to the Haghia Sophia across the park. Isn't that about 1000 years old?"

"That's what I most want to see, but I want to devote a half day to it," Phil said as we climbed the marble steps into the mosque's courtyard. The sky cast a pink glow over its white marble walls and minarets as hooded and scarved visitors scurried along the courtyard's criss-crossing sidewalks.

Once inside, Phil was astounded at the cascading domes of the softly-lit interior. It wasn't crowded, and the hushed atmosphere offered welcome peace as we pondered the monumental structure. Reddish light streamed through stained glass windows on the far side of the sanctuary. The room's vast red carpet was divided it into hundreds of small rectangles, each awaiting a supplicant.

We refused the advances of over-friendly carpet dealers as we left the mosque and walked to the Rumeli Restaurant, named after the famed medieval castle beneath the Bosporous bridge. The only patrons dining so early, we nestled into a table beside the arched stone fireplace, basking in the fire's warmth as we shared a bottle of red wine, a few *mezes*, and a plate of chicken shish-kabob. We reveled in each other's company oblivious of the cellar's brick decor and historical hangings.

"I'm sorry for yawning," I apologized. "It's not your company."

"We both have jet lag. It's probably time to head back, though I could sit here with you forever."

After a friendly farewell chat with our waiter, we strolled arm in arm back to the hotel, where Phil saw me to my door. I felt like a girl on her first date. Phil wrapped his arms around me. "Thanks for a beautiful evening." Then he kissed me.

I slept well that night, swirling in fantasies of this wonderful man. How odd it all was. How fun. How adventurous.

The next morning we woke to a winter wonderland—a blizzard. Snow was rare in Istanbul and would bring the city to a grinding halt. The hotel had central heating, but the water in the radiators had cooled by the time it reached the glassed-in restaurant on the top floor. Phil and I huddled in winter coats caressing our coffee cups as we nibbled a cold breakfast of tomatoes, cucumbers, olives, bread, and cheese, marveling at the spectacular view of Istanbul's snow-topped domes. I was pleased that Phil was accepting rather than furious about the cold.

The blizzard whirled around us as we shuffled through snow-filled streets, watching shopkeepers clear their walks with dustpans and short brooms. Orange-vested street workers labored diligently to clear the sidewalks with twig brooms as snow accumulated behind them.

"I think I'll start a snow shovel business here. I could import the foldable ones and make a fortune," I said.

"I thought it seldom snowed here," Phil replied.

"Well, I'd just set them aside until it did. Might not be a big seller, though."

Grinning snowmen appeared outside every restaurant—each more elaborate than the last, its short life a tribute to the city's fascination with snow. We wandered Sultanahmet's streets in search of treasures, targeted by every carpet dealer and tout we passed. I taught Phil to say "*Hayir.*" No.

We ducked into a cozy restaurant near the Spice Bazaar and wolfed down steaming bowls of *mercimek*, Turkey's rich lentil soup. Served with fresh lemon wedges and crusty bread, this thick, buttery dish was perfect for a snowy Istanbul day. The blizzard had calmed down by the time we arrived at the Haghia Sophia, where a short, elderly man approached us. "I would be happy to offer my guide services in English if you're interested."

"How much would it cost?" Phil asked (Ah, a careful spender!) I wondered if he lacked spontaneity, then decided it might be a good balance for my impulsiveness.

"Normally it's thirty lira each (about $21), but things are slow, so I will guide the two of you for forty." How could we resist?

A retired teacher with impeccable English, he immediately launched into a detailed and involved history of this famed edifice, often sited as one of the seven wonders of the world. He showed us the footings of the original cathedral from the sixth century.

Peppering his presentation with questions, he expertly fielded Phil's many queries. "How long did it take to build?" "Who was the sultan when it was converted from a cathedral to a mosque?" "Who is paying for the renovations?"

He sat at a mammoth egg-shaped marble fountain on the main floor to demonstrate ablutions, showed us how to make a wish at a marble column, then led us upstairs to see the famed gold mosaic of Jesus, whose eyes followed us as we walked.

"Do you know what this is?" he asked, pointing to etchings in the marble railings.

"They look like a cross between hieroglyphics and Nordic runes," I posed.

"Right! They're graffiti carved here by the Vikings. That's how old these railings are. And it also shows what an important center of commerce Constantinople was even in those times."

Three hours sped by, and as we headed outside, he said, "Let me take your photo. Is this an anniversary trip?"

Phil smiled. "Well, it's an anniversary of sorts." Yup. Our one-day anniversary. Each of us pressed a 50 lira bill into his hands—more than twice his fee, and he deserved every kuruş (cent).

Istanbul improved with a sweetheart. We snuggled together for an afternoon snooze before finding a quiet restaurant for our second dinner together—happy but exhausted.

*  *  *

The next morning at breakfast Phil took my hand. "I know it's a lot to ask in this weather, but would you go to Yedikule with me? Have you ever heard of it? It's where the janissaries, the sultan's soldiers, executed Sultan Osman II, and I'm dying to see it."

"I've never heard of it, but I'm game. Let's get directions and head out." Phil grinned and leaned in for a breakfast kiss. Gosh, he was endearing.

We found a taxi driver who knew where the Yedikule Fortress was, though the route was snow-covered once we left the main road. The entry to the castle hadn't been cleared. "Do you think it's open?" Phil asked.

"*Beklemek, lütfen,*" I said to the driver in my pathetic Turkish, holding out my hand in a gesture that indicated waiting. He nodded and turned off his engine.

"I'll check," Phil said, climbing out of the cab and tromping through the snow to the gate. He signaled for me to come along, so I paid the taxi and sent him off. A young soldier huddled over a gas burner in a tiny glassed-in office, and I did my best to communicate with him.

"*Kaç para?*" How much money?

"*İki lira,*" he said. ($1.40)

Phil paid, and he waved us on. We stepped into a vast, white-blanketed courtyard and traipsed through the deep snow around the perimeter, pushing open heavy doors to peer into cavernous dark rooms.

"Want to climb the ramparts?" Phil asked. The snow-piled stone steps had no railings, which made it all the more exciting.

"Sure—you lead." The climb was precarious at best, but well worth the panorama. We could see the old city walls climbing the hills around the city. Beyond the walls Istanbul buzzed with activity in spite of its snowy blanket. Phil took my hand. "I don't know any other woman who would have hazarded that stairway, Ann Marie. You're amazing."

"Hardly. I miss challenges in this city. All I ever get to do is walk, walk, walk."

As Phil filled me in on the history of Yedikule, I tried to focus, but it was a lot of names and information to absorb. The guard accosted us at the bottom of the stairs.

"Oh, dear. I'll bet we weren't supposed to be up there."

"Well, there's nothing he can do about it."

"*Problem var mi?*" I asked. (Is there a problem?)

"*Hayir,*" he answered, then assuming I spoke Turkish, he rattled on.

"*Anlamadım,*" I said. (I don't understand.)

He motioned for us to follow him, which we did. He unlocked and opened a heavily-studded door, hit a light switch and led us up a long stone stairway.

"I'll bet this is where they executed the sultan's son," Phil said. "That's what this castle is famous for."

Our guide stepped into a small dungeon-like room where he pantomimed putting on shackles and pointed to where they'd been chained to the wall. Then he brought us up more stairs to a wide platform on the ramparts and pantomimed strangling himself.

"See? It's exactly what I thought. This is the place. Wow! And without a word of English." Phil nodded enthusiastically as our guide explained in Turkish, Phil interjecting his own commentary in English. These two men communicated, each in his own language, neither understanding the other, but sharing their enthusiasm about this nugget of history, an event that changed the course of Turkish history.

"I'm freezing," I said as we headed back down.

"Me, too. I've seen enough," Phil agreed.

"Let's ask him to call us a taxi," I suggested, though I didn't know the right words. "*Taxi var mi?*" I asked. Is there a taxi?

He nodded and welcomed us into his tiny office, where he poured two paper cups of hot water and stirred in instant cappuccino. Heaven. Phil wasn't a coffee drinker, but he accepted the cup eagerly, just to warm his hands. When our taxi arrived, Phil tried to tip the guard, who shook his head and said "Turkish hospitality," his first English words.

That night we feasted on *mezes* and grilled lamb, *köfte* and chicken at the Hamdi, one of the best-known meat restaurants in Istanbul. My second pleasure that evening was a midnight visitor. "What took you so long?" I asked as I welcomed Phil to my bed. Not just sweethearts, but lovers.

Oh, heaven.

# 27 SHARING PHIL

At breakfast we discussed Mayu's arrival that afternoon. "It'll be hard to share you with her," I admitted. I didn't mention that sharing a room with Mayu would also end our intimacy, but we both knew it. My stomach flipped as I considered. Could I be falling in love? We'd been together only a few days, yet I hadn't been this happy in years.

We toured Topkapi Palace that morning, then Phil relaxed with his Ottoman history book while I took the tram to meet Mayu at the airport. Though we'd just seen each other, I was eager to introduce her to my new world.

"Oh, Mom! I'm so excited to be here!"

"I know you'll enjoy Turkey, Sweetie, and I think you'll like Phil, too. He's a gem."

"Oh, Mom. If you like him, I'm sure I will, too."

That was an understatement. Mayu adored Phil, and the feeling was mutual. The Halı Hotel had given us a great rate, but BRRRRR!!! Our window didn't close tightly, and frigid winds whistled into our room. After shivering all night, Mayu and I moved down to the second floor, which was actually warm. Phil stayed where he was; his windows latched tight.

We woke the next morning to another blizzard. It was blowing too much to measure, but we must have had over a foot of snow. The few shops that were open featured a Welcome Snowman, and both touts and waiters hurled snowballs at their compatriots outside nearby businesses. It's apparently contagious—Mayu and Phil ended up in a battle with them. We showed Mayu the sights of Sultanahmet, Phil an engaging and enthusiastic guide. Seeing him interact with Mayu made him all the more endearing.

Thursday morning we headed out to find an internet cafe, a formidable task in a city that had shut down. The first four were closed, but we finally found one up a dark, circular staircase. Though it felt onerous, the lights were on. The owner stood beside us chatting incessantly in halting English, but he gave us a deal: $3 for three cups of tea and an hour online.

"Mayu! My break is extended another week because of the weather!"

"That's great, Mom. What will you do with it?"

"How about if I come to Antalya with you? We'll fly down so you don't have to take the bus." Winter flights were cheap. I was low on funds, but I had a credit card, and the Antalya sunshine beckoned.

Friday morning we were relieved that the Marmara ferries were running after being grounded by the storm; I wanted to show Mayu and Phil the charms of Termal. When we arrived, the mountain spa village lay silent under its winter coat—nearly two feet of snow. Beside an open hot-springs pool, the 500-year-old domed *hamam* (Turkish bath) winked down at us, its scalloped windows graced by eyebrows of white snow. We lollygagged through two idyllic days meandering the woods and walkways along the river, scrubbing ourselves in the *hamams*, and basking in the steamy outdoor pool. It couldn't have been a better time to experience the hot springs. We were finally WARM, WARM, WARM! And the soap massages were, well...WOW! After my massage, I warned Mayu, "If he tries to massage your chest, cross your arms over yourself and say, *'Hayir!'* "

"O.K., Mom,"

"What was that about?" Phil asked.

I explained that the massage therapist, though very skillful, had focused unduly on my breasts. I hadn't minded all that much, but I was quite sure Mayu would. The man either viewed Western women as loose or just wasn't getting enough at home. Phil encouraged me to complain at the desk, but since this tourist *hamam* was a man's world, I didn't want to make waves. Mayu emerged from her massage wilted.

"How was it?" I asked.

"It was great—except I didn't say *'Hayir*," she admitted, blushing.

I hugged her. She seemed just fine, though Phil's brows furrowed. "I still think we should complain."

"Feel free," I said, grabbing my towel. "Let's hit the pool again." We floated in the outdoor pool as the sky darkened, snowflakes floating down through the mist to sting our upturned faces.

Once we returned to campus, I put Mayu in the small bedroom so I could sleep with Phil one last time. I donned my sexiest nightgown, and though it felt odd with Mayu in the next room, our mutual desire won out.

"Shhh..." I whispered. "We have to be quiet." We could have won an award for hushed lovemaking until the silence was shattered by a huge crack and a CRASH! The entire bed collapsed. We froze, breathless—still as statues.

A tentative voice called from the next room. "Mom? Are you OK?"

"I'm fine," I answered airily, then Phil and I broke into red-faced hysterics. So much for secrecy.

I couldn't stop thinking about Phil. He was a kind, positive man, and he'd been a saint with Mayu. How many men would be willing to share a new lover, especially after flying across the ocean to meet her? How could I be so lucky?

Mayu, Libby and I arrived at the Hadrianus Pension well after midnight, exhausted. A diminutive man with gray hair sat in the office watching television. He leapt to his feet when he spotted us. "Welcome to Antalya! My name is Nazıh, and I'll be your host. I'm sorry your plane was delayed, but it happens often. Let me show you to your room." Perfect English. Great.

Nazıh led us through a garden-like courtyard and into a whitewashed entryway decorated with carved antiques and woven wall hangings. Our room was upstairs, twin beds covered in sheer pale green fabric embellished with sequined embroidery. Nazıh pulled out a big, square pillow, which he placed on the floor. "For your dog. Unless she wants to sleep in her carrier." The message was clear. No dogs on the bed.

"Thank you—I'm sure she'll choose the pillow over her case," I said, knowing she'd opt for my bed. What Nezih didn't know wouldn't hurt him—she didn't shed.

"Good night," he said. "Breakfast will be whenever you get up. You're my only guests." We were asleep in seconds.

We woke around nine and wandered into the garden, a grassy courtyard with mosaic stone paths meandering among trees, flowers, and funky statuary. Orange, cherry, and lemon trees offered shade, but we wanted sun. The air was cool but heady with the scent of citrus blossoms.

"Good morning, Ann Marie and Mayu!" Nazıh chirped as he stepped from the office. "Did you sleep well?"

"Yes, thank you."

"And we're really hungry," Mayu added. "Where is the breakfast room?"

Nazıh grinned. "You can eat inside if you want, but I recommend the garden. We'll move a table into the sun by that stone wall, where you'll be protected from the wind. I think that would be best."

"Sounds great," I agreed. Mayu, not yet recovered from the blizzard, looked doubtful. "If it's too cold for Mayu, may we move inside?"

"Of course. In fact, I have something that will help. Excuse me... Ilhan and Şoat!" he called, giving instructions in Turkish before hurrying off. Two young men lifted an already-set table from the shaded patio and placed it on the sunny lawn. We'd just settled when Nazıh returned with a heavy woolen shawl that he arranged over Mayu's shoulders. Libby settled at my feet, and we all basked in the warmth of the Mediterranean sun. And yesterday we'd been in a blizzard!

"The orange juice is from this tree," Nazıh informed us. Glasses of fresh-squeezed juice were accompanied by sliced tomatoes, cucumbers, cheese, olives, bread, and eggs. And coffee—I could never get enough coffee, and theirs was delicious.

Nazıh joined us at the table each morning, and we grew fond of him. A retired army general, he was passionate about the history and culture of Turkey. Phil would have been picking his brain. "How much Turkish do you know?" he asked Mayu when he learned she'd be traveling on her own.

"I know *merhaba* (hello), *tuvalet* (toilet), and *sao* (a short version of thank you). Not really very much."

"You must learn more Turkish words and phrases. I'll teach you the ones you'll need to get around." Thus began daily language lessons. Each day Nazıh wrote out a new page of words for Mayu to learn and worked with her on pronunciation. He was a harsh taskmaster for me, too, forcing me to converse with him in Turkish a few minutes each morning. It was hard, but my Turkish improved. By the end of our week, Mayu was calling Nazıh her *Türk Baba* (Turkish Papa). In all my travels, I'd never been treated so warmly. We felt like family.

On our last day I arranged a guided tour of Termessos, the ancient city of ancient cities. Built high in a difficult pass between two mountains, it was beyond the reach of even Alexander the Great, who determined it was unconquerable. Without the threat of invasion, Termessos became a highly cultured city with sophisticated water and sewage systems, a marble mountaintop amphitheater, and countless other amenities. Marble rubble lay everywhere. "How did they get all this marble up here?" I asked our guide.

"You'll see soon enough." I felt put off, but his accounts of the city were so fascinating that I soon forgot. As we hiked back down the mountain, we came across numerous tombs—marble sarcophagi, some carved directly into the mountain. Mayu and I climbed into one for a photo.

"This is the answer to your question, Ann Marie," Kemal announced.

"Oh, my God! Part of the mountain is marble!"

"No. The entire mountain is marble, as are many of the mountains in this area. You live near the Sea of Marmara, don't you?"

"Yes, I do."

"Marmara is 'marble' in Turkish, and we have it everywhere."

That night as we bid Nazıh farewell he gave us each a shiny Ataturk pin and handed Mayu a new Japanese/Turkish dictionary. "I've arranged Mayu's bus ticket to Bodrum," he said as we shared the two-cheeked Turkish kiss that was now second nature to me.

Mayu and I went our separate ways, warmed by our beautiful week in Antalya.

# 29 DISTRESS OF THE INTESTINAL VARIETY

Mayu returned to Istanbul beaming two weeks later. "Mom! Everywhere I went they took such good care of me. I was the only person at one hostel, and for five dollars a day they fed me all three meals, I got any bed I wanted, and they took me horseback riding every day. It was so fun, Mom! I love Turkey!"

I wanted to show her more of the city that last weekend, so I booked a room at the AND Hotel. I asked my young friends Aşkın and Soner to join us on Saturday, two energetic young men who would brighten her experience.

I'd met Aşkin and Soner through a fellow teacher who taught English to adults. He'd asked for teachers to help them practice their English by letting them serve as as free tour guides, and Terri and I were the only ones who'd signed on. We'd been rewarded with fun-filled hours banging around the city with two delightful engineering students. They didn't mind that we were older than their mothers; in fact, they seemed to adore us. Aşkin (osh-KEEN) was a tall, lanky fellow with doe-eyes and a permanent grin. His best friend Söner (sew-NAIR) was shorter and quieter, but he spoke better English and his long-lashed eyes crinkled at the edges when he smiled. They were great friends, bickering like a pair of old queens. Aşkin, Söner and I treated Mayu to a whirlwind day, chatting up a storm as we rode the tram across the Bosphorus and the *Tünel* cable car up to Taksim, a trendy shopping street above İstiklal. The boys adored Mayu, and the feeling was clearly mutual. I was tickled.

First we hit French Street, a Paris-like tourist spot, where we enjoyed an overpriced cup of coffee, warming our fingers and toes in the process. After that we toured a few museums and hot spots of the city that Söner and Aşkin recommended. In spite of waves of stomach cramps, Mayu insisted on continuing through dinner and a cozy night club, but at about 11:00, she hit a wall. The boys helped us get a taxi, and Mayu and I returned to the hotel.

"Are you OK, Mayu?" I asked as we pushed into the lobby.

"I'm fine, Mom, but I think I'll go to the hospital after you leave tomorrow. There is a problem in my stomach." She was paler than pale.

"Oh, no you won't. We're going right now." The concierge arranged a taxi to the nearest hospital, where we followed arrows on the floor to a queue of patients in what appeared to be a triage line. I assumed it was a public hospital, as we passed people waiting on chairs along its dreary hallways.

As we stood in line to speak with the triage physician, I coached Mayu on English terms for stomach ailments, looking them up in my Turkish-English dictionary. A young man behind us said, "Excuse me, but I heard your conversation. Would you like a Japanese translator? My cousin speaks Japanese. I'll call him on my cell phone, and he can translate for you."

"Oh, yes!" Mayu responded, managing a smile.

When we reached the front of the line, the man handed Mayu his phone. She explained her problem in Japanese, listened a moment, then closed the phone and stepped away from the desk.

"What's happening?" I asked. "Why didn't you give the phone to the doctor?"

"He's coming to translate in person. He says he's not far away." Only in Turkey. We let others move ahead in line as we waited for our interpreter, who was there in ten minutes.

"Hello, my name is Mehmet," said the stocky young man as he shook my hand. Yet another Mehmet.

"I'm Ann Marie, and this is Mayu," I said. He spoke to Mayu in Japanese, and they approached the desk. Mayu's face relaxed as he translated her Japanese into Turkish for the doctor. "The doctor prescribed this medication," he explained, handing me a slip of paper. "You can pick it up at a 24-hour pharmacy."

I thanked him repeatedly as we left the building together. "Do you know where I might find a taxi?"

"Why don't I just drive you to the pharmacy? It won't be far, and you can catch a taxi from there."

"Are you sure?"

"Of course," he replied gallantly. "Turkish hospitality."

Though I know better than to climb into cars with strangers, this was a no-brainer. We climbed into his Mercedes. It took a while to find a pharmacy, and we learned his story on the way. Mehmet had fallen in love with a Japanese girl in Istanbul, married her and moved to Japan. When they divorced after five years, he returned brokenhearted and found a job as translator for the Japanese firm digging a subway tunnel under the Bosphorus. He and Mayu chatted amiably in Japanese, Mayu occasionally translating for me, though he was also fluent in English. When we finally found an all-night pharmacy, Mehmet went in to translate, explaining to Mayu how the medications were to be taken. We thanked him once again and headed off to hail a taxi.

"One moment," he said. "Where do you live?"

"We're staying in Sultanahmet—at the AND hotel."

"That's the hotel where our Japanese executives stay! I live near there and would happily drive you, if you don't mind."

"If we don't mind?" Who was he kidding? This was too much to believe, but who cared? "That's wonderful, Mehmet. Are you sure it's not an imposition?"

"Of course not. I'm happy to oblige."

"How can we ever repay your kindness? Can I buy you a late-night dinner, or at least a beer?"

"I don't drink, and I ate long ago. You can buy me a cup of tea, though." Tea in the middle of the night? Well, why not?

Mehmet pulled up to a security gate beside the Marmara. He spoke with the guard, parked, and walked us across a vacant parking lot beside the water. Within moments a man hurried over with a low table and three stools, which he placed on the waterfront. Stars glinted off the surface of the Marmara, dancing in the crisp midnight air as the lights of Kadiköy blinked at us across the sea. We pulled our coats tighter and a waiter appeared from nowhere with three steaming glasses of tea.

There we sat, a Japanese girl, an American woman, and a Turkish man, our laughter skipping across the waves as we shivered and sipped our midnight tea.

That taste of Turkish hospitality will forever warm my heart.

I often hopped the Sunday morning church bus to Taksim, a quick, traffic-free trip to the European side of Istanbul. Most of the riders attended the Catholic, Dutch Reform and Episcopal Churches, but a few of us went in for a meal, Starbucks, shopping, or a movie. One bus returned to campus at 1:00, and there was another at 6:00 from Kadiköy, across the Bosphorus on the Asian side.

One Sunday after a lonely Turkish breakfast of cucumbers, tomatoes, olives, cheese, bread, and egg at the Marmara Café, I wandered İstiklal. Deserted at 9:00, the street was packed with shoppers and Sunday strollers by 11:00. I headed to Starbucks to spend my last few hours grading papers. I grabbed a double Americano and climbed the stairs to the third floor of the charming neoclassical building so typical along İstiklal. I spotted Leah, a science teacher in her 30's. A pert, active woman, Leah was a delight. I sometimes joined her on her morning walk with Peter, but they left at the crack of dawn—a little early for Libby and me.

"Hey, fancy meeting you here," I said. "How was mass?"

"Oh, same old. I love the liturgy, and the old Polish priest is sweet. He always reminds us how sinful we are. Like I need reminding after last night. Probably all I really need is confession," she joked. "Come on. Have a seat."

Leah and I, both single, often talked of our search for a man. Leah had never married and frequented singles night clubs. I now had Phil, who I planned to meet again over spring break in Rhodes, but we focused on Leah's night out for a few minutes before returning to work. I pulled out a set of essays, and we worked in diligent silence until the usual street ruckus escalated to a rhythmical chant with beating drums. We peered down through the open casement near our table.

"Must be a demonstration. Look at the signs," Leah said. I grabbed my camera to catch a shot of the huge banner and people with placards displaying photos of men. The crowd was ranting, clearly angry.

"What do you suppose it's about?"

A man at the next table leaned over. "They're dock workers demonstrating for improved safety conditions at the shipyards. Those pictures are men who have died on the job. It might also be the PKK using the dockworkers as a front. That happens sometimes." His English was impeccable; it was mostly an educated crowd that frequented Starbuck's.

I wasn't surprised at their concerns, since Turkey's lack of safety regulations unnerved me. There were no barriers or cones in construction areas, just the beeping of trucks as they backed into crowds of pedestrians, who scurried out of the way. I'd seen welders working without safety goggles, workers on high buildings with no safety ropes, and jackhammer operators without ear protection.

After the demonstrators passed, Leah and I dove back into our work. We had an hour before the bus and wanted to finish our marking before evening, when we'd Skype with family and friends back home—their Sunday morning.

We finally packed up, donned our coats, and headed for the bus. İstiklal was slow going. Down the road we could see an ocean of dark heads punctuated by an occasional brilliantly-colored scarf—rare in this affluent area of Istanbul.

A few blocks up was Taksim Square, where there was often a police presence. The first time I'd seen lines of police holding clear plastic riot shields I'd been frightened—until I learned they were there to manage the usual soccer game melee. When I saw them at the Istanbul Marathon I was actually relieved, knowing it was their system of "preventive policing." That Sunday scores of helmeted police stood at attention in lines behind Lucite shields.

"Hang on, Leah. I'm going to buzz over and snap a photo of those cops. I can use it in my blog."

"Not a good idea, Ann Marie. You might get in trouble."

"I'll stand way off and use my zoom. They won't even notice." Could a tall, light-haired woman in a red leather coat be inconspicuous in

Turkey? Oh, well, I thought. I wove through the crowd on the square, searching out the best angle for a photo. There was a wide space around the queued police, so it was easy to shoot from a distance. As I framed my photo, I thought they'd noticed me, but they were staring past me. All of a sudden, they broke formation and started running— toward me! I snapped another photo, then turned to see what the ruckus was. A mob of screaming men were pushing into the square, and there I stood between them and the police. Oh, my God! What to do? Would I be arrested? Get hurt? Men of all ages raced down toward İstiklal, and I joined them. What in the world was going on?

Suddenly it hit me that I'd joined the demonstrators, some still holding signs aloft. Big mistake. We were being chased down by an army of policemen in full riot regalia— gas masks, gas canisters, guns, clubs, and shields. Oh, my GOD!

I stopped and froze, letting the crowd flow by. I snapped photo after photo, not even stopping to focus. My hands shook as I squeezed the shutter button. Once the mob diminished, I hurried across İstiklal to find Leah, my heart still pounding. What a fool I was—a lucky fool. I scanned the crowd, but no Leah. I hoped she'd gone ahead—that she hadn't been hurt. What if we missed the bus? I felt a hand on my arm and turned to see her. "Oh, thank goodness! Where were you?"

"I ran into that store with a bunch of other people. Scary! Are you OK?"

"I'm fine. Just a little rattled."

We headed up the street toward the bus rendezvous, arms linked as we shared our relief at this brush with disaster. A new troop of police gathered in the street ahead, and more filed out of an armored bus. A Turkish announcement blasted over a loud speaker, and people started running again. My heart lurched. "Now what?"

"God, I have no idea! Let's duck into this restaurant," Leah suggested, pulling at the door. It was locked. Frightened faces peered out through the glass. We pasted ourselves against the window as a second wave of police chased demonstrators down the street. One gas-masked policeman who looked like Robocop was clubbing a demonstrator as they ran. It was surreal; we'd landed in a futuristic movie. I snapped more photos, aghast at the brutality. My eyes and throat burned, and we both started coughing.

"Tear gas!" Leah yelled. "Let's get out of here!"

"Run!"

We raced up the last few blocks past Burger King and the Marmara Hotel, dodging as we pushed against the current of police and demonstrators. We were enveloped by another cloud of tear gas near the hotel; people were coughing and holding kerchiefs to their faces. The street in front of the Ataturk Center where our service bus waited was packed with armored *POLIS* tanks and giant white *POLIS* buses spewing reinforcements—police by the hundreds.

Never had I been happier to board a Koç service bus. We all shared our harrowing experiences on the trip back to campus—our quiet, calm campus beside a sheep meadow.

I learned later that the police had been there to prevent violence, since the PKK (a Kurdish separatist organization labeled as a terrorist group) had staged violent demonstrations across Turkey the previous week. They'd arranged an illegal press conference, and the police were ordered to scatter them. I did some research on the PKK, and the picture was grim. They'd used women and children as "shields" in violent demonstrations, sacrificing the innocent for their cause. Their theory was that westerners would be swayed to sympathize with the PKK if they saw news clips of their women and children being killed by Turkish police and military forces. I was aghast to learn that such things could happen in this country where I'd felt so safe.

Maybe Turkey wasn't so perfect after all.

## 31  JINXED

February was a time of reckoning, the month when international schools hired new staff. My friend John Clemens took a higher-paying position in Taiwan to fund the sailboat he was building to sail around the world. I had no interest in buying his little white Fiat, but Terri jumped at the chance. I enjoyed public transport, while she yearned for the freedom of a vehicle. John was hesitant to sell to her, though, because she had bad karma. Terri was Jinxed.

Misfortune seemed to stalk her. Not the life-and-death kind of bad luck, but minor catastrophes. When she had her hair straightened, it frizzed up the next day. When she bought a new watch, it stopped within weeks. When her new laptop arrived from the U.S., she endured a major customs ordeal that cost her $500. She'd been frazzled beyond belief and feared her computer wouldn't work once she got it home. It seemed fine, but within months it went on the fritz, and her printer kept blowing the circuit in her apartment. The Terri Trauma list goes on.

Hence John's concerns about selling Terri his car. We all feared for her, and when she couldn't get her funds transferred from the States, the writing was on the wall. More than a little worried about "The Terri Curse," John started searching for another buyer.

The purchase of a vehicle in Turkey isn't easy, and for a foreigner it's a stress-fraught, paperwork-bound journey. There are papers to sign, taxes to pay, insurance to organize, and translations to purchase —an endless cycle of travel around the city and pockets being filled (and emptied). "I'm having horrible nightmares about buying John's car," she confided one day at lunch. "Maybe I should just forget it."

"But it's all you've talked about," I said. I was happily unencumbered by a vehicle; the driving in Istanbul was treacherous at best. Terri, though, yearned for the independence of her own wheels. She hated service bus schedules and often arrived late, purse and hair flying as she raced down the hill from her *lojman*.

"Yes, but everything always seems to go wrong for me. I feel like I'm just asking for trouble."

"Think positive, Terri. You can get groceries whenever you want." How many times had I run out of milk and had to wait days for the next scheduled grocery bus?

"I have an idea," Jamilah suggested. Familiar with Eastern superstitions, she understood luck, both good and bad. She surveyed Terri with a knowledgable smile. "You're probably under the influence of the Evil Eye, and we need to perform a cleansing ceremony to rid you of it."

Terri and I exchanged glances; we weren't superstitious, but heck—we were in Turkey. We both grinned. "Why not?" she said. "What can I lose?"

"Things can't get any worse, can they?"

"Don't even think it, " Terri warned.

"The first thing you have to do is collect flowers of seven different hues," Jamilah explained, keeping the rest of the ceremony to herself. Saturday afternoon we visited the gypsy flower market near the Kadiköy ferry, where Terri carefully chose a rainbow of blooms from the sea of color that festooned the pier. Jamilah instructed her to pluck the petals and soak them overnight in water.

Sunday evening we gathered at Terri's, where Jamilah ceremoniously cut a lemon in half, scored X's in its surface, and squeezed it into the red pail of flower petals. "Mash it all together using both hands, then take a shower. Pour this water with the flower petals over yourself as a final rinse and don't dry off—just put on a loose dress, leaving the water and flower petals on your hair and body."

While Terri showered, Jamilah arranged an incense burner in the center of Terri's red evil eye rug. "The rug adds impetus to the spell," she grinned. She lit the incense, put on some Eastern music, lit a few candles and turned off the overhead light. The stage was set for a mystical ceremony. Soon Terri returned, dripping water and flower petals. In a deep whisper Jamilah instructed, "Stand over the incense and let the smoke waft up through your dress and along your body.

The curses that plague you will drift away with the smoke."

As incense swirled up Terri's body and infused the room, Jamilah and I walked in circles around her, holding *nazar boncuk* (na-ZAHR bon-JUK), blue glass "eyes" reputed to protect one from evil curses. Terri lifted her head, closed her eyes, and succumbed to the magic of the ritual.

I don't think any of us really believed in it, but we were caught up in the drama of this tradition-steeped ceremony. My initial giggles were suppressed by goosebumps crawling up my neck as we continued. Could there be something to this? I believe in the power of positive thinking, and perhaps this was similar—like collective prayer.

Turkey is a country steeped in traditions, one of which is a belief in the power of the evil eye. If you have a new car, receive an award, get a new job, or have a baby, jealous people might cast a curse on you— the Evil Eye. Turks don't admit to being superstitious, yet many entertain the possibility, and what's to lose by keeping a few lucky charms around? Every Turkish baby has a *boncuk* pinned to its crib, sleeve or diaper. Why tempt fate?

Though we made light of it, we relished the camaraderie of our shared ritual. We hoped it might improve Terri's luck, and perhaps it did. Her car purchase proceeded smoothly, but that was all. Ill fortune continued to plague her: her watches still quit, her alarm didn't wake her, and her printer never did function properly.

But next summer she'd have her own car.

# 32 ISTANBUL BRIGHT AND DARK

Istanbul burst into bloom at the beginning of March, and each morning brought the discovery of another new wildflower as Libby and I explored the fields beyond the school. The days grew longer and life brighter.

"Ms. Mershon! It's March 29th and the eclipse is TODAY!" Harun blurted before class. The room erupted into chaos even though it had been in the news for months. I held a hand in the air and picked up my clipboard. Silence. No one wanted to lose points, and I didn't want to lose control.

"Did you know people are coming to Turkey from all over the world to see the eclipse?" I asked. Hands. Lots of hands in the air. "Yes, Gizem?"

"My uncle lives in Izmir, and it's going to be a total eclipse there. Here it will be not total."

"You're right. Does anyone know how much sun we'll lose?"

"87%," answered Irem, my scientific genius.

"The school has purchased black-out glasses for each of us," I said, distributing the black-lensed cardboard frames. "You shouldn't look at the eclipse without them." We all tried them on, shocked that they were like blindfolds. More chaos.

"We're going to start with a free-write, so take out your notebooks—quietly." I wrote an opener on the chalkboard: "When I was seven..." A free write was guaranteed to settle an antsy group. They got full points for filling a page, and they could write whatever they wanted.

I wrote my own piece. "When I was seven we had a partial eclipse. I read about it in my *Weekly Reader* and prepared by punching a hole in a piece of cardboard. I watched its shadow on our sandbox bench as it transformed from a circle of light to a crescent-shaped sliver. The backyard was bathed in an eerie half-light, and the shadows of leaves on the lawn were transformed to thousands of little crescents. It was freaky, and I loved it."

Fortunately, the eclipse began during my IB class, so I didn't have to deal with the wild excitement of my ninth graders. An announcement in Turkish brought laughter, and Denizhan explained. "Everyone is laughing because the announcement says we must all put our glasses on now and keep them on until the eclipse is over. We'll be 1000 blind students fumbling down the stairs and trying to find our way outside." I joined their laughter, amused by the administration's concerns about injured retinas. Instead, we'd get broken arms and cracked skulls from tumbling down four flights of stairs. Turkish reactions tend to be large: warmth, excitement, nervousness, anger, and fear. We were instructed to close the shades tightly when we got back into the building. I knew this was overkill, but I held my tongue. Disrespect is not acceptable to Turks, especially from a teacher. We were finally instructed to go outside for the eclipse.

It was sheer joy to be outdoors on this bright, warm afternoon. Students milled around the vast school lawn, everyone using their glasses to look at the sun. Some had brought cameras to photograph each other peering skyward. I was flattered that many students wanted to pose with me. The day grew darker as the moon concealed the sun, a storm brewing in spite of the cloudless sky.

I showed some students how the leaf shadows on the lawn were transforming, and they were fascinated. A few ninth graders ran around acting frightened and yelling, "The world is coming to an end!" a behavior we squelched posthaste. A sliver of the sun shone all through the eclipse, so it was never totally dark.

I learned later that although it's always dangerous to look directly at the sun, it's even more so during an eclipse. Our pupils dilate to accommodate the darkness, which makes the possibility of retinal burn far greater than on a bright day. Because there's less light, our reflex to blink and look away from the brightness doesn't protect us. Hence, the blackout lenses.

In spite of administrative instructions I let my students take off their glasses to climb the stairs back to class. Let them fire me, I thought. Better that than broken legs.

"That was absolutely amazing!" Merve exclaimed once we were

back in the room.

"I wish we'd been in Izmir," Denizhan added. "It would be exciting to see the whole thing.

"I thought it was scary," Deniz admitted. "I can imagine what it was like in the past for people who didn't understand what was happening. I'll bet they thought the world was coming to an end."

The discussion continued, students noting when it would happen again and sharing their feelings about this fascinating phenomenon. I loved those kids—they felt like family, a closeness I'd only experienced with a few students in America.

Maybe it was my students, maybe it was spring, and maybe it was Phil, but I felt bathed in happiness. I absolutely loved Turkey.

Spring break was only weeks away, and I couldn't wait for my week on Rhodes. Susie, Annie, and her husband Mike were flying from Minnesota, Terri was joining us, and most of all, Phil would be there. Oh, heaven!

My only problem was Libby. A few people on campus were happy to take her while I traveled, but over this break all my dog-sitters would be gone. In desperation I asked my classes if anyone could take care of her. They all knew about Libby, and I'd brought her to school a few times.

It's rare for Turks to own a dog. One in twenty students might have one, while in the U.S. it would probably be more than half. Muslims see dogs as dirty creatures; the Quran warns people to wash their hands five times in sand after touching one, which might have been a wise thing in ancient times. Most cats and dogs in Turkey are street animals, surprisingly well cared for. Many people left food outside their doors for strays, and some would actually buy pet food and distribute it along the street to eager cats and dogs. You'll never see an emaciated stray in Turkey.

At any rate, I'd nearly lost hope when Deniz, one of my eleventh graders, told me she'd talked to her parents, and since they were considering the purchase of a small dog, they wanted to give it a try. Deniz was thrilled, and so was I.

We decided to try a weekend visit to make sure it would work. I wrote out clear instructions for Deniz, then met her after school with Libby safely ensconced in her little red travel case. Though Libby was confused, I reassured her. "You be a good girl while I'm gone," the farewell I used whenever I left her behind. This time she was leaving me, and on a school service bus.

I worried all weekend, hoping against hope that Deniz's family would enjoy Libby. Monday morning I waited for her service bus and was relieved to see Deniz beaming as she emerged from the bus, my wagging dog on her leash.

"How did it go?"

"Oh, Ms. Mershon! It was wonderful! Everyone loved Libby, and here's her new stuffed bunny that my mother bought for her. We can't wait to have her for a whole week."

And so began the love affair between Deniz and Libby Lou. We were all thrilled, even Miss Libby.

## 33 FRIENDS AND LOVER

When Terri and I arrived at our Rhodes hotel I barely noticed the decor. I only had eyes for Phil, and when I spotted him reading in an overstuffed lobby chair, I hurried over for a hug—what joy! We settled Terri into a cheerful seaside apartment (my timeshare unit), then Phil brought me to our room, a nondescript motel room overlooking the pool. The only good part of it was Phil. Another hug. "It's so good to see you," he said.

"That's an understatement."

We sipped beers on the balcony while Phil shared the story of his arrival the previous day. He loved the pre-season quiet, basking in the 6-foot tub with an Ottoman history book—my inquisitive, interesting lover. Oh, lucky me.

Our week was a whirlwind. Annie, Mike and Susie arrived the next morning to gleeful shrieks and hugs. I hadn't seen Annie and Susie since our tear-soaked parting in August, and Annie's husband Mike would be the perfect connection for Phil, as they were both doctors. We gathered in the apartment, opened belated Christmas gifts, and Susie broke out her martini shaker. I was afraid Phil might be aghast at mid-day drinking, but he didn't skip a beat. We all danced in the kitchen to Greek MTV. My heart couldn't have been fuller.

The next morning we hopped taxis to the ancient city of *Rhodos*, whose massive gate wafted us back five centuries. The city was built of huge blocks cut from sea coral. Knights and jousting whirled through my imagination as we explored: dungeons and cannonballs and maidens with beaded bonnets.

We began with generous fruit parfaits at a table on the city's open square. Terri and Susie wanted to shop, while the rest of us preferred to investigate historical sites. Sun warmed us as we pretended to lift cannonballs and fondled muscle-bound busts of who-knew-whom. Phil blended well with my friends, and I relished having a hand to hold.

Another morning we rented bikes to explore the island. It was easy pedaling along the shore with its cooling sea breezes, but as we began our climb up the mountain to the Filermos Monastery the road grew steeper and steeper, even with the switchbacks. It was jacket weather, but I was soon glistening from forehead to heels. (Who says women don't sweat?) We stopped to explore chapels, small stone structures, fountains, and more chapels (and catch our breath). With perfect timing, we reached the top just as Susie and Terri stepped from a taxi. Some people don't bike up mountains, but I was pleased that Phil did. We followed a dirt track dotted with stone monuments of the twelve stations of the cross. After the last one we emerged onto a high, open terrace where a modern concrete cross towered above us.

"What a breathtaking spot!" I exclaimed.

"I'll bet the sunsets are spectacular."

"We could celebrate the full moon here!" Susie said. "It's tomorrow, and if we came before dark, we could see both the sunset and the moonrise, you guys!"

Terri raised her eyebrows. "The full moon?"

"Yeah, we celebrate full moons together. It's a tradition."

"Well, then, we'll have to do it," Phil announced. This man was too wonderful for words.

The next night Terri balked at our full moon celebration. "It just seems sacrilegious," she said. "I thought it sounded fun, but I just can't drink under a cross."

We bid her a disappointed farewell, then piled into a taxi to the top of the mountain, remembering to arrange a return pick-up. (It was a long walk home). We laid a blanket near the edge of the terrace, and Susie produced plastic martini glasses, flamingo stir-sticks, flamingo napkins, and various snacks. Love that party girl! We snapped photos of each other with the sunset, the moonrise, and our picnic. We chatted, laughed, and sang our way through the evening, not forgetting to thank God for granting us the spectacular spot, good friends, and a beautiful night. We'd forgotten flashlights, but the moon sufficed, and we had everything cleaned up in time to meet the taxi.

Which didn't come.

"Do you think he misunderstood?" Susie asked.

"Or forgot?"

"Oh, if only we had a cell phone—or a flashlight. How stupid can we be?"

We waited.

Finally Mike said, "Well, we have a full moon. We might as well start walking, and if he comes up, he'll see us."

Dejected, we began the long trek down the mountain.

We'd walked a good distance before headlights shone ahead. Our driver had gotten tied up and called his friend to rescue us. Yes, there is a God, one who even takes care of those who celebrate beneath crosses.

As the week progressed, Phil sometimes chose to relax in the tub with his book rather than join us at the apartment. Though I understood, I was disappointed. I should have stayed with him, but I wanted to be with my friends. Guilt. What did I really want? Was I using Phil? Was I once again trying to squeeze too many things into my life? That tendency had contributed to the demise of both my marriage and my first romance. There they were, those damnable doubts crowding in on my perfect vacation. Piss on it. I was going to do what I wanted, and that was being with my friends. When Phil joined us, things were perfect.

On the last day Phil and I peeled away to spend a day by ourselves in the old city. He'd done more research and had some sites he wanted to see. Over lunch we had a long, painful talk about our relationship. He shared his concerns about the long-distance relationship, and I carefully skirted the issue of choosing my friends over him. Being honest might hurt his feelings, and I wanted to be loved. I loved him.

At least I thought I did.

## 34  CLINGING FRANTICALLY

Phil and I continued to e-mail daily and Skype on weekends. We never ran out of things to talk about, though we avoided the deeper conversation about our relationship. I was afraid to broach the topic, clinging frantically to my new love.

Phil bought a book about surviving long-distance relationships, and I suggested he join our kayak trip along Lake Superior's Pictured Rocks Seashore, not far from his home. I booked a layover in Michigan for a week on my way home, which cost me an extra few hundred dollars, but I knew time together was the only way to maintain our relationship. So far Phil had done all the traveling. It was my turn.

Shortly after making my reservation, I wrote this journal:

*I think Phil is having second thoughts. I've been there before. My intuition is probably right, I guess. Oh, well. He's a wonderful man, and if he decides to put up with me, I'll be a lucky woman. It's a lot to ask. I need to give him some space and see what he wants to do. I know he's waffling for a number of reasons.*

*One--he never said he loved me.*

*Two--he's been writing very short messages.*

*Three--he was distant and less warm on the phone tonight.*

*Four--he didn't say he loves me.*

*I don't think it's going to work. The long trips are wearing him out, and he needs a woman to be closer to him, to hold him. I wonder if I should give him the out or make him take the initiative to call things off.*

*What I did wrong:*

*I spent more time focusing on my friends than on him.*

*I wasn't the loving attentive woman he might have wanted. But then, that's not really me.*

*I'm hurt, and I have a feeling it will be a few months before he lets me in on his thoughts. I'm sorry for that, but I won't risk putting myself out there.*

*Life is just the pitts sometimes.*

*Oh, well.*

*Life goes on. Maybe there's a man I could be passionate about who is as wonderful as Phil, though I doubt it.*

*I'm pretty sad.*


Phil Skyped the next weekend.

"Hi, Ann Marie. How are you doing?"

"Hey, Phil! I'm great. The sun is shining, and every day is warmer. I know it'll be too hot for me soon, but right now it's gorgeous."

"I need to talk to you."

Pause... "I know."

"I'm so sorry, Ann. I just can't manage a long-distance relationship, and when you said you were flying here this summer, I started to panic. I realized I just couldn't bear to have these long separations. It's been wonderful knowing you, and I really appreciate the warmth you've shown and your generous spirit. You're a rock. You've also raised the bar for my expectations. I told you that before. I know now that there are wonderful, intelligent women out there."

"I'm nothing special, Phil. Maybe you saw me as more than I am."

"A woman who'll brave a blizzard to climb around on an old fortress she doesn't even care about? You are special, Ann Marie."

"Thanks. You're pretty special, too. I'm going to miss you."

"I'm so sorry. It just isn't right. I hope you don't hate me for this."

"How could I hate you? I'm the one at fault. I wasn't a very attentive partner in Rhodes."

"Of course you were. It wasn't that, Ann Marie."

Now who wasn't being honest?

"I'd like to stay friends," I said.

"Would you really? I'd love that. I still care about you." Never the word "love."

I didn't know what else to say.

"We can still e-mail and Skype," he said.

"I'll cancel my ticket to Michigan."

"That's a good idea." I waited for an offer to reimburse me, since he'd been in favor of the idea initially and had a lot more money than I did. It didn't occur to him, though, and my pride wouldn't let me mention it.

"I'm truly sorry to do this, but it's just not the romance I need right now."

"Take care," I said, my throat constricting. "So long."

"Take care, Ann. I'm sorry."

Tears welled as I signed off. I needed a good cry, and it came.

We shared a few e-mails over the next few weeks, then nothing. He blocked both my e-mail and Skype accounts.

The end.

# 35 AYVA IS QUINCE

"*Ayva* is Turkish for quince," John explained as we drove into the Aegean village of Ayvalik. Full of quince.

"I think it should have been called *Zeytinlik*," I said. "Every street has an olive oil shop."

"We have to pick some up before we leave—it's the best olive oil in Turkey." John maneuvered the car up a winding cobbled street barely wide enough for his tiny Fiat (soon to be Terri's). He squeezed between crumbling stone buildings and tucked the car into a space beside a public fountain—a brass spigot in a carved marble wall. Five little boys welcomed us with eager grins, keen to pose for photos but leery of Libby. I always got a charge out of that—she was anything but fierce.

We stepped into the vestibule of the *Taksiyarhis,* removing our shoes to set them with others lined up inside the door. The low-ceilinged lobby was piled with ornately-patterned Turkish pillows, its stone walls and sparkling wooden floor decorated with bright-patterned kilims and carpets.

"Welcome to our home!" Emine said with a warm smile, repeating each of our names in turn as she took our hands in hers. A man in loose gray *şalvar* pants entered the room. "This is my husband Ali." He smiled as he sat to register us in the ledger. Then Emine led us up a winding wooden staircase to the whitewashed second level. There we found a sparkling kitchen that opened onto a grape-arbor balcony with tables, couches, and pillows, all in the cozy, ornate style of the Turkish lounge. We were entranced.

Our room was up another wooden staircase—a spacious room surrounded in casement windows that opened out over red tile rooftops, two ancient churches (not mosques), and Ayvalik's bustling harbor. A heavy wooden table sat on a square carpet in the center of the room, and a single bed graced each wall. Perfect. John, Nora and I dumped our backpacks, headed for the rooftop terrace, and sipped

Efes beers as a cool sea breeze soothed our travel-weary bodies.

"OK, enough sitting," Nora announced as she stood and stretched. A striking, leggy blonde thirty years younger than John and me, Nora's spark kept us in motion. We strolled down the cobbled street, Libby sniffing for cats. As we approached the harbor, an officious announcement exploded from loudspeakers. My heart raced. "What is it, John?"

"Just do what everyone else does." There was a staticky pause as cars stopped and people stepped out to stand in the street. The loudspeaker blared the Turkish national anthem while everyone stood at rigid attention, many with hands on their hearts, some singing along. All this for National Youth and Sports Day, which I later learned is also Ataturk Commemoration Day. The Turks' passion for their founder never ceased to amaze me. After a moment of silence, people climbed back into their cars and Ayvalik reverted to its usual chaos.

We explored the marina, picked up a few souvenirs, and discovered spots for coffee, *mezes*, and finally dinner. We danced with the locals to live music that reminded me of Zorba. The Greek influence in Ayvalik was clear—the music was brighter, the people carefree, and the churches open.

I woke early the next morning and crept out to explore the streets with Libby. A few blocks up our narrow lane I heard a booming voice call *"Si-mit! Ye-mek!"* before a lanky young man strode around the corner with a green box of *simits* (big bagel-like sesame rolls) balanced on his head. I bought one for 30 *kuruş*, about 20 cents. It was fresh, crusty—and delicious. Libby agreed.

Later that day I was reading on the terrace when I heard another voice call, *"El-ma! Şeker el-ma!"* An elderly man in a woolen vest and cap sat on the corner beside a basket of bright red candied apples, which sold quickly. Turkey's street vendors never ceased to charm me.

After dinner that evening we relaxed on the pier watching a fisherman drag a dead octopus back and forth across the concrete like a mop. His friend kept pouring water over it, apparently to clear its ink. Sadly, our Turkish was so bad that we couldn't ask.

We found a candlelit table nearby and ordered a glass of tea as the last rays of sun disappeared into a dark sky behind the island of Lesbos. We moseyed back up to the pension, where a young couple lounged among the balcony pillows. The girl sang as her boyfriend played his guitar, and we settled in with our books, more entranced by their music than our reading.

"Are we bothering you?" the girl asked.

"Absolutely not," Nora answered.

Big problem to have a live starlight concert to finish our Ayvalik weekend.

# 36 ONE DOGGONE POINT

June finally arrived, and with it the dreaded finals. My students were more distraught than I was over the ordeal, and we all heaved a sigh of relief once exams were over and grades posted. Little did I know, the struggle was not yet behind me.

"Ms. Mershon?" Ninth-grade Elif peered up at me through a haze of tears, her brown eyes reflecting both sorrow and hope.

"Yes, Elif?"

"Ms. Mershon, could you please give me just one more point on my exam? One point would make my grade for the whole year a 4 instead of a 3. Please?"

"Elif, I don't hand out points—you earn them." Tears welled.

"Turkish teachers are much nicer than foreign ones. I mean, I love you Ms. Mershon, but American teachers are so hard. Turkish teachers understand the system."

Maybe she was right. The Turks had grown up with this system that totally defied logic. Why was I so obstinate? American education left much to be desired, but at least I understood the rules. I'd never been a strong proponent of either testing or grades, which made this even more difficult for me. I hated to do it, but I buckled anyway. "I'll tell you what, Elif. I'll go over your exam one more time myself and have it moderated by another teacher to see if we missed any points. They need to be earned, though—I refuse to just hand you extra points."

Elif beamed. "Oh, thank you, Ms. Mershon! Thank you so very, very, very much!"

As I reviewed Elif's exam, I found two items where I could add a point on language usage. Though she hadn't been a stellar student, she'd worked hard, and I felt I may have graded a bit harshly (though remember, I'm an easy grader). I shared the changes with my department chair who supported them. Elif now had two more points on a 100-point exam. Nothing, really.

I went back to the computer to re-enter her grade, and lo and behold, she was right. Two tiny points in a year's total of nearly a thousand raised her yearly grade from 69.3% to 69.5%, which would round up to 70—a four. I e-mailed Elif, who ran up to the office to give me a huge, tearful hug. So Turkish.

I loved teaching in Turkey but felt professionally compromised by their grading system. Their policies drove me bonkers. Not only were the grade levels too broad, but failing students could take a grade-changing exam and have that exam grade averaged equally with their entire yearly grade. It infuriated me. We made grade-changing exams difficult, but I felt it was a disservice to students who worked hard all year. I also prayed that I'd never have to rely on a doctor who'd squeaked through school on grade-changing exams.

# 37 PLEASE, LOVE TURKEY

In spite of my frustrations, I was eager to share Turkey's magic with my son Ross and sister Laura. I hoped their visit would take my mind off Phil, who I still pined for.

I caught a 3 A.M. ride to the airport with a teacher who was leaving for the summer, consequently arriving four hours before Ross's flight. Libby and I snoozed in a coffee shop easy chair, then headed down to meet him, only to find that his flight was delayed two hours. I waited a third hour outside customs, craning to see inside each time the doors opened. No Ross. Could he have missed his plane? I was just leaving to check with the Delta counter when I spotted a Marlins baseball-cap emerging through the doors—my handsome Florida son.

"Oh, Ross! Thank God you're here!" I cried as I hurried over. He dropped his duffel and wrapped me in a big bear hug. I hadn't expected the swell of emotions, but my tears flowed.

"Don't cry, Mom. It's great to see you. It was a tough trip. We got delayed in Amsterdam, and then I forgot to stop and buy my visa, so I had to go through the passport line twice. But I'm here. You look great."

We checked into the Kybele Hotel, my favorite in Istanbul. Like many hotels, every room featured Turkish embroidered bed covers, fringed pillows and carpets as well as ornate antiques and bright ceramics, but the Kybele was also bedecked with small glass lamps hanging by the hundreds from every ceiling. The lobby welcomed us with a blaze of lanterns of every color, shape and style, and our room had over 100 lamps that transported us to the world of Aladdin.

Ross and I dropped off our bags and caught a ferry up the Bosphorus, a relaxed first-day outing for my jet-lagged son. We reveled in the cooling breeze as we caught up on each other's lives. Ross looked healthy, and his bright eyes and winning smile showed me he was in a good place. He'd been through hard times, and it warmed my heart to see him happy. He was in love and asked my advice about moving in with his girlfriend. I recommended caution, but what does a mother know?

The churning waters of the Bosphorus mesmerized us, both great lovers of water. While I love to kayak, canoe and swim, Ross surfs. "These houses are fantastic," he said. "You'd have to use scaffolding to paint them, though, all those stories. They must be really expensive." His comments reflected his Florida paint contracting business.

"There's a lot of money in Istanbul, and this is probably the most affluent part of the city."

"What's the deal on the deserted ones? They look like they're going to collapse in on themselves."

"Those are centuries-old Ottoman houses. Turkish law protects them, so if someone dies without willing the house to an heir, no one can buy it or fix it up. Some have numerous owners who can't agree on who's responsible, so the house just sits with the wood rotting until it finally disintegrates. It's heartbreaking."

Ross stood to check out something ahead on the European side. "Is that a castle, Mom?"

"That's the Rumeli Castle. The Ottomans took control of Constantinople around 1500 using this castle. They changed the country from Christian to Muslim." Far beyond the castle we disembarked at Anadolu Kavaği, the ferry's last stop. We hiked up a winding road to the ruins of Yoros Castle, once the site of an ancient temple to Zeus. It offered a spectacular view of the Bosphorus, though, and we found a shady spot where we could see up to the Black Sea and down to Istanbul's distant skyscrapers, many miles away. We watched massive barges and tankers carrying goods to the Black Sea. "Each ship has to take on a local pilot because the currents are really crazy here," I explained. "I guess there are 17 turns to navigate, and each one has its own idiosyncrasies."

"Cool."

We watched tiny red tugboats sidle up to each ship for the pilot to disembark. As a surfer Ross understood currents. We cooled off with a frosty beer on our way back down the mountain, then caught the ferry back to the hotel. It was odd sharing a hotel room with my 27-year-old son, but he'd have his own room once Laura arrived. "I have to take a nap, Mom. I can't stay awake any longer."

"Oh, no you don't. You have to stay up as long as you can. The only way to beat jet lag is to put yourself right on the new schedule. A nap will mess you up."

He looked at me dubiously, eyes at half-mast. "I'll try."

Neither of my sons had traveled overseas, always too busy with sports when I'd encouraged them to join my student tours to Europe, so they knew nothing about jet lag. We dined on *mezes* and *köfte* (ground spiced meat), then strolled through Sultanahmet until Ross was in a walking stupor.

Laura arrived the next day, and in spite of grueling heat we explored the Blue Mosque, carpet shops, and the Grand Bazaar for the next few days, always finishing with cold beers in the shady courtyard of the Medusa Restaurant near our hotel.

We flew to Selçuk, where we stayed at the charming ivy-clad Bella Hotel. Laura and Ross loved the breezy third-floor terrace restaurant and lounge, complete with traditional Turkish pillows and *nargile* (water pipes). It overlooked the ruins of St. John's Basilica and Ayasaluk Castle, but our favorite feature was a nest of baby storks just across the street. We marveled as they practiced flying from their nest to the nearby cathedral and castle ruins. The quiet, lazy pace of Selçuk was refreshing after the bustle of Istanbul. Although I'd been to Ephesus twice, I took them on a tour. Laura and I were fascinated with its history, told through its marble arches, walkways, and two-tiered library. Ross was interested, though too impatient to listen to our guide.

We made three trips to Şyrince, the nearby mountaintop village. Laura and Ross loved their *gözleme* (a huge paper-thin "crepe" grilled with cheese and spinach or a spiced potato filling). We also imbibed the area's fruit wines, explored the tiny gift shops, and marveled at the houses and pensions lining the narrow stone streets. I brought them to the old spoon carver, whose toothless grin once again warmed my heart.

The day before our departure Laura announced, "I think we should find an earlier flight back to Istanbul. I don't want to miss the plane home."

"If we fly back to Istanbul, we'll be stuck at my apartment, which is incredibly boring—and HOT!"

"I don't care. I don't want to miss the plane. We have to get back." She sounded almost frantic. I was confused. I'd thought she was enjoying herself, but she'd been away from home two weeks, the previous one at business meetings in Belgium. She probably missed Erin and Matt. Getting back to Istanbul earlier wouldn't get her home any sooner, so it made no sense. "I'll check to see if there's a later flight to Istanbul in case we miss ours, Laura. That way you won't have to worry." Ross wisely stayed out of the discussion.

"I just don't know!" Laura said, her voice a little shrill, especially for my pragmatic, organized sister. There was another flight after ours, but she still insisted on driving to the airport three hours early. I'd never seen her like this, but my intuition told me not to push it. Laura had a strong will, and I was the easy-going one. Or so I thought.

Instead of spending the night at my apartment as I'd planned, Laura made reservations for us at the Airport Sheraton. She wasn't going to take any chances on missing her plane. I called Cebryil to see if he could drive us a day earlier. It was Friday rush hour, so the trip took three hours, much of it sitting in stalled traffic as vendors walked from car to car peddling water, *simit*, balloons, and toys. Cebryil doesn't believe in air conditioning, and it was hot. I was miserable.

"Did you tell the hotel about Libby?" I asked.

"No. I didn't even think of it. Sorry."

"Oh, well. We've never been turned away before." I zipped Libby into her case and pulled out the shoulder straps, hoping they'd think it was just a backpack.

Laura and Ross heaved sighs of relief as we entered the glitzy, western hotel. "Oh, it feels like home!" Ross announced.

I felt exactly the opposite. We'd spent a week reveling in Turkey's traditional charm, and they preferred the sterile, pompous atmosphere of a luxury hotel. I was hurt.

"I'm sorry," the security guard informed me, pointing at my

backpack. "We don't allow dogs in this hotel."

"What? Well what would you suggest I do?" I was frantic. Would I have to sleep outside?

"You can leave your dog in the baggage room," the concierge said dismissively. My heart fell. I didn't want to guess what hell this would be for her—and for the lobby personnel. I reluctantly handed her case to a bellman, who talked to her soothingly as he walked off. She yelped and cried and yelped some more as he closed the door. I doubted she'd quiet down.

I lay awake all night thinking about how much I'd grown to love Turkey and its lovely people (except for the Sheraton staff). Who would have guessed that a country could steal my heart in just ten months? I tried to focus ahead on my Minnesota summer—kayaking, swimming, and canoeing with the people I loved.

And I imagined Libby, yelping and crying in that lonely, dark baggage room.

Talk about mixed feelings.

Still struggling with conflicted feelings about leaving Turkey, I burst into tears when I saw Annie at the airport. My best buddy for over 25 years, I'd missed her. Friendships buoyed me, although I was convinced that was the reason I'd lost Phil. If I'd learned anything in the past year, it was to live in the present and make the most of each moment. No regrets, I'd told myself as I pocketed the still-pulsing pain of lost love. At this moment I was with Annie, and we talked nonstop on the two hour drive home.

I was struck by the North Shore's lush landscape. Had it always been so green? "Don't you love the solglimt?" Annie asked, referring to the glint of sun across Lake Superior.

Eileen and Dad met us at their door, and Eileen had crafted one of her signature welcome signs: "Welcome Home, Dear Ann and Libby!!!" adorned with sunburst smiley faces. Her enthusiasm astounded and often overwhelmed me. Dad reminded me repeatedly over the summer that I needed a man in my life. Well, I'd tried.

Once settled in at Dad's, I learned that my renters were bailing. They'd neglected to inform me that they'd purchased a house —like it was a surprise? Our negotiations were ugly, and I felt rotten about it. Friends pitched in to help clean the house (which was filthy), and I began the search for new renters. If I didn't find someone it would mean no traveling the next year.

In spite of the drama, I had a wonderful summer, including time with my sister Laura and her family in Minneapolis, a summer canoe trip with family, and swimming and paddling whenever I could. My summer sparkled with the warmth of sunshine, friends and family.

The highlight was our Old Fogies kayak trip along Michigan's Pictured Rocks National Lakeshore in August. Mike and Annie and I, along with friends Dick and Jini, drove all day to Munising, where we unloaded all our gear onto the beach. "Don't worry," Mike assured us. "It's less than an hour to Grand Island, and there are a few campsites on this side. We'll be fed and in bed before dark." Sadly, the first sites were taken. "Plan B," Mike announced, "will be to stop for a snack and forge on. Sorry, you guys, but no supper. The next site is on the back of the island, about four more miles." We arrived in the dark, dragged out our gear and set up with headlamps.

The next morning I headed bleary-eyed up the latrine path and found myself face to face with a sleek black bear who eyed me as she munched on blueberries. I deferred. I don't mind peeing in the woods. After we'd all imbibed on our particular versions of coffee (mine dark and strong), Jini laid out a breakfast of granola, yogurt, and fresh-picked blueberries. YUM!

We packed up and paddled across South Bay to shore, where limestone cliffs were eroded into fantastic shapes by wind, water and sand. Dwarfed  in our little vessels, we paddled awe-struck beneath multi-colored rainbows painted by ground water seeping through the cliff face.

That evening Dick laid out appetizers of canned oysters and crackers on a huge rock. As he prepared dinner, a young man in a park uniform surprised us. "I hiked in to warn you about an impending storm. We expect 7-10 foot waves tomorrow, so if you don't get out ahead of the storm, you should plan to sit tight for a few days." We were impressed that he'd hiked in over a mile just for us.

Mike took out his weather radio and he and Dick listened intently to storm warnings. "Let's go to bed early and get up at 5:00," Mike said. "The wind usually doesn't increase until mid-morning, so at least we can get further down the shore."

At 5:30 the waves were already high, so we crawled back into our sleeping bags. After a leisurely breakfast of blueberry pancakes, we agreed to hike along the shore to Chapel Rock, six miles. The wind whipped us as we followed the ridge of sheer limestone cliffs, a breathtaking view accosting us at every turn.

Mike, Jini, and I cavorted in the five-foot waves at Chapel Rock. Jini and I had bathing suits, and Mike was hilarious high-stepping through the waves in his gray briefs. I've never had to work so hard to keep myself afloat, and when we headed back to shore the strong surf crashed over us, challenging us to reach the beach without being knocked over. The sun shone bright on Tuesday, but the waves were even higher. We dallied over breakfast and spent our second wind-bound day exploring the shoreline, lying in hammocks, and reading.

The wind finally abated Wednesday, and we paddled 14 miles to make up for lost time. That week left me bushed yet grateful for my adventuresome friends. Too soon I'd be leaving for Istanbul, a place that fascinated me but offered neither adventures nor deep friendships. Not yet, anyway.

Our Full Moon Celebration was the summer's grand finale. A small group of women friends gather on the beach with firewood, snacks, and "adult beverages" to celebrate the full moon as it rises over Lake Superior. That morning Annie called from work. "Want to sleep out on the beach tonight?"

"Absolutely. The bugs should be gone by now, and it's our last chance. No tent?"

"No tent. We'll sleep under the stars."

The evening was warm, the company delightful, the moonrise splendid, and the bugs few. After the others left, Annie and I dragged out our Therm-a-rests and sleeping bags and settled onto the pebble beach.

"Thanks for doing this, Ann. I'm going to miss you. When you're gone I have people to do stuff with, but no one like you. Not a bosom buddy.

"I know, Annie. This has been harder than I expected. I love Turkey, and I love teaching there, but I need a buddy. Even a man would do," I laughed. We talked long into the night but finally dozed. I woke to a light mist on my face.

"Annie?"

"Yeah?"

"I think it's raining."

"I know."

"Oh, well."

"You're the only person I know who'd do this."

"Yeah, me too. Night."

After a few hours of fitful sleep, still warm in my sleeping bag, I ventured a hand out to feel the surface—sopping. Oh, the miracle of fiberfill.

"Are you awake?" Annie asked.

"Yup. My bag is pretty wet."

"I think I slept about three hours."

"But it was heaven."

"I agree, good buddy. Better get up, though. I have to get to work."

"It's 5:00, Annie."

"Oh, my God. Can you get back to sleep?"

"Not a chance."

We talked our way through the sunrise, then piled our wet gear into my car and headed for town. I brewed coffee while Annie showered, and as I drove home I fought back tears. How many people score a friend like mine—and for 25 years? She'd even promised to find renters for my house.

I lay awake my last night thinking and worrying. Worrying and thinking. In spite of some bumps, it had been a beautiful summer. I treasured my time with friends and family but was disappointed I hadn't seen my son Dustin, who lived in California. I'd felt pulled in fifteen directions and worried about finding renters for my house. Did I really want to go back to Turkey? My stomach churned as conflicting thoughts roiled through my mind.

When I hugged Dad and Eileen goodbye the next morning the tears began to flow, and I sobbed through every farewell. What a change from last year, when I'd been light-hearted and eager. This time I wasn't buoyed by the excitement of a new adventure. Home meant people who loved me.

Istanbul was fascinating and challenging—and lonely.

# 39 BACK TO—OH, NO!

When Libby and I arrived at Ataturk Airport, I feared Cebryil might have forgotten the arrangements we'd made months earlier. Had they been clear? I couldn't trust my Turkish, but he was a reliable fellow...

My anxiety dissolved when I spotted him standing among the customs crowd, his gentle smile a warm welcome. Outside we were pummeled by the blazing August sun, but as we drove Cebryil ignored his air conditioning; he really believed that drafts and cold air cause Bell's palsy. I cranked down my window as we forged through the congested streets. I'd cope. I couldn't help but smile as we drove across the Bosphorus, huge cargo ships gliding beneath us—I was home. Once we'd left the concrete congestion of the city behind, I was shocked to see the countryside parched a dull brown. Istanbul looked anemic after the lush forests of Minnesota.

Libby and I arrived at my *lojman* to find furniture pulled away from the walls and black stains streaking up from swollen, cracked moldings. My Turkish carpets were rolled up in the bedroom. What was this? I assumed it was exterminators until a note on the counter caught my eye.

*Ann Marie:*
*Welcome back!*
*Your lojman was flooded when a radiator release valve burst. Your cleaning lady discovered it, and we did our best to clean it up. Good luck!*
*Ileyn*

That black stuff growing up my walls was mold! If I hadn't already depleted my supply of tears I would have cried. I did what any self-respecting woman would do. I walked out.

Up the street I discovered Jacqueline sipping a beer in the shade on her front stoop. Wild red tresses framed her round, freckled face. A French Canadian, Jacqueline had taught French at Koç for years.

"Welcome back, Ann Marie! Hi, Libby, how are you, sweetie? Did you have a good summer? Want a beer?"

"Oh, Jacqueline! I had a wonderful summer, but you should see my *lojman*! It's a mess—an absolute dump. I just had to get out of there—and yes, I'd love a beer."

Jacqueline disappeared inside, returning with a cold Efes. "What happened? Did someone break in?"

I recounted the details. "My silk rug is ruined. It's all bled together. I can't believe it. I wish I hadn't come back!"

"Have you told Marnie? She and Tony are back. I'm sure they'll help you. The school should certainly be responsible for the damage." I was distraught, but talking about it helped. We finished our beers, then I walked down to the Paulus's. Marnie hadn't heard about my plight, but she was sympathetic. She insisted that I stay for dinner, and the evening with them soothed my conflicted soul. Little do we realize the value of kind gestures.

"We have a new teacher I think you'll enjoy," Tony announced at dinner. "Dee is a southern belle—well, a little tougher than that—and I think you'll like each other. There's also David, an American man about your age who you may enjoy, too. I want you to sign on for a third year." I'd told him the previous year that my major difficulty with Turkey was the lack of close friends.

"I don't feel all that positive about staying on just now, Tony. The mold in my apartment is horrible. There's even orange fungus growing from the baseboard in my bedroom. And my carpets are ruined—even the silk one you guys paid for in Selçuk." I blush to recall the whine in my voice.

"I'm sure the school will cover your damages," he said. "Take your rugs to Adnan & Hassan in the Grand Bazaar, and they'll help you, then give me the bill."

"I appreciate that, Tony, but what about the mold?" He told me to contact Aşkin, the building and grounds director.

I felt better. Maybe it wasn't the end of the world. Tony cleaned up the dishes while Marnie walked me over to meet Dee, who I liked immediately. A bright woman, she was right on my wave length—

liberal. Her brilliant smile, friendly laugh and sparkling blue eyes exuded warmth, wisdom and honesty. She pulled out a bottle of wine, and the three of us settled in for some quality girl time.

Dee and I had differences as well as similarities. She loved to cook (that wouldn't be me) and I loved to exercise (that wouldn't be her). We had similar teaching philosophies, though, and we both loved to read and travel. Hope, hope, hope.

When I returned to my moldy *lojman*, rather than giving in to despair, I dug out my rose-colored glasses and gave myself a talking to.

"OK, Ann Marie, time to buckle down, muster up, and face another year here. It will be what you make it. The teaching is great, and you'll dive back into writing and exercising every day. Find someone to walk with in the mornings, get your writing group going again, and make a point of connecting with Dee. If you don't get renters, you'll just have to budget. You can do it. Tomorrow is a new day."

I moved into the smaller bedroom, which had less mold and overlooked the hills of Istanbul. By the end of my first week back, things were looking up. The walls were still stained, but Askin had promised repairs.

# 40 SECOND TIME AROUND

It felt like old home week when the teachers returned to campus. We were like high-schoolers reconnecting on the first day of school. I had to admit, Koç employed exceptional people; the filter of international teaching makes for an interesting group. Serge and Sue's twins (now four) were exuberant about walking Libby, and Annie and Koray's 5-month-old twin boys were beyond adorable. We had new neighbors to fill the *lojmans* of those who had moved on, though I'd miss John Clemens, now in Taiwan. Workshop brought new faces, including Dee and David. I hoped people wouldn't expect me to "hook up" with David and was relieved when he introduced us to an attractive woman that first afternoon. "This is my Particular Friend, Kerime (CARE-ee-may)." Though an odd way to introduce a lover, the message was clear.

We waded through the obligatory bilingual staff meeting—repeating everything in two languages was an unfortunate reality at Koç. Next time I'd bring knitting.

My luck was turning. Annie wrote that she'd found some renters, so I'd be able to travel after all. I wanted to explore Turkey, and maybe I could coax Terri and Dee to join me.

I smiled as I cut through the long line of service buses delivering students. The excitement of the first day of school always lifted my spirits. The day began with my beloved IB kids. "What a joy to see you again! I look forward to another fun and interesting year together." Now seniors, they grinned, reflecting my pleasure at our second year, a requirement of the International Baccalaureate program. "You'll be relieved to learn that I attended an IB training during workshop so we won't be so much in the dark about the program's expectations." Laughter. Last year had been like Blind Man's Bluff as we felt our way through the IB requirements. Now I had a handle on just what it entailed. I explained the units we'd be studying, the two essays they'd have to submit to IB, the projects they'd need to complete, and the oral exams that lay ahead, giving each of them a chart I'd prepared to lay it out clearly. IB was a daunting program, but this group had been both kind and patient with me as I'd stumbled through it. I'd been confident with my teaching and consulted with other IB teachers, but the system had seemed labyrinthine. Now I got it.

My two ninth grade groups were better behaved and spoke better English than last year's Newfies. Now that I was familiar with Turkish names, I learned theirs more quickly, though I again enlisted my camera. Only two of my three classes were new to me, so the transition was easy.

After a rough landing, I was on my way.

The tour director missed our flight (damnable Istanbul traffic), our first indication of trouble. Marnie had invited me to join her on a tour to the Euphrates, and we sixteen tour members landed in Malatya with no inkling of what to do next. We hopefully scanned the tiny airport, relieved to find a small, grizzled man holding a FARIT sign (Friends of Archeological Research in Turkey). We weren't so thrilled, though, when we saw his dented bus.

Sky darkening, we set off on paved roads that soon deteriorated—as did our driver's caution. The moon was nearly full, lending a surreal quality to the craggy, rolling landscape. We shrieked as the bus careened around steep mountain curves and shielded our eyes as massive boulders loomed in our path. At one point the moon revealed no road ahead. Just a path.

"Oh, my god! We're going four-wheeling!" someone cried.

"In a BUS!" another laughed.

We jostled, bounced, and flew from our seats as our driver navigated his short-cut to our destination. After an hour of back-road bouncing we emerged on smooth pavement that wove along beside the Euphrates, a murky moonlit trail glowing below us. The peaceful river soothed our souls after the horrifying journey.

The small city of Kemaliye was a welcome sight. After lugging our bags up a long flight of stone stairs, we stepped through an ornate wooden door into a lobby adorned with multi-colored carpets, kilims, and tasseled pillows. Another flight up, our spacious room opened onto a vast balcony. Though it was nearly midnight, Marnie, Lorna and I wandered out to marvel at the river glittering in the moonlight.

"Here's to a relaxing adventure," Marnie joked as she raised her wine glass.

"And to leaving the short-cuts behind!" Lorna added with a grin.

The next morning I woke early and headed out to explore the

village. I passed a woman in an embroidered scarf and *şalvar* (skirt-like pants) shelling walnuts by the side of the road, and she insisted I take a handful. "*Çok teşekkürler*," I said, wishing I knew enough Turkish to do more than just thank her. Moments later an older woman strolling the path invited me for tea. Turkish hospitality. I refused her invitation because of our hotel breakfast but regretted it. Never again would I pass up an opportunity to glimpse the lives of these kind people.

At breakfast we learned our tour director had caught a morning flight, delaying our trip to Divriği until noon. It was a brilliant, warm day, and someone suggested we wander up the street to visit an artisan who made door knockers.

Kemaliye is famous for its hand-crafted door knockers, and the walls and ceiling of the shop were hung with hundreds cleverly crafted from pounded metal. They ranged from plain to ornate, and many featured two separate knockers, a large one for male visitors and a smaller one (below it, of course) for females. Since the men's knocker made a deeper sound, it alerted the women of the house to cover their heads or hurry up to the harem level before a man entered their home.

On the way back we passed an ancient fountain carved into the rock with an ornate brass spigot and a battered cup hanging from a chain. How many people had stopped to refresh themselves there over the centuries?

Mr. Greenwood finally arrived and introduced our academic guide, Dr. Scott Redford, a medieval archeologist from Georgetown University. We climbed into two vans for a ride to eclipse the past evening's horrors. Kemaliye had been cut off from the west by the Taurus Mountains for centuries, and in the late 1800's members of the community decided to tunnel to the other side. It took them 130 years to chisel a road through ten kilometers of rock using only hand tools, breaking through the wall at intervals to light the tunnels. Many of the tunnels were named after men who'd fallen to their deaths in the process. Designed for donkey carts, most of the road was only wide enough for one vehicle. In the late 1990's the Turkish government intervened to finish the last few kilometers with heavy equipment, completing the road in 2002. Little did we know that our route is considered one of the most dangerous in the world.

I'd traveled mountain roads through the Rockies, the Alps, and Cost Rica, but they were nothing like this. The tunnels were narrow and rounded with rough-chipped walls and no hint of pavement. (Why pave solid rock?) Our van careened out of the first tunnel onto a narrow track on the mountain's edge—what? No safety barrier?

"Oh, my goodness!"

"Look how far up we are!"

"God, save us!"

Curses and prayers resounded as our van navigated high above the Euphrates (*Firat* in Turkish). Comments evolved to shrieks and screams at each precipice or wild turn. Some passengers cowered in their seats while others just covered their eyes. I have to admit that I found it exhilarating but knew better than to show it, so I suppressed my glee. Even that abated, though, when my heart lurched to see the Euphrates hundreds of feet straight down. I finally realized this was no carnival ride and that my life was in peril. At long last we emerged from the tunnels onto a smooth tarred road.

We were treated to another hour of heart-stopping vistas through stark, mountainous countryside, finally arriving at Divriği (dee-VREE-yee). Dr. Redford explained, "This is probably the least visited tourist destination in Turkey, although it contains one of its greatest treasures (obviously because of the danger involved in GETTING there). The Ulu Mosque and Hospital portals are the finest examples of Seljuk stone carving in Turkey." The entrances' intricate, exuberant designs fascinated me. Soaring 40 feet above the doors, the carved stone featured every shape from botanical to geometric in deep relief.

We squinted in the bright sun, trying to soak up Dr. Redford's enthused explanations. "The adjoining buildings were constructed during the crusades between 1228 and 1229, and they portray an incredible mix of styles, ranging from gothic and Islamic to baroque. The variation in style is so unexpected that some have questioned its authenticity, but when you review medieval history, it becomes clear that the Euphrates was a border between the Byzantine, Roman, and

Ottoman cultures. War-torn nearly every year from the seventh century on, this area drew soldiers and craftsmen from both Europe and Asia."

As the late sun painted the western sky, we headed home. The quickest (and most fearful) twelve raced to the van with the older driver, while we remaining six rode with a younger fellow who looked about fourteen. We regretted it. He drove like most teen-aged boys in spite of our frantic warnings.

We were again treated to expansive views and then the hair-raising trek through the mountain tunnels. My heart raced as we careened through the tunnels far too fast, and at one point, skirting the mountain between tunnels, one of our front wheels slipped off the edge. I caught my breath, tensed, and looked down, anticipating my life's end with a plunge into the Euphrates. I screamed. We all screamed. Miraculously, Junior swerved and got all four wheels back onto the road. He was nonplussed, but the rest of us were laughing hysterically—with both fear and relief. Thankfully, darkness finally enveloped the van and we couldn't see the perils ahead. Three riders abandoned the van a few miles from Kemaliye to walk the rest of the way in the dark. I stayed on, certain that the worst of the ride was behind us. I was shaking too much to walk anyway.

There's nothing like glimpsing the end of your life to make you appreciate the people around you (and to put a little mold into perspective). I still have warm feelings for friends I made on that trip.

Not so for our young driver.

May I never see him again.

To begin our second week of school (and give myself a breather until I could catch up from my packed weekend), I had my ninth graders write short biographies of themselves. At the beginning of the previous year many of my ninth graders could barely produce a paragraph, but this year they all managed a cohesive page—whew! We had plenty of work ahead, but for the most part they were eager, capable students. I love it that Turks have high respect for education—and educators. The public schools paid poorly, but teachers were esteemed in society and treated well. There are even luxury hotels, *Öğretmen Evi,* available only to teachers and at minimal cost. But I digress.

I was concerned about one of my students, a ninth grade boy who just couldn't settle down. Burak was a tall, handsome, athletic boy, and he was surprisingly popular, though I'd seen him bully some of his classmates. He was so impulsive that he didn't think before he spoke, and his comments to peers were often hurtful. I was familiar with hyperactive students and had some tricks up my sleeve, so I gave them a try. I seated Burak off to the side of the class beside Erdem, a solid student who was willing to help keep him on task. I made a point of stopping often at his desk to check on his progress, and I let him take an occasional stroll through the halls. All fingers crossed. The ninth grade dean was well aware of Burak's issues and had offered to intervene whenever necessary. Unfortunately, I always had him in the afternoon, a time when he was hard-pressed to contain himself. Mornings are generally easier with hyperactive kids. I knew Burak would be a challenge.

My IB class started their year with *1984* by George Orwell. Most of them had already finished the novel and loved it. What? I remembered being deeply disturbed by it in high school. I think those kids were pre-programmed to love everything. I put them into small discussion groups, and they argued animatedly about themes and characters.

Amazing. Seniors weren't expected to put much effort into schoolwork their senior year because they'd be cramming for the spring Ö.S.S., the college entrance exam. A few of them planned to attend foreign universities and wouldn't take the exam, but most devoted their weekends to *dersane,* the official Ö.S.S. cram school.

Another bright spot at school was our ninth grade team, which was downright inspiring. Our meetings were a forum for sharing creative teaching ideas and brainstorming new approaches, and we agreed to institute the six traits program, a method for teaching and evaluating writing that I strongly supported. I credited Annie Özsaraç, our new team leader, for the stimulating changes. An American married to the ninth grade dean, Annie was eager to bring creative innovations to the curriculum.

School was off to a great start, but it was soon eclipsed by my travels. Now that I had renters, I could afford to explore Turkey. Each new destination illuminated the warmth and beauty of my adopted country.

# 43  OH, FOR A CUP OF TEA!

On our first three-day weekend, Dee, Terri and I flew to Trabzon on the Black Sea. "Oh, Lord in Heaven!" Terri screeched, clenching my wrist. "We're going to crash into the water!" Dee and I craned to look out her window as our plane descended and saw only azure sea below us. My stomach lurched, but the other passengers seemed calm—at least as calm as Turks are at landing, already unbuckling their seat belts.

"There's no announcement, and no one seems upset," Dee said as she reached across me to pat Terri's arm. It turned out the Trabzon landing strip stretched along the beach between the Black Sea and the Pontic Mountains, the most picturesque airport setting imaginable. We picked up a rental car and headed for the city, unclear about the directions we'd been given to our hotel. I wished we'd gotten a map.

As we looped through the city center a third time, Terri quipped, "Well, we're getting the grand tour of Trabzon." Frustrated, I stopped to ask directions of a middle-aged man sitting outside a shop, probably chuckling that this was the third time he'd seen these dippy tourists drive by. I knew just enough Turkish to communicate our plight, which must have sounded like "Teacher I am from Istanbul lost our way please Nur hotel know you?" I got the idea across, though. I understood most of his directions, but when I tried to repeat them back he offered to drive us there. Worked for me. Dee and Terri weren't impressed at my decision, but what could they do?

"My name is Arif," he said, starting the car. "I am at your service. Do you know your gas gauge is low? I can take you to a gas station." And he did. The clerk at the Nur Hotel, yet another Mehmet, teased and cajoled us as we checked in.

"Can I drive you back to your store?" I asked Arif.

"Of course, but I will drive," he insisted. He offered to guide us through the city the next day and gave me his card. Lo and behold, he was a doctor.

We settled into our rooms, then trekked off to find a late lunch. The city square was a vast shaded tea garden, its tables populated by men and women chatting. "Get a load of that," Dee said. "It's such a habit to sit in the tea gardens that they do it even on Ramazan when they can't drink tea."

We walked through the city peeking into restaurant after restaurant —all cold, dark, and empty. No food in sight, even for Christians. We finally discovered a tiny *lokanta* (restaurant) with chickens roasting on a rotisserie and a few men eating inside. "SCORE! We might be heathens, but we can eat!" Dee exclaimed. We shared a roasted chicken, salad, and *sutlaç* (rice pudding). Yum.

After a few hours exploring the city's ancient churches and mosques, we found a small restaurant that was open. When we asked for tea, the waiter smiled and guided us to an upstairs room where patrons chatted at empty tables. They served us tea but refused payment because it was Ramazan. We left a big tip, which I hoped wasn't an insult.

Back at the hotel we trudged upstairs to our rooms. "I brought a bottle of wine," I said. "Interested?"

"So did I!" Terri and Dee chimed, laughing. We gathered our tiny water glasses and Dee produced a bag of pistachios for cocktail hour— and probably dinner. "*Şerefe!*" we toasted as the call to prayer blasted through our open window. The neighborhood mosque's loudspeaker was mounted directly across from our window.

"Don't worry," Dee yelled, covering her ears. "It'll be over soon." We sipped and nibbled, waiting for the Arabic verses to end. It continued longer than usual, so I closed the window, which hardly helped. We smiled and waited.

And waited.

And waited.

Not only did we wait through the call to prayer, but through an entire sermon. We watched through a mosque window as men with crocheted beanies on their heads stood, bowed, stooped, bent their heads to the floor, stood again, and repeated the entire sequence over and over as the sermon droned on.

"This is getting old!" Terri yelled.

"Must be the Ramazan Holy Day Service!"

"Yes, and it's being blasted to the entire city through our room!"

"I think I'll go back to my room!" Terri yelled. Her tiny room was further from the loudspeaker. Dee and I braved the hour-long sermon, then talked late into the night. No point in looking for dinner.

Saturday we drove to Üzüngöl (long lake), an alpine lake high in the Black Mountains. We'd been warned that weather along the Black Sea was usually foggy and rainy, but the sun shone bright in an azure sky. After driving a half hour along the Black Sea shoreline, we turned into the mountains along the Sulaklı River. Lush green mountain slopes were dotted with tiny villages, their minarets reaching into the blue. "There must be a mosque for about every 50 people," Dee commented.

We passed a number of Koran schools and noticed that most of the men we saw wore crocheted skullcaps, rare in Istanbul. We stopped to watch a young girl and her little brother drive a cow and calf through an alpine meadow. The girl was about ten, dressed in a long skirt with her hair tied back in a scarf. She pulled the cow along while her brother cavorted and occasionally slapped its flanks with a stick. At one point she pressed her shoulder to the cow's side to make her turn. It was adorable.

At long last we reached the picturesque lakeside village of Üzüngöl, which reminded me of Grandfather's Alp in *Heidi*, but with minarets. We passed a woman pushing a wheelbarrow piled with hay and another toting a huge load of wood on her back. More women stooped in a nearby field. "So where are the men?" Dee asked. "Do the women do all the work here?"

An elderly man leaned against a fence at the roadside. Thankful for my rudimentary Turkish, I asked if there was a restaurant nearby. He shook his head then pointed across the lake, indicating that we might find some food there. Most of the tourist restaurants were closed for the season—or perhaps just for Ramazan. Who knew?

We parked near the Mosque and began to walk along the lake

keeping our distance from cows scattered along our walk. Though the village seemed deserted, we found a log-sided restaurant where a bearded man with a red bandana around his head chatted with a black-suited waiter.

"*Merhaba,*" I said to him. "*Nasilsiniz?*" (Hello, how are you?)

"I'm just fine," he answered in perfect English, grinning over his neatly-trimmed white beard. "Are you looking for lunch?"

"We are definitely looking for lunch, and it's not an easy business this week," Dee answered. "Is there any chance we can get a meal here?"

"I'll see what I can do," he said, then spoke to the waiter in Turkish.

"They'll bring you a meal," he said. "Sadly, I have to be on my way. Enjoy!" He picked up his backpack and wooden staff, then trudged off into the mountains. We soon sat before a meal of freshly grilled trout, fries, vegetables, and bread. Sheer heaven. We were the only patrons in the restaurant, which could easily serve 150. We felt guilty that the staff had to prepare and serve (and smell) such a delectable meal when they could neither eat nor drink until sunset.

After an afternoon of hapless wandering, we drove back down to the coast. We spotted a large restaurant and tea garden along the highway. "This looks like a tourist spot," I said. "They should certainly have tea." The hostess shook her head at our request, but invited us to step in and enjoy their view. The restaurant, perched on a bluff above the sea, had a breathtaking panoramic view.

"Hey, you guys, it's only an hour until sunset, and they'll serve dinner then—how about staying?" Dee suggested. We made a reservation then trekked down their hundred-plus steps to the beach where we watched the sun paint and repaint the clouded horizon. We returned to a restaurant full of Turks sitting patiently at tables. They seated us by the window, where we waited another twenty minutes, tantalized by the delicacies laid out before us.

A large family sat at the next table, and the father nodded to us when the call to prayer signaled the sunset. Time to eat at last. We feasted on a platter of fried anchovies, lentil soup, bread, salad, and dessert. As we finished, a scarved woman from the next table brought us a bowl of roasted hazelnuts, an area specialty she'd brought from home. And at last we were served the tea we'd originally stopped for.

Sunday dawned sunny again—miraculous for this grey corner of Turkey. We headed to the Sumela Monastery, built into the side of a mountain, a mere hour away.

I opted to hike up to the monastery while Terri and Dee drove up. Oh, for a friend who loved exercise! I was invigorated as I followed a rushing stream that tumbled over rocks on its plunge down the mountainside. The Sumela Monastery hangs from a sheer rock face hundreds of feet from the ground, and I had a variety of views as I grew closer. Near the top I met another hiker, a Swiss man who'd spent the past three years biking through Europe and Asia.

"What have been the highlights of your trip?"

"I have to say it's been the generous hospitality of Romanians, Armenians, and Turks. In fact, the Armenians were particularly warm and hospitable—a major change from the Swiss. We're so reserved!" I agreed about the Turks, who had proven their generosity to me time and again. I'd have to get to Armenia some day, but the border from Turkey was closed because of the Ottoman's notorious massacres in the early 1900's.

Our woodland path finally emerged on a long stairway carved into the side of the cliff. At the top a stone arch opened onto a courtyard, where Dee and Terri sat on a ledge at one side. "Hi, Ann Marie. Have you seen much of it yet?"

"I just arrived," I said, introducing my new friend. Dee guided us through the monastery, its focal point the Rock Church. It was a small chapel carved into the mountain, embellished with medieval religious frescoes both inside and out. "What a travesty that they're so marred by nicks and bullet holes," I said.

"Shepherds, soldiers, and teens have defaced them," Dee explained. She'd taught art history and understood the politics as well as the art. "Muslims felt it was their duty to destroy Christian relics—such a travesty." A Trabzon Travesty, I thought to myself. It was too tacky to say out loud.

Sumela was like a small stone village, its breathtaking views far surpassing the structures themselves. It was established in the fourth century by two priests who discovered an icon of the Virgin Mary in a mountain cave and built the monastery there to protect it. The entire country had once been Christian.

I was awed by the incredible faith I witnessed, from the ancient Christians who risked their lives to save an icon to the current Muslims who fasted for a full month. Though I'd recently turned my back on organized religion, these insights stirred my latent spirituality. So much to think about.

# 44 THE CAVE HOTEL

Libby nearly wagged her tail off when I picked her up—such joy to be loved, even by a dog. My apartment walls had been painted in my absence, though shadows of mold insinuated through the white. The carpeting was still nasty, so I e-mailed Aşkin suggesting they remove or replace it. No answer, as usual. He wasn't quick with e-mails.

I slid back into my school routine, cajoling my reluctant seniors to focus on their studies, at least until second semester when I knew they'd quit working completely. We finished *1984* and launched into a global issues unit on poverty. I divided the class into small groups to research the causes of poverty and the ways wealthy nations exploited resources and workers in developing countries. Their assignment was to create presentations to share their findings, and I knew they'd be good. They dove into their task with gusto. They may have gotten lethargic, but compared to American students they were still stars.

My ninth graders were rolling along fine—except for Burak. The poor fellow couldn't focus to save his life and had quickly become the bane to my existence. He was easily the most seriously ADHD (attention-deficit hyperactive disorder) student of my 31 years of teaching. He'd enter the classroom (usually after the bell), execute a pull-up on the door jamb, and things would deteriorate from there. When he wasn't singing, he was drumming on his desk or climbing on a window sill to adjust the shades. Really. Poor guy. No one should have to live with that kind of energy. Sadly, Turkish schools don't have special education, so we teachers met regularly to plan interventions to help him. Koray, now the ninth grade dean, offered to supervise him when he got out of control. We'd devoted the first quarter to getting him to class on time, and our next goal was to have him arrive with materials. My day often ended with the challenge of managing Burak's class, which exhausted me. No wonder I was eager for another travel adventure.

\* \* \*

The big celebration at the end of Ramazan was near the end of October, and a group of us headed to Cappadocia over the break. It's spelled Kapadokya in wonderfully-phonetic Turkish, the language where every letter always makes the same sound. Dee and I were joined by Sarah Boyd, a Fulbright exchange teacher we'd met from another school. With Ramazan ending, we'd be able to eat and drink to our hearts' content on this trip. Terri was off on a road trip in her new car.

We entered the Kelebek Pension through a carved stone archway onto a plaza overlooking the magical city of Göreme. The city itself was carved from massive stone formations like shaggy-mane mushrooms, the area's famous fairy chimneys.

On our right intricately carved wooden doors led into two fairy chimneys, part of our cave hotel. Potted geraniums and ancient pottery jugs lined our path as we climbed two flights of stone stairs to an open terrace where people chatted and ate at sun-warmed tables. The view stopped us in our tracks: hot-air balloons floated overhead above the panorama of fairy chimneys, tile-roofed stone houses, and a khaki landscape of fantastical formations.

"Can you believe it? This is phenomenal!" Dee said.

A cheery young man with a shock of dark hair across his brow approached us. "Welcome to the Kelebek," he announced in a gravely voice. "My name is Mustafa. Help yourself to breakfast, and then you can come through the lobby to check in."

"Thank you. We will." He hadn't even asked if we had reservations! We dove into the sumptuous breakfast buffet of breads, vegetables, dried fruits and olives as well as made-to-order omelets. (I love olives and always left at least twenty pits on my plate.) We found tables outdoors and basked in the bright morning sun as we feasted and sipped strong coffee. I'd stumbled on heaven.

Later we migrated to a bright office overlooking another view of the city. We sat on a lush black leather couch as Mustafa checked us in. "This hotel is made from the centuries-old cave home of the Yavuş family, which was carved from rock and fairy chimneys here overlooking Göreme," he explained. "Ali has decorated each room in the traditional Turkish style. We hope you enjoy your stay, and please let us know if we can help you with anything."

He handed us an ancient key on a carved wooden fob and guided us back down to a door off the terrace. "Oohhh! This is darling!" Dee crooned. And it was. The ornately-carved bed had a coral chenille spread with white nubbins and tassels. Matching drapes were pulled back from wide double windows above the bed. Turkish rugs and antique tables contrasted with the soft limestone shades of the carved dome ceiling. Tiny alcoves were carved into the walls for candles, and a wrought-iron dressing table welcomed us with bottles of water. My trepidations about dark cave rooms were dispelled in this bright haven.

Dee chose to read while Sarah and I headed off on a hike. Cappadocia is a   network of valleys carved between three extinct volcanoes, and because of the area's ongoing erosion, the terrain is ever-changing. The rock formations range from 40-foot tall towers to mushroom-like lumps, most carved at one time or another into dwellings. Sarah and I explored the Pigeon Valley several times, thrilled to clamber through the valley's other-worldly rock formations, exhilarated as we discovered each deserted cave home or chapel. Cappadocia boasts some of the world's earliest Christian churches, some dating back to the eighth century. On a guided hike through the Rose Valley, we rappelled down a steep incline with climbing ropes. It was a blast, reminding me how much I missed outdoor expeditions. Sarah shared my sense of adventure, and I hoped we'd get together more. All fingers crossed.

Between excursions we lounged at tables or balcony cushions on the hotel's terraces, gazing out over the town sprawled around a monstrous fairy chimney, reputed to have been a Roman tomb. Staff were on hand to serve our every need, and on a rainy afternoon one of the hotel's four Mustafas taught us to play tavla (backgammon).

Wandering the village one afternoon, we ran into Allana, another Koç teacher. She'd flown to Göreme with us but stayed in a hostel. "Hey guys, want to do a balloon ride?"

"Sure, but isn't it expensive?"

"Absolutely," Allana said. "It usually costs 200 Euros, but I've been negotiating with a guy over there, and he's willing to do it for 200 lira each if we can fill a balloon. That's about half price if we can get ten people."

The next morning we roused at 5:00 A.M., dressed in our warmest clothes, and walked down the dark stone stairs to meet a 5:30 van. "Brrrr," Dee said. "This is not my idea of a good time." Floridian to the core, cold temps undid her. A toasty van delivered us to a building for breakfast then to the launch site, where over 20 balloons lay on their sides in various stages of inflation. The air was suffused with the repeated shhht of propane as flames heated the air in the balloons. They glowed in the early dawn light, lending an eerie, ethereal atmosphere that intrigued yet frightened me. My anxiety mounted as we wandered through the maze of inflating balloons. At last we found our balloon, hovering straight above its mammoth basket.

"How are we going to get in there?" Sarah asked. The six-foot high wicker basket was divided into five inaccessible compartments. Before anyone could answer, one of the men bent over on all fours and another took her hand so she could step up on the man's back to climb into the basket. Once we were all in, they loosened the tethers and we lurched into the brightening sky. My stomach somersaulted a few times, then settled as I watched, amazed, at the scene unfurling beneath us—a terrain sculpted in stone. We rode across a moon-like landscape of varied land formations ranging from fairy chimneys to small mountains to gently eroded slopes like wind-sculpted sand dunes, many with doors and windows carved into them.

At first we were one of a crowd of balloons, but our driver split off, maneuvering between two tall fairy chimneys—goodness! We sailed down along the Rose Valley, where hundreds of tiny alcoves were systematically chiseled into the rock, always near a doorway and windows. These alcoves were carved for pigeons, their droppings gathered to fertilize the vineyards. "Look, Ann Marie!" Sarah exclaimed. "I think we're going down!" Our balloon was drifting down onto a hillside.

"What in the world? It can't be over yet." Two men jogged toward our balloon and reached up with bunches of wildflowers, handing blossoms to each of us. They called something in Turkish as we drifted skyward.

"How sweet was that?" Sarah crooned. I settled a daisy behind my ear, wondering what they'd said. After an hour we descended again, this time to a truck waiting in an open field. Our driver settled our basket on a trailer, the balloon floating down beside it. Two men helped us down as others set up a makeshift table with a tablecloth, juice, and champagne. We toasted to a beautiful morning and a delightful ride—at the special Koç discount.

We returned to the Kelebec for breakfast, then wandered the town and surrounding countryside, always welcomed with smiles. I met an elderly man outside a mosque who showed me through the sanctuary, proudly introducing me to his son, the Imam, or spiritual leader. When I asked to take his photo, he grinned, but his response was vague when I showed him the photo in my camera. When I realized he couldn't focus on it, I handed him my reading glasses He grinned when he saw his image. Did he even own reading glasses? I insisted that he keep them, and he nodded sagely then handed me a copy of Islam and Christianity.

We were invited into the homes of local women whose intent was not only to show off their ancient abodes, but to sell needlework. We'd been warned not to be taken in, yet I felt differently. I have so much, and they have so little. Anyway, I was curious. Our first invitation was from a young mother dressed in sweats (rare in Göreme), who proudly explained that her cave home was over 200 years old. I bought a small necklace and şalvar for a whopping $12.50). We visited two other women as we explored the Pigeon Valley. The elder one,  Fatma, treated us to tea and snacks in her well-cushioned outdoor gazebo before bringing out her needlework. Though she looked well over 70, she was the same age as I was, 57. Life wasn't easy for the Turks, though I must admit, it couldn't have been too terrible amid the splendors of Cappadocia.

# 45 AN UNEXPECTED VISIT

My *lojman* got some long-awaited attention the week I was gone. The plaster walls were sanded and repainted, the carpeting replaced with laminate flooring, and new mouldings installed. Goodbye, mold! I gleefully moved back into the big bedroom and laid my carpets on the new "wood" floors. Adnan and Hassan had arranged a fine refurbishing of my silk carpet, though its pastel tones had been transformed to deeper shades.

My entire world felt brighter, including school. We were making headway with Burak. With the support of Koray he was getting to class on time—a humble beginning. To his credit (and my chagrin) he had perfect attendance. I worked out a system for him to "escape" to the hallway to complete his work with a peer, one of a few diligent students willing and able to keep him on task. He made every day a challenge, though I imagine it was more difficult for him than for me.

My IB students entertained and enlightened us with creative presentations on world poverty. Their enthusiasm continued to astound me. I learned that half of the children on the planet live in poverty. How could I have missed that fact? I also learned that 80% of the people in the world live on less than $10 a day and half on less than $2.50 a day. I'd seen photos of starving children in Ethiopia and Bangladesh yet had no idea how routinely American industries exploited them.

One memorable presentation was an interview of an African native who'd been injured in a Nike factory accident. Take a starving community and offer people a dollar a day to make shoes in a sweatshop with no benefits and no safety precautions, and you make a huge profit. If someone gets hurt at work, fire them. The more I learned, the more infuriated I became—as did my students. It was a life-changing awareness for me. (I would later spend a month volunteering at an Ethiopian orphanage and sponsor a young Ethiopian man through college.) I admired my students, too, for framing their depressing presentations with humor. The interview with the African worker was conducted in an invented dialect with an interpreter and they had us all laughing hysterically in spite of the devastating realities of the situation. Gosh, I loved those kids.

I received an e-mail from my Australian niece, Laura, in late November. She was traveling in Italy and Greece and planned to join me in Turkey for Christmas.

*Dear Ann:*

*Italy is lovely, but the men are horrid. I've had enough pawing to last a lifetime, and Yvette has found me a cheap flight to Istanbul. I'll be there on Friday, so I need directions to your apartment. I hope it's not a problem for you to have me arrive early. I can't wait to see you.*

*Love,*

*Laura*

Needless to say, I was thrilled. Laura (named after my sister) had lived with me in Grand Marais for a year, and we were close. Friday was Teacher's Day, so I arranged for her to be my guest at the big dinner celebration. I sent directions for her to meet me at the Fenerbahçe Club, much easier than finding her way to the Koç School. A seasoned traveler, she'd be fine.

Friday dawned sunny and warm— Istanbul Indian Summer. At school I discovered my Teacher's Day gift, a large black umbrella with my name engraved on its wooden handle. The day was business as usual, except for long-stemmed roses delivered by student council members, red carnations at lunch, and an assembly in the auditorium. I was touched to see the students welcome 25 retired teachers by applauding enthusiastically as they filed to the front row. Typical teachers, some of them made quite a show of bowing and throwing kisses to the students. It brought tears to my eyes, reminding me how very important relationships are between teachers and students in Turkey. Each teacher was presented with a plant, and the presenting students took the teacher's hands, kissed them, then bent to touch them with their foreheads, a traditional sign of respect for elders in this culture. More tears.

I couldn't wait for the party that evening, mostly because Laura would be there. She stood waiting beside the entrance to the Fenerbahçe Club decked out in a full ruffled skirt and a felted black cardigan. "Oh, Ann! I'm so glad to see you!" she cried, enveloping me in a bear hug.

"Sweetie! How long has it been? How I've missed you!" Tears again.

"Three years. Can you believe it?"

"Well, I'm glad you hated those lusty Italians, because now I get you for longer! We'll start making up for those three years right now. You look fabulous." Wild brown curls framed her healthy, freckled face, and her eyes were bright with anticipation. I held my arm around her as we entered the ballroom.

We ate, danced, and drank our way through an enchanted evening. Our waiter, Ismael, was quite taken with Laura. He refilled everyone else's wine glasses without a word but repeatedly asked her (in Turkish) if she'd like more. She learned the word *"biraz"* (a little) and always indicated an inch with her fingers. He preferred it that way, since a short refill gave him more opportunities to return. When the clock chimed twelve, a group of us hurried to catch the service bus to Taksim and a taxi to a Sultanahmet hotel. No school the next day.

8:30 came too early, but we managed to shower, dress, eat, and board the tram to meet Edda for her "Hans Around the Bazaar" tour. Though I'd already seen much of what she showed us, her command of history and the ancient areas of Istanbul fascinated me. Edda pointed out a birdhouse on the side of a *medresi* behind the Beyazit Hamamı (an ancient Turkish bath). "I'm sure this is the loveliest bird house in Istanbul. See how the sparrows flit in and out of the compartments of their miniature mosque? They love it!" she said. "The Ottomans believed that caring for birds was a way to earn their way to heaven." We donated to a footless beggar sitting on the sidewalk. After the tour we had lunch, made a few stops at the Grand Bazaar, and visited Harem 49 to look at rugs. Hüseyin, now a friend, convinced me to buy a kilim that caught Laura's fancy, telling me he was funding half of it by charging so little. What a charmer. Actually, I trusted him implicitly. Jamilah had introduced us, and I knew he was honest. In fact, he hired young assistants from rural Turkey and gave them English lessons as they worked out their apprenticeships.

We were settling into my *lojman* Sunday evening when I heard a knock at the door. "Welcome back, Ann Marie," said my neighbor Füsün, who stood holding a covered plate. "I wanted to share some of these delicious *hamsi* with you and Laura. We had too many. Please enjoy them!" She refused to come in, so Laura and I sat down to enjoy a repast of tiny fried butterflied fish fillets, about an inch-and-a-half long. They were beyond delicious, and I didn't have to pull together a meal. Ah, friends!

# 46 SEIZED!

I heard moaning in the kitchen early Monday morning and got there just in time to break Laura's fall as she lurched forward. I laid her on the floor, kneeling beside her. Had she fainted? Her head jerked backwards and her body convulsed.

"Oh, my God! Laura! Laura!" She was having a seizure! My mind raced. What do you do? Hold her head—keep her from hurting herself. Tip her head back. I couldn't remember anything else. I knew not to shove a spoon in her mouth—thank goodness for first aid classes. My heart pounded as she struggled against me, then finally relaxed.

"Are you OK?" I asked as she opened her eyes.

"What happened? Why am I on the floor?"

I explained as I settled her on the couch, then called my department head. "I'm not coming in today, Roger. My niece just had a seizure and I need to get her to a doctor. Can you get someone to cover for me? I don't have class until period three. Can I bring her to the school doctor?"

"I'm so sorry! Calm down, Ann Marie. It's no problem here. We'll cover your classes, and I'll transfer you to the school doctor right now. Good luck, and don't worry." The doctor was busy at the elementary school, so I threw on a coat and ran down the hill to wait until she was free. She promised to send a nurse up to my *lojman*.

I ran back to the apartment where Laura lay on the couch, deathly pale and listless. "Do you want some ibuprofen?" I asked her. "Some water?"

"No medicine, but water would be good," she said weakly. Bless her heart. She sure didn't need this! The nurse arrived, checked her vitals, then said he'd arrange an appointment with a neurologist. She'd need some tests, and the sooner the better. A student had broken his ankle, so we could catch a ride to the Amerikan Polyklinik with him. Laura pulled on a skirt and sweater, stepped into her tennis shoes and donned a light jacket. The weather had been warm, but clouds were moving in. I should have grabbed more clothes, but of course all I could think of was getting Laura to a doctor. We'd be in a warm car.

The neurologist recommended that Laura have an EEG and directed us to a med-tech lab in the city. Since Laura wasn't a Koç student, we were on our own for transportation. Navigating the city was a challenge, as I only knew public transport from a few places I frequented. We spent the entire day traveling from clinic to lab to clinic by train, tram and, when I was at a total loss, by taxi. The day grew colder, my wallet more empty, and poor Laura could barely stay awake, much less warm. I wrapped my pashmina around her shoulders and sat close to her. Why hadn't I grabbed more clothes? I felt helpless, wishing I spoke more Turkish and frustrated that I didn't know the city better.

She'd probably suffered an epileptic seizure, but there was no sign of brain damage. She was supposed to take it easy for a few days and have further tests once she returned to Australia. Relieved, we finally headed back to campus, exhausted. We walked to a nearby train station and waited shivering for the next train. When we got off at Pendik it was already dark, and I knew Laura was too tired to manage the crowded mini-bus. Though I had only a few lira left, I called Cebryil. I had a hard time communicating our location in Turkish, but a man standing nearby helped me. We were chilled to the bone by the time he arrived.

I guess the good part of all this was that Laura was with me when she had the seizure. What would she have done alone in Italy? It had been a rough day, but we'd weathered it together.

Laura regained her strength in a few days and felt ready to launch on her planned month-long tour of Turkey. She caught a bus to Cappadocia and would 'wing it' from there, promising to be back for Christmas.

# 47 THE DECISION

Teachers were all buzzing about contract renewals—who would stay and who would leave? It seemed too soon to face the question, yet Tony needed decisions about the coming year. International hiring fairs would begin in February, and it was time to post positions. I had until December tenth to decide.

I'd planned to stay on a third year, but I was waffling. The mold in my *lojman* had been disheartening, and I was disappointed that Aşkin had put me off in my requests for repair. The school had paid the cleaning bills for my carpets, but they'd lost their splendor. And then there was Burak. I'd grown to like him, but his energy was wearing me down, day by day. I wasn't sure I could face another year. The biggest issue for me, though, was friends and family. Did I want to stay?

I decided to "try on" each option for a week.

The first week I pretended I'd be staying. I woke each morning trying to focus my mind on new explorations of Istanbul, more travel, and another year with Dee. She and David would be back, both good friends. Terri was leaving, and it would be sad to say goodbye. She'd wormed her way into my heart. I wanted to visit Thailand and maybe do a Safari like the one Jacqueline had raved about it. I hadn't been to London yet, and Easy Jet had just begun reasonable fares there. Travel was one of the great perks of teaching overseas.

Getting up at 5:30 was a drag, though, and I spent too much time alone. Whose fault was that? I needed to be more pro-active about making plans to connect with people. I'd make it a priority for the rest of this year and the next. The next year at Koç.

Libby and I walked up to meet Leah for our morning walk.

"What have you decided about next year?" I asked.

"I'm staying on, but I've decided to move off campus. I'm a little worried about the expense, but I think I can swing it."

"How would you like a weekend roommate to share expenses?" I asked. "You could camp here with me on weeknights when you need to stay late."

"That would be awesome, Ann Marie. I hadn't even considered that option."

"Well, if I stay I'd love to do it. I'd rather live on campus, but a place in the city on weekends would make life perfect. I'm thinking seriously about staying."

"Oh, I hope you do! We'd have such a great time!"

Hmmm... Another year at Koç....

The next Monday I switched hats. I pretended I'd be returning to Minnesota, just to see how it felt. When my alarm rang at 5:30, I thought about sleeping in every morning. Oh, heaven! I'd rejoin the morning walk with my neighbors and exercise in the afternoons with Annie—biking, hiking, skiing, and paddling. Oh, how I missed that. All I ever did in Istanbul was walk, walk, walk—usually alone. And snow! There was something cozy and comforting about a few feet of snow in my yard, and I'd be able to ski and snowshoe all winter—a full five months in my neck of the woods.

I'd missed two years of Erin and Matthew's growing up, and I knew Laura would be thrilled if I came back. She was my rock; we'd grown close in the twenty years since Mom died. I admired my little sister, an up-and-coming executive who stayed on top of everything in her world. Her accomplishments boggled my mind, and I often thought that if Mom could see us, she'd be proud of us both, different as we are.

My heart lightened as I considered the freedom of retirement and the warmth of the close relationships back home. But would I miss teaching? Would I miss my students? I'd miss the travel, which I certainly couldn't afford on a teacher's pension.

I thought back to a conversation I'd had with John Clemens the previous year. He'd mentioned Teachers on the Move, an organization that sets up long-term subbing for international teachers. With Teachers on the Move I could teach overseas for just months at a time and have the best of both worlds.

I liked that. I'd leave at the end of the year.

Sorry, Tony.

# 48 YAHŞİBEY CHRISTMAS

David invited Dee and me to join him with Kerime (his Particular Friend) for Christmas at their home in the tiny Aegean village of Yahşibey (Yah-SHEE-bay). David, Dee and I often connected for trips to town or a meal on campus, and Christmas together sounded lovely. I e-mailed Laura with directions to join us there.

We rented a car and left right after school, but we missed the 6:00 ferry across the Marmara and didn't arrive in Yahşibey until the wee hours. Kerime was waiting up for us in their ultra-modern stone house. A fire blazed in the fireplace, and Christmas lights blinked all along the living room's curved stone wall. Welcomed with the usual Turkish hugs and kisses, I felt immediately at home. Laura was already asleep, so I had to wait for morning to hear about her travels. During the night she blurted, *"Cok Guzel!"* (wonderful!) in her sleep, so I figured the news would be good.

We woke to a brilliant sun in a cloudless sky. The scent of fresh coffee, the crackling of new logs in the fireplace, and a sparkling plate of Christmas cookies welcomed us to the new day.

"Today we'll celebrate Christmas Eve a day early," David announced as we breakfasted on crusty bread, cheese, cucumbers, tomatoes, and olives. "Kerime has to teach on Monday, so we're moving Christmas up to the 24th. We have to drive back to school on the 25th."

"Why do you have to teach on Christmas?" Laura asked.

"I'm a Turk teaching in a Turkish school, and Muslims don't celebrate Christmas. Koç gets the day off because so many of the staff are Christian, but I have to head back to Izmir on Sunday. I'm sorry, but it can't be helped." I was disappointed. Kerime's gentle warmth brightened the house.

A baker in a nearby village would roast our lamb in his wood oven, and while David and Kerime delivered it, Dee, Laura and I marveled at the parade of traffic heading up and down the cobbled street by the house—two brightly-decorated horse carts, scarved women in *şalvar*, and a herd of sheep and goats trotting home for lunch. That afternoon David and Kerime took us on a walking tour of their village, an ancient settlement perched low on a mountainside overlooking the Aegean. "There are about 150 residents here," Kerime explained, "and their ancestors before them."

"There are only a few new homes," David added. "We had our house built by a local architect who designs stone and concrete houses that blend with the originals. He uses the coolness of the rock but adds lots of glass facing the sea to take advantage of the view."

"Which is stunning!" Laura exclaimed as she perched on a rock wall overlooking the sea. "I love it here!" That girl warmed my heart; her enthusiasm for life was sheer joy. We continued our stroll past goats tethered to trees and cows lounging in vacant lots. We could have been in any century the way Yahşibey's people and animals shared space so equally.

After our walk we hopped into the car and drove to the neighboring village of Bademli to retrieve our roast lamb. We passed a small window advertising fresh-pressed olive oil, and Kerime coaxed us inside. A man in a white coat handed us each a tea glass of pale-green oil. Were we supposed to drink a whole glass? I ventured a small sip. "Oh, my goodness! This is delicious! I need bread to dip!" We each purchased a 2-liter tin, which the owner decanted from a stainless steel vat, the only feature in the tiny shop. Further down the street we purchased dinner vegetables from a vendor, then stopped for tea. "This place is famous for their almond tea," David said. "You have to try it. *Badem* means 'almond,' and it's one of the main products in Bademli." We crowded around a small table and ordered five cups.

"*Yarin*" the waiter informed us. Tomorrow.

We settled for plain tea.

On Christmas Eve we feasted on garlic mashed potatoes, fresh steamed Brussels sprouts, steamed carrots, tender, flavorful lamb, and rich, dark gravy. After dinner we gathered around the fireplace, celebrating the warmth of friendship around the evening fire. Too full for dessert, we sipped mulled wine as we opened our Turkish gifts: textiles, *rakı* (the Turkish liqueur), ceramic tiles, and scarves.

Sunday morning we stopped once more in the Bademli tea shop for the promised almond drink before Kerime had to leave. *"Yarin,"* he once again informed us. Tomorrow.

Right.

It reminded me of Coconut's Bar and Grill in Cozumel, where a sign announces, "Free margaritas tomorrow." Always tomorrow...even on the Aegean.

# 49 PRAGUE? WHY NOT?

New Year's break brought another long weekend, and the Keetmans had arranged a trip to Prague through a Turkish tour company. I'd purchased tickets for both Laura and myself, and Dee and Terri signed on as well. We were all eager to see this famed city.

Never mind that we had to leave campus at 3:00 AM. Never mind that it was drizzling when we landed. Never mind that we didn't get enough sleep. Never mind that it was a Turkish tour. It was fun.

First off, Prague is colder than Istanbul. A lot colder. Our warm coats and scarves were packed in suitcases beneath the bus, so we braved the elements in what we'd worn on the plane. We began our five-day sojourn with a walking tour through a chilling rain, heads down under umbrellas as our guide explained the sights in Turkish. The medieval Prague Castle huddled behind a screen of grey mist. Fortunately, the rain subsided before we arrived at St. Vitus' Cathedral, its many-pointed spires reaching to the heavens. Fleur-de-lis dominated the coal-darkened marble, repeated on every facet of its tall visage. Our guide led us down through narrow cobbled streets to the Vlatava River, interrupting his Turkish narration with an occasional broken English translation.

We gaped, gasped, and shivered our way across the Charles Bridge, reveling in its myriad statues, musicians, and artists. I loved the broad pedestrian bridge, more art fair than historical site. Painters and jewelers stood shivering beside booths along the bridge, and at one end a group of elderly men in down jackets and earflap hats performed jazz beneath one of the bridge's many statues. Beyond the bridge we spotted a Christmas market, probably open until New Year's Day. "Anybody up for some brats and mulled wine?" I asked.

"I'm in!" Laura cried, and a few of us peeled off to warm our innards.

"I can't believe how scrumptious this tastes," I said, wiping grease off my chin. "I'm in hog heaven." I never realized how good pork tasted until I went months without it. Our hotel, located a short train ride from the city, had quaint shuttered windows and pastoral scenes hand-painted on its stucco walls. Laura and I scored a spacious, cheerful attic room.

Sunday dawned clear, and Dee, Terri, Laura, and I took a train to Kutna Hora, a town famous for its Bone Church. "I'm disappointed," Laura complained when we approached what looked like every other church. "I thought it was constructed of bones."

"Oh, my God!" Terri exclaimed as she stepped inside. The interior was macabre, its entry arch decorated with sculls artfully interspersed with crossed bones, and below it hung an ornate crucifix composed entirely of bones and skulls. The church's entire décor was crafted of the femurs, skulls, fingers, and ribs of 40,000 skeletons. A monstrous chandelier hung from the dome, reputedly including every bone of the human anatomy.

"Look at this, you guys," Laura said. "A coat of arms made of bones!" Tiny finger bones formed intricate arrangements in each quarter of the shield, and the crown of bones and tiny sculls above it must have been from children. I hovered between revulsion and fascination.

"This is too weird for me," Terri announced as she snapped close-ups of skull candelabra lining the walls. According to legend, the chapel's graveyard was a popular burial place for Central Europe's aristocracy after an abbot sprinkled Holy Land soil over it. When the graveyard became overpopulated, older remains were exhumed and stored in the chapel. Some resourceful monks apparently fashioned those bones into the chapel's present decor. In any case, the Bone Church was beyond gruesome.

That evening everyone gathered in our big attic room to toast in the New Year. Fireworks exploded both above and below us; it felt like we were caught in a night-long battle. The noise escalated at midnight, when resonant bass voices wafted from an open window across the street singing "Auld Lang Syne" in Czech, and I watched, aghast, as a drunken man scrambled out the window to perch on the roof's steep ceramic tiles. I wished I hadn't noticed.

On the last day we visited the Jewish Ghetto. Our private guide, Rose, was a sprightly woman well over eighty who fascinated us with data and stories about the Jews of Prague as she led us through synagogues, streets, and the Jewish Cemetery. "I'm going to take you into the Pinkas Synagogue, but you must not take any photos," she warned. "Please show your respect with silence, and I'll answer your questions after we leave." We filed silently through a sanctuary with walls covered in meticulously penned names—wall after wall, arch after arch, floor to dome. I needed no explanation. These were Prague's Holocaust victims. The implications were overwhelming; silent tears streamed down our cheeks.

Rose walked us around an ancient Jewish cemetery crowded with crumbling tombstones that tumbled over each other. Hitler's troops had annihilated 77,000 people, 85 percent of Prague's Jewish population.

"Where were you during the war?" Dee asked.

Rose paused a moment. "Those were difficult years for me. Most of my family was deported early in the war, but my father and I managed to hide away in a dark basement. We had people who brought us food, and we spent years down there. Near the end of the war we were discovered and sent to the Terazin Concentration Camp. My father and I survived, but we never found the rest of the family. I was one of the lucky ones."

What could we say? Once again we stood silent, respectful of this woman who had dedicated her life to sharing the horrific realities of Prague's Jews—her people, her story.

# 50 LOVE THOSE FELUCCAS

I agreed to arrange a semester tour for Terri, Dee, three younger teachers and myself: two weeks in Egypt and Jordan. We were astonished to find that we were the entire group with a bus and tour guide to ourselves. Who knew? After two days exploring Cairo, our endearing guide Mustafa settled us on a train to Aswan, promising that we'd be met by another guide for our Nile cruise. We found the angular Aiman cockier than our sweet Mustafa, but he was knowledgeable. We kept close watch over him near our beautiful red-haired Leslie; he clearly had designs on her. Western women are viewed as loose in the Middle East, and we didn't trust him.

We watched dark, bare-bottomed children cavort in the Nile while their mothers scrubbed laundry on shore. I don't know whether I was more struck with their poverty or their happiness, but I was moved. The river, laced with date palms, offered a welcome respite from the surrounding desert, where I assumed they spent much of their time.

It goes without saying that 4000 years' worth of pyramids, tombs, and temples are awe-inspiring. I did my best to absorb all the historical information of the Luxor Temple, the Valley of the Kings, and the Temple of Karnak, but it all blended together in my mind. I loved the metaphor of the scarab beetle rolling its dung ball along as a source of food while it traversed the ground, the sun god rolling the sun to make it shine on earth—a heavenly cycle of life.

My favorite, though, was sailing on feluccas, primitive boats that have navigated the Nile for centuries. A felucca has one sail hanging on a rope from a single mast, and one man pilots the boat, which can hold as many as 12 or 14 people on benches along the perimeter of its wide, flat bottom. We'd enjoyed a few felucca rides as a part of our Aswan tour, and when we had an afternoon free in Luxor, we decided to hire one on our own. Allana negotiated a great price—the equivalent of nine dollars each for a two-hour trip to Banana Island, half of what the captain had requested. The handsome young Captain Fox hoisted the sail, and it hung limp. He rowed out of the marina using rough twelve-foot 2x4 oars dotted with chips of long-gone paint, ineffective at best. He assured us he'd catch some wind out on the river. Our guide took one of the oars, working up a good sweat. No hint of a breeze. Captain Fox removed his sweater and shirt and rowed in his t-shirt, heading across the wide river to a group of motorboat ferries, hoping for a tow.

No dice.

Captain Fox stripped down to his boxers, kicked off his shoes, hopped off the boat and began towing us along the shore. "Please stop," Dee begged. "We'll help row back over the river."

"He promised to take you to the banana plantation, and he's a man of his word," Aiman translated.

"Maybe he can get that water buffalo to tow us," Terri said, but he strained past it, sloshing through the muddy riverbank. A few broad-lipped camels regarded us curiously as we passed, but Captain Fox continued, determined to earn his fee.

"I feel rotten," Leslie said. "I hate just sitting here while he's working so hard."

"Don't go there," Allana warned. "He knew there was no wind when he took us on."

"Yeah, well that doesn't make me feel any better," I said. Aiman stood on the bow waving a white scarf as boats motored by. A tugboat finally approached towing two other feluccas and sidled up to grab our tow rope. "The Nile Felucca Choo-Choo" Dee quipped as we followed along in line.

Sadly, all good things must come to an end. Our tow rope came loose, and we were stranded again, this time in the middle of the river. Captain Fox finally allowed us women to "man" the oars, taking turns until we reached shore. Our intrepid hero jumped off to tow us again.

We finally reached the docks at Banana Island. Captain Fox pulled on his jeans and escorted us up a steep path to the plantation, where we were treated to a nearly-serviceable restroom, a tour, and a bunch of tiny, sweet bananas. When we returned to the boat Captain Fox had scrubbed down the decks and pulled out a little stove to brew tea.

"Is this tea made from Nile water?" Allana asked, critically inspecting the ancient china and cloudy glasses set out for us.

"Oh, yes. It is very good," Aiman assured her.

"I don't know. I don't think it's a good idea to drink the water from the river," Allana warned. She was a biology teacher and knew what she was talking about.

"Isn't it OK if it boils for ten minutes?" Terri asked.

"In the Boundary Waters they say all you have to do is bring it to a boil to kill all the bacteria and microbes," I offered. " Of course, Egypt isn't Minnesota." Allana turned down the tea, but the rest of us sipped it as Captain Fox swabbed the deck, tied up the sail, and put his shirt back on.

"Have you arranged a tow back?" Allana asked. Captain Fox shook his head and pulled out the oars. We took turns rowing back downstream to the marina. The sky burned gold beyond the palm trees by the time we bid Captain Fox a fond farewell, each folding a tip into his hand. He'd been no fool. We'd negotiated a great price, we'd had a grand adventure, and he'd earned four times the fare he'd negotiated.

# 51 SINAI SUNRISE

The next day we joined a police-escorted caravan of vehicles from Luxor to the Suez Canal, where our beloved Mustafa met us for the ferry ride across to the Sinai Peninsula. We relaxed all day at a beach hotel near Sharm el Sheik before our planned hike to view the sunrise on Mount Sinai. At 2 A.M. our van lurched into the darkness, reminding me that this excursion involved some sacrifice, the first being sleep. Little did I know.

I was just dozing off when we stopped at the first of many roadblocks. "Give me your passports, then stay in the van and DON'T talk," ordered our security guard Khalef, a clean-cut man in a tweed sport coat that concealed an automatic weapon. I yearned to snap a photo of the six armed guards but decided not to tempt fate.

We passed through four more roadblocks on our way to Sinai, clearly one of the most protected sites on the planet. Mustafa explained, "The weather has turned cold, and the peak of Mount Sinai will be snowy. I'm also sorry to also inform you that because it is Sunday, St. Catherine's Monastery will be closed."

"That's terrible!" Dee complained. "That monastery supposedly has the burning bush of Moses inside."

"Well, I'll see what I can do, but it's doubtful we will be able to see it. The good news is that few tourists will be climbing Mount Sinai because of the snow and because it is Sunday." Worked for me. I had no desire to share the mountain with the hundreds who trek it nightly to see the Sinai sunrise.

"Have you ever climbed it?" I asked.

"No, I haven't. My tours are usually limited to the mainland. I'm looking forward to it. I've also never seen snow."

"Snow?" Terri gasped. "Did you say snow?" Apparently she'd slept through Mustafa's warning. The van pulled into a dark, empty parking lot, and we stepped into the frigid night.

"There's no way I'm hiking in this cold," Dee announced. "I'd love to climb Mount Sinai, but not in these conditions. Unlike the rest of you, I'm from Florida. I'll wait in the van." I couldn't believe my ears. Dee, the art historian, was going to pass this up? She'd been fascinated with every site so far, and this one trumped them all, at least in the realm of biblical history.

"Me, too," parroted Terri. "I have no burning desire to do this hike. I'm already freezing, and it's going to be even colder up on the mountain. I'd rather sleep for the six hours you guys'll be hiking. I wish I'd stayed at the hotel."

Well, there was no way I was going to miss this opportunity, and I was desperate for exercise. I had ear muffs and gloves, layers of warm clothes, and my camera. I would see the sun rise from the top of Mount Sinai.

Mustafa, the three younger teachers and I followed our mountain-goat guide up the dark path. Mahmud was dressed in hiking boots, a hoodie, a few light jackets, and a checkered Arab scarf. He had the only flashlight, so we stuck close to him in the inky darkness. The path was relatively smooth but eventually grew steeper and rockier. "How high is the mountain?" Leslie asked.

"It is 7,498 feet, and the hike is six kilometers each way. I hike it two or three times a day, so I know it well. Near the top the path turns to stairs, but we should have some light by then."

"I'm really cold," Mollie complained, puffing as she climbed. "Do you know what the temperature is up here?"

"It's about five degrees Fahrenheit, but the wind chill is lower. I don't know what it is exactly."

"Well, I'm from Minnesota, and I can assure you the wind chill is well below zero," I said, navigating yet another switchback. The stone path was now snow-covered, and we slowed to avoid slipping on the ice.

"Hey, snow!" Mustafa cried. He leaned over, grabbed a handful and rolled it into a snowball. "I've never seen it before! This is wonderful—but so cold!" I knew what was coming. Our laughter rang through the night as we pummeled each other with snowballs.

We passed a camel sleeping near a small stone hut. "Many hikers rent camels for the trek up the mountain," Mahmud explained, "but because of the snow, the camel tenders are not out. No camels for you." Within an hour my tennis were soaked from the snow—not the best climbing gear. We passed more rock huts, panting with the effort of the climb.

"These are refreshment stations, but they are closed from the weather. I think one will be open further up the mountain." We trudged on silently, praying for a break from the bitter wind. We'd hiked another hour before Mahmud led us inside a square stone hut and lit a kerosene lantern. A young Bedouin man was huddled in a huge fuzzy blanket in the corner. His hut was like a miniature convenience store with snacks, candy bars, coffee, and tea on display. Lovely beaded purses hung from the rafters, also for sale. The man lit a gas burner and Mustafa treated us all to hot drinks and candy bars as we chatted with Mahmud and the shop-tender. Once we'd finally warmed up, we braced ourselves and headed back into the cold. The path grew steeper, icier, and more difficult. We picked our way carefully up the icy mountainside, thankful for a hint of light in the sky as we began climbing rough stone stairs.

"These are The Steps of Repentance," Mahmud told us.

"How many are there?" I asked.

"749." I began to repent my decision to climb Mount Sinai. It was tough!

"You could have climbed the entire mountain by stairs from the monastery," Mahmud added. "One monk built that stairway as repentance for his transgressions—3750 stairs."

"Oh, my God!" Allana exclaimed. "No, thank you!"

"He must have committed some pretty major sins," Leslie added. Snow swirled around us as we climbed, and true to Mahmud's word, the sky lightened as we passed a rest room made of thin bamboo poles, an oddity on the stark stone of the mountain. I was thankful I hadn't been drinking water.

At long last we reached the summit, where a small stone mosque (12th century) stood beside the Chapel of the Holy Trinity (4th century), built of massive stone blocks. Snow swirled around us as we stood in the clouds hoping for a hint of sunrise. We discovered a group of Egyptian students huddled beneath blankets on the lee side of the chapel. They invited us to join them and practiced their English with us as we all shivered, waiting for the sun to rise.

Which it didn't.

The sky got a bit brighter, but our Sunrise on Sinai was a non-event. All we could see was fog, snow, and each other.

The climb down was risky at best. Though the light was better, it's always harder to maintain footing on a downhill slope, especially in ice and snow. About halfway down the mountain the sun emerged through the clouds and we were treated to broad vistas of the craggy, rock-strewn mountains. The light cast a rosy glow on the world of brown rock. Sinai's terrain was rock, rock, and more rock—wrinkled and dusted with snow. There was no vegetation except an occasional cypress planted beside a camel hut. The sun energized us, and of course, it was less work going down. Tears filled my eyes as I read the engraving on a stone pedestal: "May Peace Prevail on Earth."

We met Terri and Dee at the van, and somehow Mustafa wheedled our way into St. Catherine's Monastery. We got to see Moses' Burning Bush—a massive weeping rosebush. More important to me, though, was that St. Catherine's houses a Christian church, a Jewish synagogue, and a Muslim mosque within its walls. All three faiths share the Old Testament, and at least in that one monastery they cohabit peacefully.

Peace on Earth.

# 52 PETRA—UNFORGETTABLE

There are two reasons I'll always remember Petra. The first was our guide, Mahmud—the memory I prefer. Half the men in Jordan were named Mahmud, much like there the many Mehmets in Turkey. A clean-cut, charismatic fellow in his 40's, Mahmud began with tales of his childhood. "I grew up in old Petra, and my father tended camels and goats. We were very poor, but of course I didn't realize it. I wore a shirt with no pants or shoes, and I remember scaling the walls of the exclusive Petra hotel. I never knew whether I'd be rewarded with bread or pelted with stones, but if I got bread, I would run home to share it with my family. I had a happy childhood, even though we were often hungry. We didn't know anything else."

"Did you live in one of the caves?" Terri asked.

"In the winter we lived in a cave house, but in the summer my mother preferred to live in a tent." We'd seen many of these long, black Bedouin tents along our drive.

"There were nine children in our family," he continued, "and for some reason my father chose me to attend school. None of my brothers or sisters had to, and I thought it was unfair. Every morning my father would say, 'Just one more day,' and I would cry as I trudged up the Siq to the main road, where someone would usually let me ride in their cart." The Siq is a canyon 3/4 of a mile long, an ancient rock crevice probably formed by an earthquake. It's a narrow meandering road between steep, red stone cliffs eroded into fantastic formations by desert winds blowing sand through this awe-inspiring cleft.

"One summer day when I was twelve, I was tending our flock in the hills when some soldiers came to me. I didn't speak their language, but they indicated I should follow them. I was confused—afraid I was in trouble or some terrible thing had happened. They left someone to watch my animals and brought me to my father. Their interpreter explained that I had done well on an exam at school and King Hussein wanted to meet me. Of course, my father insisted I go.

"I was taken to the palace in Amman, a full day's journey. I was wearing my only clothes, which reeked of goat urine. King Hussein was kind as he explained that twelve students had been selected for their exam grades, and I was one of them. The others had already visited the palace, but it had taken them longer to find me. He would buy me new clothes and cover my expenses for a prep school in England, then university. I was honored, but I didn't want to leave my family. The king promised to fly me home twice a year, and eventually I agreed to leave Petra."

"I was the only one of my siblings to get an education," he explained. "I chose to pursue a degree in history so I could return to Petra to share our history with foreigners like you. The government has resettled everyone into new homes outside of Old Petra, but my mother still lives in her tent all summer. When I'm overwhelmed by the stress of the modern world, I visit her tent and bury my face in the clothes she saved—I find great peace in the smells of my childhood." I was moved to tears by his story. What a difficult yet beautiful life these people had enjoyed compared to my sterile, comfortable existence.

We walked down the same Siq Mahmud had taken to school each day. As we meandered along the deep rock crevice to Petra's treasures, horse carts flew by us. "Lazy tourists," I thought. Not us.

Rounding the last curve of the Siq, I was staggered by the splendor of a towering red temple that glowed in the morning sun. Vendors accosted us with postcards and books, while camel-tenders offered transport on their drooling dromedaries. Mahmud waved them away and sat us down for our lesson on the Petra Temples. "You may recognize this temple from *Indiana Jones and the Last Crusade*," he said. "You must understand that the Holy Grail was never located here. That part was fiction. The temple itself, though, is real. It was most likely a tomb." When he took us inside, I was astonished that it was just a shallow cave; the ornate, pillared facade carved into the red rock was the whole show.

Mesmerized by the collection of temples and caves carved into the red cliffs, we continued to explore on foot, passing scores of small vendors scattered along the way, eking out a living by selling handmade trinkets and jewelry. "I want to point out this shop in particular," Mahmud said. "This is a women's cooperative established by Queen Noor. When she married King Hussein in 1978, single women were considered the dregs of society, unable to work or appear in public unchaperoned. Many widows and single women were forced into prostitution if a male relative didn't offer to support them. Queen Noor's cooperative craft shops offered these women a way to support themselves and gain respect."

As we browsed the shop, Mahmud sat with a milky tea. When I asked what it was, he told me it was spiced tea with camel's milk. "Could I order one?" I asked.

"It's not a good idea. The camel's milk is very rich," he said. The man who'd driven us through the Wadi Rum sand dunes the previous day had quipped that he had to drink camel's milk to keep up with his three wives.

"Oh, I have an iron stomach," I replied. The tea was exquisite: rich, smooth, and delicately spiced.

After completing our purchases, we explored the valley's many caves, snapping photos of wide-eyed Bedouin children and young camel-tenders. They all opened their palms for a coin afterwards, and of course I obliged, still stung by the story Mahmud's childhood. We lunched at a lavish buffet of Mid-Eastern fare spread across long tables, thankful to finally sit down. Then we wandered the less busy areas of the valley, keeping a careful eye on the time so we wouldn't miss our afternoon cooking lesson.

Thus began my second noteworthy Petra memory. As we walked, my stomach began to grumble. Should I make one last WC stop before the Siq? I decided not to bother—I'd be fine. My friends paused for last-minute purchases, but I forged on. My stomach was complaining and I needed to hurry. "Horse cart, lady?" someone asked. Tempted, I waved him off. I wanted the exercise.

I increased my pace as the grumblings advanced to pressure. Gastronomically explosive pressure. I sped on, searching frantically for a rock or tree to squat behind. This was the wrong time and the wrong place—sheer rock walls rose twenty feet on both sides. I tensed to fight the inevitable, but my efforts were in vain. There was nothing I could do to prevent the onslaught. I was just thankful to be wearing jeans. Nothing would show.

Wave after wave of cramps racked my system. Relieved that few people were walking the Siq, I raced ahead, passing them all. I prayed for a break in the rock: a fissure, a boulder, even a shrub! Something trickled down my leg. My face burned. Was it the lunch? The camel's milk? This was a new experience for me—I was the child who'd had to drink prune juice every day. Why me? Why now?

I pulled off my jacket and tied it around my waist, hoping to cover any telltale stains. Oh, for a break in the rock—or a hole to climb into. I hurried on, completely abandoning any hope of control. Nature was taking its course.

"Ann Marie! Ann Marie! Wait up!" Terri panted as she hurried to catch me.

"You don't want to come near me," I warned.

"Why? What's wrong?" she said. It didn't take long for her olfactory senses to detect the problem. "OH, NO! What happened?" I explained my plight, then lifted my sneaker to display stains on my white socks.

"Oh, Ann Marie! I'm so sorry! What can I do to help?"

"Nothing, I'm afraid. You don't have to walk with me, though. I think I'd rather be alone."

"No—I'll stick with you. What was it? Do you have any idea?"

"I think it was the camel's milk."

"Oh, dear."

"Yeah, dumb move."

The interpretive center was still open, thank God, and they had modern toilets. I raced for an open stall, ripped off my jeans, and wadded my underwear into the bin. Now what? I soaked my red-and-white cotton scarf in the toilet and began the mammoth task of cleaning myself. It seemed impossible, though with repeated flushing I was finally clean. But my jeans! I scrubbed at them with the wet scarf, not caring how wet they got. If there was any way I could have stayed in that stall forever, I would have. I was beyond humiliated.

Eventually the toilet would no longer flush—I'd pushed Petra's plumbing to its limit. Sighing, I pulled on my slightly-cleaner-but-odiferous wet jeans, tied my jacket back around my waist, and waddled out. Terri was waiting. "I told the others we won't be going to the cooking lesson; I said you felt ill. I also found us a taxi."

"Oh, Terri. You're a dear. How can I ever thank you?" I said, all too aware of the fragrance surrounding me. Images of Linus' friend Pigpen enveloped in a cloud of dust came to mind, only this wasn't dust. We found our taxi and I buckled in, careful to sit on my jacket. Terri rolled her window down and announced, "We've been around animals all day. We probably smell terrible." So thoughtful. I rolled mine down, too. The driver said nothing, and we paid him double the fare. As I stepped out, I was mortified to see a stain on the back seat. I hoped the tip would help. We hurried into the lobby, and I stood far from the desk with my back to the wall as Terri asked for the key.

"I apologize," the attendant said. "You must move to a different room. Can you be ready in five minutes?"

"NO!" I blurted.

"I'm sorry—there is a problem with the air conditioning and we need to close the room down."

"We'll need a half hour," I said.

"We'll call you when we're packed," Terri added. Bless her heart. I was desperate for a shower, unwilling to wait even five minutes. When we got to the room, I stripped and jammed my clothes into a plastic bag, then reveled in the joy of clean, hot water and soap, soap, soap purging every inch of my skin.

Feeling human once again, I packed for the move. In our new room I filled the tub with piping hot water and poured in my soiled clothes for a major laundering. Not only was it a filthy task, but an exhausting one. I took a break and stepped out to inform Terri of my progress only to find her standing on a chair with her head out the window.

"Oh, Terri!" She turned to me, blushing. We both broke into hysterics.

"I'm so sorry—I just couldn't take it another second," she apologized.

"Trust me, I understand."

The others returned from their cooking lesson raving about the meal. I went without dinner that night, too embarrassed to share my trials with the others, at least not yet.

Our final adventure in Jordan was an afternoon at a Dead Sea luxury hotel where we were free to enjoy the restaurants, spa and waterfront.

"What should we do first?" Mollie asked.

"Let's get our suits on," I suggested, eager for a swim.

"Great!" Mollie, Allana, and Leslie chimed.

"Not interested," Dee said.

"Me, neither," Terri added. "It's too cold. I just want to relax and have a little lunch, then shop a bit. You guys go ahead."

I couldn't believe it. Just like Mount Sinai, I thought. They'd passed on the primo adventures, the things I most loved. It would be me and the young teachers again. Maybe I'd just never grown up. We grabbed towels and headed for the water to find a beach of black muck.

"Ick," Leslie moaned. "What's this?"

"I'll bet it's the mud the spa charges a fortune for," Allana said. "It's hard, though. You can walk on it."

I dropped my towel on a beach chair and stepped over the muck into the Dead Sea's lukewarm water—weird. We waded easily out to our waists in this tepid bath.

"OK, you guys," called Allana, ever the intrepid leader. "One... two...THREE!"

We all dove in, then exploded back up out of the water laughing hysterically, rolling like beach balls on the surface. Floating in the Dead Sea was no problem. If you've ever wondered what it's like to be a cork, swim in the Dead Sea. It has the most densely saline water in the world: 33.7%—nearly ten times that of most oceans. I float easily, but in that water I couldn't sink.

Mollie lay on the surface with her arms and legs straight in the air, giggling. "Hey, you guys. Try this—if you can keep from rolling over!" There was no way you could drown in the Dead Sea. Even floating on our stomachs, we merely had to turn our heads to take a breath. We ran into a film crew slathering themselves with mud and joined them. Allana agreed to be buried in the thick black paste, and soon we were all covered in grey muck, the same stuff people pay big bucks for. Not only was it free, but it included a bonus of laughter therapy.

Terri and Dee missed the highlight of the day, but what they didn't know wouldn't hurt them.

Yup, I'll never forget Jordan. In spite of the most humiliating experience of my life, I loved it.

I returned to school renewed from my adventure—and flat broke. I was saved by the hearty Turkish lunches at school, free for teachers. Between that and the street market, I squeaked through the rest of February.

I seduced my ninth graders through *Romeo and Juliet* with skits, role-plays, and games. Most of them actually enjoyed it, much to my amazement. The language was a challenge for them, but I framed it as a puzzle and they were hooked, especially the math whizzes. They enjoyed creating modern versions of important scenes, utilizing slang they'd learned from American movies. We had a blast.

Sadly, my seniors were checking out. They were obsessed with the upcoming ÖSS exam, so I tried to pull them together with a world poverty project—the "So what?" of our past unit. "When you learn something about life or the world, it doesn't mean much unless you do something with it," I explained. We'd discussed the value of micro-loans and the impressive efforts of Nobel Prize winner Muhammed Yunus, so they decided to raise money for to his Grameen Bank. Denizhan offered to do some research and learned that Grameen accepted no donations. Another student discovered Heifer International, a charity that gives livestock to people in developing countries. The class set goals, organized committees, and developed action plans. It was slow going, but they slogged through in spite of the ÖSS workbooks concealed on their laps.

The   March doldrums were brightened by a visit from my brother Steve. A professor at St. Olaf College in Minnesota, he'd arranged a few days in Istanbul after an Economics Conference in Kiev. I booked a hotel for us in Sultanahmet, and his enthusiasm energized both of us as I showed him my favorite mosques, museums and bazaars. Steve raved about everything, but he was most entranced with Musa Başaran's carpet studio.

I'd met Musa the previous year through Jamilah. On my first visit to his studio he'd opened his door saying, "Welcome! Come in and take off your clothes." Our laughter had laid a foundation for what was to become one of my most precious Turkish friendships. Musa designs kilims of captivating designs in vibrant colors. Steve's favorite was a modern pattern of swirls and curls in a bouquet of shades. Mine had always been his tulip design, a textured background with fine silk tulips woven into the center, but I loved all his work.

After piling the studio floor with scores of silk and wool kilims of all sizes and designs from classical to modern, Musa explained his process. First he'd create designs in his head, then weave them with hand-dyed silk. He showed us the materials he used for his natural dyes, and we watched, fascinated, as he dropped samples of clay (sienna), chamomile blossoms (yellow), and dried insects (red) into water-filled tea glasses. The color swirled magically through the water, transforming it to rich shades. He showed us his huge stainless-steel dye vats outside, and we saw yarns drying in the sun before being stored in his basement room, a weaver's dream. "We can't make so many different colors with natural dyes," Musa said, indicating the 20-30 open sacks of yarns in rich, earthy tones. "These are all the colors I can create. After I design something, I deliver my sample and yarn to women in a village near the Aegean. They weave the kilims in wool, choosing their own variations in color."

"How long does it take to weave one?" Steve asked.

"Depending on the size and pattern, anywhere from a few weeks to six months. They do most of their weaving in the winter when they aren't needed in the fields. I pick up the kilims in the spring, and my brother Haydar checks them over for flaws then combs and knots the fringe. After that's done, we carry them up to the terrace to burn off loose fibers and straw with a blow torch. Would you like to see?"

We climbed an endless spiral staircase up six flights to a penthouse plaza overlooking the Marmara. "This view is amazing!" Steve said as he stepped to the railing. The incredible panorama was Musa and Haydar's reward for hauling heavy kilims up all those stairs.

After they torched off loose threads and straw, they sent the kilims out to be cleaned and pressed. Musa sold directly from his studio;

customers found him by word of mouth. "I don't sell to carpet shops because I don't want anyone to copy my designs."

As Steve paid for two kilims, he commented, "I can't believe I'm doing this. I'm usually hard-pressed to part with my money, but these are a treasure."

We were bushed by the time we picked up our packs for the trek home. Although the trip back took three hours, it wasn't expensive:

Tram to Karaköy: 1.5 Turkish Lira (just over $1)
Ferry to Hydarpaşa: 1.5 Turkish Lira
Train to Pendik: 1.5 Turkish Lira
Mini-bus to Koç School gate: 1.25 Turkish Lira
Exploring Istanbul with my brother: Priceless.

# 54 FAREWELL, DEAR HEARTS

My IB students had brightened my life for the past two years, and it was time to bid them farewell. Koç seniors were excused from school in April so they could devote their spring to preparations for the ÖSS, the three-hour exam that would determine which schools they were admitted to and what majors they could pursue. Less than a third of students taking the exam qualify for places in Turkish universities, so the pressure was on. They would focus all their energy on exam prep for the next six weeks.

I wanted to do something special to say goodbye, so I held class in my *lojman* on their last day to celebrate our two years together. A few of the girls came early to help whip up topping, slice strawberries, and serve up the rich flourless chocolate tortes I'd baked the night before. They took over my kitchen with the same gusto they'd applied to nearly every task I'd placed before them. I adored those kids. At first Libby was thrilled to have company but was soon overwhelmed by their number and retreated under the bed. Imagine my small living room with 22 students and their aging teacher. Everyone squeezed in, chatting happily. They were nearly free. Well, so to speak.

In my 32 years of teaching I'd never had such a close relationship with an entire class. Of course, I'd been frustrated with them occasionally, as I'm sure they'd been with me. We'd bulldozed our way through the IB program together, and they'd impressed me with insightful class discussions, thoughtful analytical writing, and inventive presentations.

"I want you all to know that I'm really proud of you for raising over $500 for the Heifer Project. Your bake sales and raffles have purchased a cow and a goat for poor families in Africa, which will help their entire villages. What do you think you'll remember the most from our two years together?"

"I'll remember going out to watch the eclipse," said Kadir, whose great passion was science.

"I loved it when Zeynep played Paris Hilton with her naughty little dog!" laughed Denizhan.

"Remember when Iraz came wandering through the room like a homeless person, glaring at everyone and stealing our pencils?" laughed Nazlı. "That was hilarious!"

"How about Selim Can the Macbeth Mafioso? He was exactly the right character. It was a perfect translation for Macbeth, too," added Begüm, who invariably added a note of insight.

"Could you ever forget Haluk as the African worker?" Ezgi laughed. Just the mention of it drove us all to hysterics. Haluk blushed. He'd been the poor African worker interviewed by TV commentator, Merve. Gözde had served as their translator, and the interview had gone something like this:

Merve: "Can you tell us what it's like to work in the Nike factory, Haluk?"

Gözde (turning to Haluk): Bflsgek sniavlin shrockbuosd nvidlsint, Haluk?

Haluk (nodding): Fbgilsienrs ageidlgn dfsdkge aaslkfinv doigs. Teiosidn vfdiong eowinef bldisdonfi goind geont!

Gözde (turning back to Merve): It is very difficult. We work long hours and we do not get time to even have lunch.

Merve: How much do you get paid?

Gözde: Slibvengiber shnedlesiz...

As the actors continued their gibberish (half the interview), our chuckles grew to uncontrolled laughter. We were soon holding our stomachs, tears streaming down our cheeks as the presenters remained in character playing out their charade. I'm amazed that none of us wet our pants (as far as I know). It was easily the most hysterical moment of my teaching career.

Together we'd weathered Henry Miller, George Orwell, Shakespeare, global issues, comparative commentaries, mock orals, and oral exams. These shared experiences were our bond.

Many teachers cheered at the departure of their seniors while I shed tears. O.K. I admit that even my twenty-plus proteges had been a challenge this last semester. They hid workbooks in their laps, and it took me forever to get class started. Sometimes one or two of them even fell asleep, a behavior I'd never tolerated, but I knew they were burning the candle at both ends. Their lives were ruled by the upcoming exam, and at that point English class was mere fluff. I'd done my best to prepare them for the upcoming IB exams, but they hardly cared. Only four were headed for foreign universities.

They posed on my front steps for farewell photos, and as I hugged each of them goodbye, I knew I'd miss them. They'd enriched my life, and I hoped I'd done the same for them.

## 55 A HESITANT PROPOSITION

Edda was offering another tour, this time around the Sülymaniye Mosque, an edifice beyond edifices. Marnie agreed to join me and suggested her driver bring us in early that morning. Not quite caught up from all my travel expenses, I appreciated saving the cost of a hotel. I was also saving for a bang-up retirement trip after school ended.

As usual, Edda's walk transported us back centuries to ancient Constantinople. Istanbul's largest mosque, Süleymaniye was built by Mimar Sinan, the famed Ottoman architect. He supervised the construction beginning in 1550, often sipping tea in a corner of the vast sanctuary. When asked why he slurped so loudly, he explained that he used the echoes to test the acoustics of the structure. Sinan designed 100 mosques in his 50 years as Chief Architect, starting at age 50. Oh, to be so prolific—and until age 100! It gave me pause to consider my paltry contributions to the world. The mosque sat on a hill overlooking Constantinople, an edifice built to honor Sultan Süleyman, reputedly the greatest of the Ottoman sultans.

Edda gathered us inside the mosque's cemetery. "These large buildings are the tombs of Süleyman and Hürrem," she explained. "Hürrem was a slave in Süleymaniye's harem, and she won more than his heart. She ousted his previous favorite and manipulated him into marrying her (uncommon for sultans). She tricked Süleyman into believing that his first son, Mustafa, was plotting to steal his throne, so Süleyman had him strangled before his eyes. Hürrem's son, Selim, became the next sultan, and he lacked the leadership skills of his father. Known as Selim the Sot, his reign initiated the downfall of the Ottoman Empire." Her story piqued my curiosity about this amazing woman, enshrined in an ornately tiled mausoleum, slightly smaller than Süleyman's beside it.

The mosque's exterior and courtyard boast exceptional grandeur, and its interior is beyond belief. The vast sanctuary has numerous stained glass windows on its marble walls, with domes cascading down seemingly from heaven. In spite of the hushed interior, we could hear whispered conversations from across the sanctuary—astounding acoustics.

Edda then guided us through back streets to a number of Byzantine churches dating back ten centuries. She always incorporated a snack break into her tours, and that day it was the Vefa Bozacisi (1876), a *boza* bar. It looked like an Irish pub but dispensed only one item: *boza*, a non-alcoholic drink made from fermented sweet millet. A white-capped man with a broad mustache and an engaging smile looked like a soda jerk as he scooped thick, yellow *boza* from a marble terrine into glasses. He arranged them on the bar, sprinkling each with cinnamon. We helped ourselves, found seats at tables, and tentatively sipped. I liked the thick, custardy drink, but others were put off by its sharp tang. As we sipped, Edda explained, "When I was a child a *boza* vendor would walk the streets each evening, calling '*Boza! Boza!*' He would pour out the drink from a canister that he carried on his back, washing the glasses with water from another container at his side." A nut vendor circulated among us, sprinkling roasted chickpeas into our hands. We dropped them into the *boza*, yet another taste and texture to enhance our culinary adventure.

Bottles of vinegar and ornate mirrors lined the walls of the bar, and a small case held the obligatory picture of Mustafa Kemal Ataturk, the Father of Turkey, along with the silver-ornamented glass he'd used when he visited this bar. (He was a greater aficionado of *raki*, Turkey's anise liqueur.)

After the tour, Marnie and I joined Edda for a bowl of the local specialty, *fasuliye*, a stewed bean dish featured at restaurants across from the mosque entrance.

As we indulged in this delicious meal, I brought up something I'd been considering. "It makes me sad that so few people get to experience the magic of your walks, Edda."

"It is as it is," she replied. "I cannot do more than I do."

"I have a proposition, though. Would you like to collaborate on a book of your walks? I'm a writer and a photographer, and I'd love to make these walks available to tourists who don't know you. As your friend, I get to join your walks, but what about the thousands who might want to do them on their own?" Was I being presumptuous?

"What a wonderful idea! I'd love to!"

I was dumbfounded. Edda knew nothing about my writing skills yet was willing to take a chance on me. We set a meeting to discuss the project, and I pounded out a book proposal and visited English bookstores to identify prospective publishers. My first choice was Çitlembik, an Istanbul publishing house that produces a variety of books on Turkish culture and tourism in both English and Turkish. I shot off my proposal, expecting to wait the usual six months for a response. I got a call the next week from Nancy Öztürk, Çitlembik's owner. She was excited about the project and wanted to sign us on immediately.

Little did I know when I proposed the idea that it would be the beginning of a treasured friendship with Edda.

# 56 SCAVENGING

With about a month left of school, spring fever hit hard. Our ninth grade team racked our brains for a way to hold the students' interest through a poetry unit and finals, what boded to be an excruciating month. When Heather suggested having students create video versions of poems, we actually clapped. It might just work. First we needed to teach the techniques of filming and editing, and we designed a video scavenger hunt to practice these skills. Teams of students were given a double period to film short clips from a list of items like 'sleeping in an inappropriate place,' 'kissing a fish,' 'playing leapfrog,' etc. We gave them the list ahead of time so they could prepare (like learning to play leapfrog), but they could only film during their designated 80 minutes. The kids had such a blast doing it that we teachers decided to create our own.

After that project each team had to recreate a poem in video form. They read scores of poems before choosing one, analyzing it, and creating a storyboard for their production. Many planned elaborate scenarios, devoting weekends to filming in the city while others went for simplicity, keeping their project within the confines of school. The videos were surprisingly professional, and everyone enjoyed the process (well, mostly). Not only that, but they stayed on task for the entire month. Amazing!

We teachers were so inspired by their enthusiasm that we decided to stage an Academy Award-like ceremony, the Golden Ram Awards (koç means ram). Each class selected its best video for the competition, giving us ten finalists. Our awards, The Teachers' Choice and The People's Choice, were two plastic rams sprayed with gold paint. The esteemed hosts for our ceremony were David, who actually had a tux at school, and Duygu, who wore a glittering gown.

We showed the winning videos as awards were presented, and the highlight of the event was the teachers' scavenger hunt video. We'd filmed David kissing a warty old fish in a public market, and all of us "sleeping in an inappropriate place" on couches in Director Tony Paulus's office. We all dropped off to sleep, snoring loudly as he lectured us about motivating our students.

I had naively agreed to edit our clips using iMovie, which I'd never used. After seemingly insurmountable technical problems, I finally pulled it together, thanks to the generous assistance of Alexander Best, our department's young computer-tech savior, just in time to premier it for the students as the grand finale of the Golden Rams. The kids went ballistic to see their teachers dancing the Halay, a traditional Turkish folk dance. There's something about English teachers doing anything Turkish that really sets them off.

[Our video is posted on You Tube: "Koç Teacher Scavenger Hunt"]

I couldn't leave Turkey without attending a soccer game, and time was running out. Most of my boys lived for soccer, launching into chants at the mere mention of a team's name. I asked Murat, my most obsessive Galatasaray fan, to help me buy tickets.

"Ms. Mershon. You do not need to buy them. We have extra tickets for every game, and I know my parents will give some to you."

"Murat, that's unbelievable. Are you sure?"

The next day Murat brought me an envelope with three tickets for the final derby match between Istanbul's top two rivals, Galatasaray (Gah-lah-TAH-sah-rye) and Fenerbahçe (Fay-nair-BAH-chae). When I asked David to join me, he was hesitant, and when I suggested it to Duygu, she said, "Are you crazy? This game will be a disaster and could even be dangerous." A positive and adorable Turkish teacher, she was usually game for anything, so I was shocked. I explained that I had first-class tickets on the lower level, and they both reluctantly agreed to join me for my maiden voyage into Turkish Soccer-dom.

The boom of distant cheers filled the air as we stepped from the metro, though the stadium was blocks away. We passed through two stages of security where female guards inspected our bags and grinned at us, saying *"Yabanci"* (foreigner) and nodding us on. They only expect problems from Turks—overzealous fans. My heart pounded, partly in anticipation and partly in fear for what might lay ahead.

The stands were packed; most of the fans had been there for hours, standing on their seats and revving up with chants and cheers. Our seats were in the fifth row near the center line. Galatasaray and Fenerbahçe were Istanbul's arch-rivals, and in recent years Galatasaray had been stronger. This year, though, had been Fenerbahçe's year. They'd won the national championship, and this game was a derby match—a post-season game between rivals.

I was shocked to see the field ringed with police, most helmeted and many with riot shields. It felt otherworldly. The stands teemed with red and yellow-shirted Galatasaray fans except for a small section on one end reserved for the yellow-and-navy-shirted Fenerbahçe fans. Their single section of seats was ringed by a 12-foot chain-link fence surrounded by helmeted police in rows three deep. The next section of seats was empty, and another legion of helmeted police and fence insulated the Galatasaray fans beyond it. Unbelievable.

I could tell that my soccer experience would would be less about the game than the fans. When the game started the field was clear, though within moments people started pelting players with plastic water containers (no water bottles allowed in the arena, as they make dangerous missiles). Regulations say that the officials will call a game if anything is thrown on the field, but the behavior continued. The field was strewn with plastic containers.

A few minutes into the game, Fenerbahçe scored. The small enclave of yellow and navy went wild. Galatasaray chants redoubled. Moments later Fenerbahçe scored again. The red and yellow just couldn't get the ball past their goalie, who made some spectacular saves. I was awed by his kicking, too, nearly the distance of the field every time he thwarted a goal. Galatasaray played with near frenzy to make a goal before the half, but it didn't happen even with the roaring encouragement of their fans.

After half-time the police formed a tunnel with their shields to protect the Fenerbahçe players as they re-entered the field. I was stunned that they had to provide that kind of protection. After all, it's only a game—isn't it? The tumult in the stands increased. Everyone in the upper decks stood on their seats, scores of water containers exploded on the field (many on players), and soon fans were lighting flares in the crowded upper balcony. I was aghast.

Play continued as fans threw flares onto the field. The air reverberated with chants and the entire arena exploded into flame. Firecrackers, rockets and flares blazed throughout the stadium, but the clock kept ticking. How could the officials allow behavior like this? The hazards were horrendous for both players and fans.

Finally, the officials stopped the game. After about ten minutes of total chaos, the smoke lifted and there was a warning on the loudspeaker. The game continued. Unreal. Not long afterwards, all the police ran to one end of the field—another delay in the game. Players donned their warm-up suits and kicked balls around the field as the rest of us wondered what was happening. Apparently a referee had been attacked, because there was a warning that teams and fans would face serious consequences if officials were attacked again. This might mean clearing the stands before the game continued, fines against the team, or the termination of the game.

Wonders never cease. The game continued, and the fans settled down. Just a little. Galatasaray finally scored, and the game ended 2-1, another Fenerbahçe win. By the end of the game, people were smashing their plastic seats and throwing fragments onto the field—seat shrapnel.

Most of the seats were demolished by the time we left. The streets outside were lined with riot police wielding shields, some in plastic armor. "Robocops," David quipped. It's an odd feeling to be so guarded—ominous safety, I'd call it.

"I don't understand what makes soccer fans so crazy," I said once we were back on the metro.

"I think it's the hot southern European  temperament," David replied.

Duygu had a different take. "The sporting arena is where Turks vent all their pent-up frustrations. They really don't have any other outlets."

"And why didn't the officials just call the game?" I asked.

"Because terminating a derby match means a guaranteed riot. This was nothing compared to what it could have been," Duygu said. "We were lucky."

Really?

The Galatasaray fans did face consequences. The next season they played their first eight home games to an empty stadium.

# 58  RETIRE? REALLY?

Even Istanbul has arts events, and I was thrilled to attend a gallery opening for a Koç teacher's artist husband. His paintings were a splash of historical and political commentary, many washed in darkness, both visual and emotional. John Chandler, the previous Koç director who'd hired me, stopped to chat.

"What are your plans for next year, Ann Marie?" I wondered why he asked but assumed he hoped I'd signed on for a third year. He'd moved to Robert College, but he apparently cared about his recent hires.

"I've decided to retire, but I hope to do long-term subbing internationally. I'll sign up with Teachers on the Move and send letters to the best Turkish schools in case they have short-term openings. We had two second-semester positions at Koç this spring, and Tony filled them both with Teachers on the Move."

"I may have a position for you at Robert," he said.

"I'm not interested in a full year. I really want to be home, and I'm working on a book."

"What are you writing?"

"I'm collaborating with Edda on a guide of her walking tours."

"That's impressive, Ann Marie. This position would only be for the second semester. I have a teacher who turns 65 in January, and according to Turkish law she has to retire. The position may be filled by someone returning from service, but I won't know until summer. If he doesn't, I'd like you to fill the spot."

Robert College was an elite prep school in one of the most beautiful areas of the city. I'd attended a carpet show there with a group of Koç teachers, and the park-like campus dazzled me as we drove up the hill. The ivy-league quintet of campus buildings overlooked the Bosphorus, and we were shown the adjacent alumni country club. Robert was the renowned zenith of Turkish education, and I would have given blood to teach there. "Sounds great," I said, struggling to reign in my excitement. Oh, my goodness.

The conversation turned to the art show, everyone's summer plans, and the upcoming election. My mind raced. Could I be so lucky? That position would be perfect. I wanted to ask what my chances were, but I didn't want to be a grubber.

Saying goodbye was harder than I'd expected. I had mixed feelings about leaving Koç, both students and staff. I knew I'd miss Dee and David. They had another year on contract and would probably stay on longer. Terri was leaving for a position in Mexico, and I'd miss her bright smile and genuine kindness. And then there were the students. Because of the chaos of finals, I hadn't gotten to say goodbye to my ninth graders. It's impossible not to fall in love with these kids, even the wild and crazy Burak, who gave me a hug when he spotted me in the hallway on the last day of school. He'd pulled himself together and squeaked through the second semester with the lowest passing grade. In Turkey if a student fails the first semester and passes the second, they pass for the year. Burak was a bright boy with an unfair disability, and I was glad he'd passed. Everyone had pitched in to help him— Koray, his teachers, his parents, and his peers. We all cared.

Our beloved bartender Şakır Bey was also retiring. We'd developed a warm relationship over the past two years, each other's "Genç arkadaşim." The Community Center would seem empty without Şakır's ready smile, Turkish lessons, and piping hot French fries. We had a gala celebration at the Social Center for everyone who was leaving— catered, of course. I received a watch encased in an etched lucite cube as well as endless hugs. I'd miss these wonderful people, though I knew I'd return to visit, hopefully the following spring.

As I faced the end of my sojourn in Turkey, I recalled comments from before I'd left Minnesota two years earlier. "You'll never come back," a Turkophile acquaintance had proclaimed. He'd been wrong; I was heading home.

"You'll fall in love with Turkey, I promise," Uygar had said. Wise beyond his years, he was right. How could anyone live in Turkey without having it steal their heart? Certainly not me.

"Your experience overseas will change you," my former sweetheart had said even before I chose Istanbul. Was he right? Had I changed? I felt like the same person, the same teacher, the same adventurer. Yet my view of the world had shifted, as had my view of America

Many Turks commented that my weekly missives had shown them Turkey through the eyes of a foreigner, encouraging them to both scrutinize and treasure their world: the call to prayer, the sparkling Bosphorus, the sun setting over distant hills, the occasional Christian church, the bustle of a street market, even a beggar along İstiklal.

I realized, too, that I now viewed America through a different lens. I'd listened to student presentations about the negative influences of media in their lives and others about U.S. corporations exploiting third world workers. How many times had Selim Can prefaced a remark with, "I mean no disrespect, Ms. Mershon, but America...useful"? I'd heard countless diatribes against the War in Iraq and even attended an antiwar rally. I'd worried about the impression America was making on the rest of the world. It wasn't pretty.

The world's disenchantment with America was not just about the war; it was also about broken promises, hidden agendas, and exploitation. People no longer believed that America was an honest nation acting according to altruistic values.    I found that heartbreaking. It was a real eye-opener to view America from across the pond. I can't even count how many times people said, "How could your country vote for Bush a second term?" My only response was that I hadn't.

Had I changed? Was I seeing the world more clearly? My experience in Turkey had been positive. I felt safer in Istanbul than in Minneapolis; in Turkey people reached out to help. I'd once seen a burgeoning street fight where two elderly men stopped it by stepping in and scolding the fighters. Never in America.

The Turks had been warm, the warmest people I'd ever known. 'Turkish hospitality' isn't just an expression, it's a way of life. We interacted as individuals, not as representatives of a particular country or faith. It wasn't me that the Turks disliked, it was my government, its war, and its Machiavellian capitalism. When will we all realize that we

are one people who worship (or ignore) the same god?
One can only hope.
Goodbye, Koç.

# 59 BLUE CRUISE

My retirement celebration was a month of travel beginning with a Blue Cruise (*Mavi Tur*), a sailing trip along the Mediterranean. Friends and family joined me for this grand adventure, including my son Dustin and his sweetheart Aly, Jana and her best friend Beate, and Susie. What joy to celebrate with people I loved. Dee invited her daughter and son-in-law, and Terri joined us with her son. There were also a few more Koç teachers and friends from the States. After a few days touring Istanbul, we flew to Fetiye the night before sailing.

Our sailboat, the Sevi 5 (*sevi* means love) was a beguiling craft of glowing teak, both inside and out. I was glad to see thick sleeping mattresses strapped across the deck; I couldn't bear the the thought of being confined in the below-deck heat. The boat had a little perch out beyond its prow, and Gene (a former student and friend) immediately straddled it, eager to lead us across the harbor and out onto the sparkling Mediterranean. We also took turns in a hammock that hung from the mast. Captain Atilla, who spoke excellent English, guided us through the *gulet* and demonstrated how to flush the pump toilets. Though it looked easy, we weren't the most gifted students and often had to sheepishly summon Atilla's assistance below decks.

First mate Orhan and second mate Söner completed our crew. I was skeptical about our 19-year-old chef, but Söner proved to be a master. At mealtimes the sixteen of us gathered around a long table on the back deck. The first night Söner served us platters of grilled fish fillets, pasta swimming in olive oil and herbs, spiced boiled potatoes, and cucumber and tomato salad. YUM! Every meal rated an easy ten.

For five days we lolled, swam, slept, read, and played cards as the Mediterranean's turquoise waters and mountainous scenery slid by. Three or four times a day Atilla would pull into a little bay or lagoon and we'd dive and cannonball into the Mediterranean's clear, warm water. One day our leisurely lunch was interrupted by shouts. "Come to the bow of the ship. Come now!" Atilla yelled. Oh, my God! Were we sinking? We raced to the foredeck.

"Look, there!" he said, beaming. Four dolphins cavorted along with the ship, leaping within feet of the hull, then diving to repeat their performance. They'd race ahead of us, then fall back to work their way up along the side of the ship again. I was tempted to join them but didn't want to spoil the magic, and my lunch was waiting.

On the Fourth of July Söner emerged from the hold with a late-night snack of fruit-kabobs and a watermelon studded with sparklers —our personal celebratory fireworks.

We visited a few coastal villages along the way. One was Kaş (Kosh), famed for an ancient Roman theater and ornate tombs carved into the marble mountainside. At another small island we were met by village women carrying baskets of handwork: embroidered scarves, dolls, hankies, napkins, and necklaces. Scarved and dressed in bright calico şalvar, they guided us up the island's steep stone-paved streets through a maze of small shops and up to a castle ruin. I chuckled as we passed the 'I Am Here Café.'

A woman named Şerefe (Share-AY-fay, "cheers") walked with me, pointing out items of interest. Between her limited English and my limited Turkish we discovered that we were the same age, though her children were older than mine. She had nine grandchildren, while I had none. Her life had been much harder than mine, but she lived in Paradise. I bought a few small items from her basket and tipped her for guiding me up the mountain. She was half my height and twice my weight, so it was no easy task for her. As we parted, we kissed each other's cheeks. Ah, those Turks.

"What town was that?" I asked Atilla as we returned to the boat.

"I'm not sure. We call it Castle Town."

"What about the restaurant called Simena?" I asked.

"That's just the name of the restaurant," he answered, dismissing me. I later learned that Simena had been the island's Greek name.

"Tonight you can all go to the Pirate Bar," Atilla announced. I thought he was joking until he added, "After dinner a boat will come to pick up any who are interested." This was for real!

"Are you joining us?" Susie asked.

"Sorry—I have to stay with the boat. Pirates, you know," he smiled.

After dinner we donned our finest hot-weather duds and boarded a barge-like motorboat that held 30 people on benches and seats arranged around its carpeted deck. It delivered us to the Smuggler's Inn Pirate Bar, a thatched-roof affair tucked into a tiny cove beneath a high rocky crag. We were amazed at this open-air night club in the middle of nowhere, but it served the many Blue Cruises that came through. A generator provided power, and the only real drawback was the outhouse. We tried to avoid it, but when one drinks beer elimination is inevitable.

Though it took a while for us to get up the nerve, Susie pulled us onto the thatched-roof dance floor, where we danced and sweated up a storm, occasionally pausing to cool off in thatched sitting areas scattered in the nearby jungle. "Cool off" is a relative term. It was hot.

All good things must come to an end, and on the fifth morning we waved farewell to our crew and hopped a service bus into Demre, where we'd find transport to our next destinations, which were many. It broke my heart to say goodbye to Dustin and Aly, who were heading home. They wanted to stay, but their flights were set. I swallowed my tears and looked to the adventure ahead. Susie, Jana, Beate, Shelly (a Minnesota teacher) and I would visit Antalya then drive back along the Mediterranean.

# 60 BACK ALONG THE MED

As our tiny bus bumped down dirt switchbacks through a forested mountainside, my mind raced. What had I gotten us into? These friends had trusted me, and I was leading them to the middle of nowhere. I'd reserved treehouses, for cripes sake. We finally lurched to a stop before a huge sign: WELCOME TO BAYRAM'S TREEHOUSE PENSION. We clambered off the bus, dropped our bags and backpacks and gawked. Young travelers chatted at wooden dining tables in the mottled shade of an outdoor commons. Thatched platforms held young people sipping drinks as they lounged on cushions around low tables.

"Where's the bathroom? I sure hope they have plumbing," Shelly said, looking dubious.

"Looks more like outhouses and sun-showers," Jana commented.

My guilt turned to defensiveness. "We're supposed to have a private bath in our treehouse, and I requested air conditioning." Was I whining?

"There's the office," Susie said, picking up her suitcase and marching off. "Maybe they have beer." The attendant was friendly and spoke excellent English. He explained that they had 20 treehouses and 60 bungalows, many with air conditioning. We followed him through a maze of tiny cabins with rough wood siding, and when he opened the door to ours, there was an audible sigh of relief at our bright, clean room and spacious, white-tiled bathroom.

"How much is this costing us?" Shelly asked.

"$23 a night each, including breakfast and dinner."

"Perfect!" Susie said. "I love it!" Gosh, I loved that girl. Once settled, we headed back to the commons for a cold one. My laptop was in great demand, as we hadn't checked e-mail for five days, and Bayram's had wireless—in the middle of nowhere at the foot of Mount Olympus. Who knew?

That night we bussed to the top of the mountain to see the Chimera, where flames supposedly spew straight from the rock. We hiked a steep, rocky path with occasional stone steps—in the dark. We didn't have flashlights, and relying on the beams of those following us was dicey at best. At last we emerged on a rocky field dotted with campfire-sized flames jetting from fissures in the rock. Both eerie and incredible, it featured in many myths. Who wouldn't be tempted to explain this as the ire of angry gods?

The next morning we enjoyed a typical Turkish breakfast beneath the shade of lush ficus and fig trees then followed the path to the beach, stumbling across ancient ruins on our way through the woods. We saw sarcophagi draped in vines, arched entries to nowhere, and marble pillars lying in the weeds. The sizzling beach sand hurt our feet, so we settled in the shade of a benevolent olive tree. We swam and slept. Heaven.

That night after dinner a full moon drew us to the beach.

"Oh, damn!" Beate yelled when she tripped over a rock and fell face first on the path. Jana laughed, assuming the sand had cushioned her fall and that her ire was over dumping her beer. Beate didn't get up, though. She rocked back and forth cradling her ankle. Jana apologized, and Shelly suggested she soak it in the cool water of a nearby mountain stream. We all dangled our feet in the cool water as we finished our beers in the moonlight. We helped Bea hobble back through the woods to the clinic, a white trailer with a red crescent on its side. As we approached, two men quickly wrapped up the meal they'd been enjoying at a low table outside the trailer. *"Acelem yok,"* I assured them. (No hurry.)

"No problem. We were finished," the doctor said as his friend waved goodbye. "Can I offer you some bread or salad? I'm afraid that's all we have left."

"No thanks—we already ate."

He examined Bea's ankle, slathered it with salve, wrapped it with an ice pack, and gave her ibuprofen. He charged a nominal fee for his services, assuring Beate she could pay later. "Now I must offer you some tea or coffee—or maybe a beer?" A doctor offering us beer? I hesitated, unsure of the protocol.

"Beer sounds great," Susie ventured, raising her eyebrows.

"Excuse me. I'll be right back." He strode across a ravine to a small stand and returned with five beers. Not only that, but he offered Susie his last cigarette. Yup, Turkish hospitality.

After tucking Beate in with a mountain of pillows, Susie and I trekked off to find the Orange Bar, tucked beneath some nearby cliffs. "Oh, my God!" Susie said. The building was two stories high with colored searchlights radiating from its roof. Once inside we realized there was no roof—the club was a shell open to the sky. Music rocked the surrounding cliffs, and myriad stars supplemented the light show. Every table was packed, but no one was dancing.

"Well, let's show them!" Susie said, plopping her beer on an open table. We stepped onto the dance floor alone, much to everyone's amazement. Soon it filled; all they'd needed was a push, which we'd gleefully supplied. We danced our sandals off, sweating and grinning the night away. Around 2 A.M. we dragged our weary bodies home, giggling as we stumbled through the dark to our cabin, where Shelly snored contentedly.

Antalya was beautiful but blistering. We stayed at a funky old pension run by a charismatic surfer who memorized our names immediately. We spent the day wandering Kaliçi, the old city, its heat pounding our skin. I suggested a boat ride, but the rest wanted to explore the old city's countless boutiques. "We've just spent five days on a boat!" Shelly snapped. We were all a little short that day.

Susie and I   split off to find an air-conditioned restaurant. Our waiter teased and chatted with us, promising second beers "on the house." What a deal! He served our free beers in liqueur glasses.

The next morning I stumbled bleary-eyed to breakfast in the pension's walled courtyard. "Happy birthday, Ann! Here's to a beautiful day for a wonderful friend!" Jana led me to a table set with champagne, mini-cakes, a candle and a collection of small gifts. I was abashed, embarrassed, and tickled. Every day reminded me how precious friends were.

We rented a car and headed for Kalkan along nearly 200 km of breathtaking, winding roads skirting the Mediterranean. It took nearly

an hour of meandering narrow city streets to locate the Balıkçı Han,
but once we found it we were thrilled. Located at the edge of the city
on a mountain stream, its six rooms faced the water. There was no
concierge, but the rooms had been left unlocked for us. A young man
on the street offered to carry our luggage, and when we tried to tip
him, he refused. "Turkish hospitality," he said. "Enjoy your time in
Kalkan!"

The next morning we congregated on the shaded patio overlooking
the stream. Durmuş, the caretaker, had arrived early to prepare
breakfast in an open-air kitchen beside the patio. We feasted on olives,
*beyaz peynir* (white cheese), *taze kaşar* (regular cheese), sliced
tomatoes and cucumbers, bread, homemade preserves, melons, and
individual omelets. The terrace was a secluded, quiet spot. Except for
the buzzing cicadas. Jana occasionally shook the tree to quiet them for
a moment of peace.

Our next stop was the Saklikent Gorge, sculpted of marble. Because
of Bea's ankle, Susie offered to stay with her to relax on cushions at a
waterside restaurant while Jana, Shelly, and I explored the gorge. We
paid our 3YTL ($2.25) to get in, then followed a wooden walkway
hanging on the cliff wall just above the water. A huge Turkish flag
fluttered overhead, an oddity in this wilderness setting; patriotism
abounded in Turkey. The walkway ended at a maze of more pillowed
restaurants perched over the water. Ignoring them, we forged across
icy, knee-deep water that soon waned to a warm trickle. Rock
formations swirled above us, each turn revealing more fantastic forms.
A young man helped us up a difficult spot and joined us. Shelly was
immediately uncomfortable with it, but Jana and I decided to go with
the flow (pardon the pun). As we chatted, I explained that we had no
money to pay him.

"No problem," he said. "Just come a little further. I'm happy to help
you." I assumed he was just being friendly, but when we decided to
turn back to join our friends, he grew angry. Just then a woman
coming downriver stopped, raging. "Don't let anyone help you. They
help you up the waterfall, but then they won't help you back down
until you pay them. You can't get back down alone, and they want a

lot of money! I'm furious! If I want a guide, I'll hire one!"

This certainly wasn't the Turkish hospitality I knew. It had to be illegal, and I hoped the authorities fought it, but then again, maybe not. It made me sad.

# 61 AH, THE GREEK ISLANDS!

After a week driving the coast, Susie and I bid farewell to the other three, eager for our two-week tour of the Greek Islands. Susie caught a horrific flu bug that held us at a seedy hotel in Izmir a few days, and just as I'd decided to admit her to the hospital her fever turned and she felt well enough to travel. We caught an afternoon ferry to Chios, and Susie rested at a little coffee bar while I checked for a room at a nearby budget hotel. The lobby was up about a million marble steps, but heck...at this point our coffers were lean.

We checked in and borrowed a few chairs from the dining room to squeeze onto our miniature balcony, where we dined on snacks from our backpacks. We watched buxom women ride by on mopeds, long-bearded priests glide past in long black cassocks and round caps, and old women hobble along in grandma shoes—probably to church. Before we knew it, a sliver of moon appeared over the next building. We toasted it with a glass of apple wine from Şirince.

The next morning Susie brought a few cups of steaming coffee to our balcony perch, and I opened a guidebook. "Here's something about a little village in the south of Chios. It says it's a mastic village, whatever that is. Or maybe we should visit a monastery. What do you think?"

"I don't know," Susie admitted. "I'm thinking maybe a beach."

We returned our chairs to the dining room for breakfast, where a man smiled at us across the tables as we ate breakfast.

"Do you know anything about Chios?" I asked.

"Absolutely," he said, eyes sparkling as he approached our table. "How can I help you lovely ladies?"

"We only have one day here, so what should we see?"

"You are in luck," he answered. "I'm here from Athens on business, but I grew up here. I can tell you the most interesting things to see. In fact, I'd be happy to show you around. I have some business to take care of, but if you'll meet me later this morning, I will happily be your guide." Was he a little too eager?

Susie and I looked at each other. "Why not?" she said.

"It's 8:30 now," he said. "I'll meet you back here at 11:00. Be sure to pack your swimming suits. There are some lovely beaches on the island. My name is Takis. I'll see you in a few hours." Probably in his 50's, his handsome boyish face was dominated by a wide smile.

We met in the lobby, suits in hand, and Takis greeted us with cheek-kisses. He then gave us one of his five cell phones. Our friend Shelly would have been suspicious from the get-go, but we naively dove in with all four feet (and Susie's floatie).

We strolled through a park, where Takis posed for photos with each of us, his arm around our waists. Cheeky? Fun. He explained that he'd treat us equally, no matter what. Hint number one: beware of "touchy" fellows.

We waited while Takis ran yet another personal errand, then he treated us to coffee at a tiny cafe on the pier, where his kissing commenced. One for Susie, one for Ann Marie. Total equality. I could see Shelly shaking her head.

He mapped out our day, noting numerous stops for food and entertainment. Obviously a planner, he explained that he managed the catering for a large Athens hotel. He made copious apologies about his battered '82 Volvo. "I'm sorry it has no air or radio. I have a better car in Athens, but this was my father's car, a little older than my elder daughter." Our ride up the switchbacks to the other side of the island was hair-raising at best, but we clung to the door handles as the muffler clanked at every bump. We screamed up over the mountain and down the other side, where the air was blistering. As we descended, a sprawling white building emerged between hills along a beach. "Is that a convent or a monastery?" Susie asked.

"I will take you there," Takis answered. "I think you will love it. It's called the Cathedral of Saint Markella, and it's very important on this island." I was sorry I hadn't brought my guidebook, but Takis knew a lot. We entered the chapel through a pair of intricately carved wooden doors. The splendor of the interior stopped us in our tracks, our eyes immediately drawn to a gilt and white frontispiece lit by a golden chandelier beneath a dome decorated in brilliant religious frescoes that could have been painted by Michelangelo. Takis led us through the church, kissing each shrine as he explained that people purchase silver and gold icons to hang in the church as they pray for healing. In one corner a tall cabinet held hundreds of gold and silver rectangles pounded with the shapes of arms, legs, hearts, and people with ailments. "People purchase these and place them on this icon of Saint Markella," he explained. "We believe that she has the power to heal all ills."

"And who is Saint Markella?"

"She is the patron saint of this island. Her father was furious when she became a Christian, and he decided to punish her. She ran away across the island, then climbed a tree out of his reach. In his fury, he set the tree on fire. She jumped from the tree and ran to the beach, where he chased her. She prayed for a safe haven in the rocks, and a crevice appeared large enough for her body, but not for her head." He paused, eyes wide. "Her father grabbed her hair and cut off her head. Each year on Saint Markella's Day you can see the blood and the hoof prints of her father's horse in the rocks beyond the beach. My granddaughter is named Markella, and her christening will take place in this cathedral next month. This is why I am here now," he explained. "I am making arrangements for the celebration."

"Next Sunday will be Saint Markella's name day, and people will walk 50 kilometers from Chios Village, over the mountains, and down to this beach to pay tribute to her." Outside the church a woman was crawling up the long walkway on hands and knees. Takis bought each of us a cross and a medallion. Equal treatment. Hint number two—beware the bearers of gifts.

We all dove into the chilly sea, a refreshing break from the midday heat. Susie and I relaxed in the shade while Takis settled in the sun, answering calls on each phone—one for his daughters, one for his wife (who he said was divorcing him), and the other two apparently business phones. Our cell phone rang, and Takis grinned up at us, a mischievous twinkle in his brown eyes. We were within easy talking distance.

After drying off, we wandered to a little beach restaurant where Takis treated us to a lunch of fried cheese, Greek salad, crusty bread, and fresh grilled fish. He ordered grilled octopus, which he devoured with gusto. Susie tasted it, but allergies and revulsion kept me from indulging. Takis distributed frequent kisses, and true to his word, neither of us got more than the other. Hint number three: beware the proffering of kisses.

Takis left to take care of some business in a nearby village, but we weren't invited (red flag). We lollygagged on the beach for a few hours, smooch-free. By 4:00 we had the beach to ourselves. We walked back up to the restaurant to wait for Takis, who had called twice to say he loved us both and wanted to know if we loved him. We shared a beer until he returned with more kisses. He was definitely looking for more action, poor man. On the drive home, he stopped at a little beach bar for tall, frosty beers. "What do you think the chances are that he's actually getting a divorce?" Susie asked. A rhetorical question. Boyfriend for a day.

The drive home was quiet. Totally exhausted, we were marveling at the sunset tinting the sea when Takis pulled into a gas station. He pumped gas for a few seconds then brought the attendant out to meet us. His American conquests. Hint number four: beware of men showing you off.

We got back to the hotel around 9:45 and invited Takis for wine on our balcony at 11:00. We'd treat him to dinner and dancing, the least (and most) we could do.

We sat across from Takis at dinner, as we'd had our fill of kisses. After a scrumptious meal of souvlaki, fried potatoes and bread, we headed off for some dancing. The first club was packed, so we continued down along the harbor. Takis walked far ahead of us, probably to make sure no one he knew was working the next clubs. He said it was because of the divorce. Susie and I plied him with drinks to get him on the dance floor, to no avail; we danced by ourselves until 3:00 A.M. "Good night, Takis. Thank you for a great day," Susie said as she closed the door on his expectant face. We broke into giggles and collapsed into bed.

When we met him at breakfast and thanked him again, there were no kisses. I wondered if he was pouting, then realized the hotel owner was a family friend. He offered to take us into the room one by one for a good-bye kiss, which we prudently refused. Shelly would have been right. He had only wanted one thing.

Our next stop was Mykonos, on a ferry so busy we had to hunt for space but finally found seats in a huge salon that reeked of sweaty feet —thousands of them. Those backpackers' feet outstank anything my teenaged sons had ever generated.

I woke to bustling noises in the salon and peered out the window—lights!

"Is this Mykonos?" I asked another passenger.

"Who knows?" he yawned, then rolled over and went back to sleep. I raced into the hall to ask an agent. "Yes, this is Mykonos, and you'd better hurry if you want to get off; we only stop for fifteen minutes."

We grabbed our bags and raced off the ship onto a vacant pier.

"What? Where's the bus? Where are the taxis?"

"They must have all left," Susie said as she lit a cigarette. "We might as well start walking."

"Want to ride?" someone called. Damsels in distress, we were thrilled to see two dark-haired young men in a convertible jeep. They must have thought we were younger, but when they saw we were old enough to be their mothers, they were undaunted.

"You bet!" Susie said, dropping her cigarette and stomping it out. They squeezed us, our bags, and Susie's floatie into the back of the Jeep.

"Where are you from?" I asked as we sped off down the road, doubtful that Greeks would be so kind.

"We're Turkish. We work on that cruise ship, and we're free for three hours so we're going into town for some excitement."

"*Merhaba. Nasilsiniz?*" I said. They laughed at my Turkish, tickled to chat with me. No wonder they'd been so kind. How many young men would pick up a couple of middle-aged women? They spent a precious half hour of their evening trying to locate our hotel.

"Gosh, you gotta love those Turks," Susie said.

The Apollon Hotel was the second floor of an old house overlooking the harbor, absolutely darling. We felt terrible about arriving at midnight, but a light gleamed from inside. I knocked, and through the lace-curtained entry I spotted a sprightly old woman hopping off an antique daybed to greet us. She must have been 80, dressed in a loose black dress with a deep v-neck, a knitted shawl thrown over her shoulders. She grinned and embraced us warmly. "My name is Maria. Welcome to my home. My family living here hundreds of years, and I'm happy sharing it to you. How was your ferry ride, good?"

Maria's high-ceilinged parlor brimmed with antiques, pillowed rockers and curio cabinets. Family photos covered the walls, and the ceilings were hung with finely-etched glass lamps. She showed us to our room, demonstrated how to use the shower, and handed me a huge key. "Are you needing anything more?"

"No, thank you, but I think we may go out to find something to eat," Susie said.

"Good food is everywhere. Mykonos busy all night. This key for front door. I'm to bed. Please come in quiet; I have other guests."

We adored Maria, as we loved our unforgettable friend Takis. In fact, we loved everything about our Greek Island tour, except that it wasn't long enough. Is it ever?

Once home, I devoted every morning to writing and making maps for the hans guidebook, rewarding myself with afternoon swims, paddles, and hikes. I booked a November flight to take care of final book details in Istanbul, and just days later I was offered the position at Robert College. Oh, heaven!

My heart swelled as our plane descended to my beloved second home, even though the November skies were gray. I stayed with my friend Leah, who'd moved to a bright city apartment that she shared with Dee on weekends (my previous plan). The living room had two plush red couches, and her spacious yellow kitchen boasted a dishwasher, a luxury in Istanbul. We chatted non-stop for two days, catching up on each other's lives before Leah left on a trip, leaving me alone for the next week. November can be dreary in Istanbul, but I set a busy schedule of shooting final photos, checking walk instructions, and revising the book each evening. My son Dustin had compiled a music selection for my iPod, which kept me company on my hour-long walk, ferry, and tram back and forth from Sultanahmet. It was lonely, but I managed.

Thank God I had Edda, my tiny dark-haired dynamo. I never understood how she could remember so many facts—all of them fascinating. We tested the second walk together one morning, perfecting the directions and double-checking street names and building locations against my maps. We also conducted interviews for feature articles, as we would include some of Edda's more interesting friends along the walks. Most of them spoke only Turkish, but that didn't seem problematic. My favorite was Turan, a shy mustached cobbler who set up shop each day on a street corner beneath the shade of a massive plain tree. He sat behind a treadle sewing machine and repaired shoes. When it rained he put up a big umbrella, and in the winter he kept a charcoal hibachi burning beside him. Turan's father had passed the business on to his son—low overhead.

The next day (forecast cloudy with a slight chance of rain) Edda and I met near the Spice Bazaar, umbrellas in hand. As we hiked up the steep, narrow Çakmakçılar Yokusu, the clouds dropped a deluge of rain, transforming the cobbled street to a river. We trudged up through water streaming over our ankles. "Let's duck into this restaurant, Edda. I'll buy you tea," I suggested, hoping the tide might ebb. We shook the water off our coats and umbrellas, then dissolved into laughter as we poured water from our shoes. Never has a hot cup of tea been so welcome.

Later that week Edda invited me to her penthouse apartment, a treasure-trove of old furniture, photos, and relics from her parents' lives—a veritable antique shop. I was mesmerized by her panoramic view of the Golden Horn and the domes and spires of Sultanahmet. We spent the afternoon reviewing photos and clarifying details, our laptops side by side on her kitchen table. "What else do we need to do?" Edda asked.

"I want to include pronunciation guides for each of the sites. I hate it when people mispronounce Turkish names. People don't know that C is pronounced like J, but if they have the phonetic pronunciation for each site, I'll feel better—even if they don't care. We can go item by item. You say each name carefully, and I'll write it out phonetically. What's the first site?"

"It's the Taş Han," Edda said.

"TAHSH hahn," I spelled, slowly repeating the name. Edda giggled as she looked at my phonetic interpretation.

"Next is the Laleli Camesi."

"Can you repeat it again and emphasize the accented syllables a bit more?"

"LahLEli CaMEsi."

"Lah-LAY-lee Jah-MAY-see," I wrote as I repeated it slowly.

Edda giggled again. "It looks so funny that way—is that really how I said it?" I repeated it from my phonetic spelling.

"So odd," she laughed, "but I guess it's right."

Names sounded goofier and goofier as we labored over their phonetic spellings. Turkish is already phonetic, so our challenge was translating it to spellings unmistakable to English speakers. My interpretations grew more ludicrous, each one more confusing. It wasn't long before we were both laughing hysterically—tears streaming down our cheeks, stomachs aching. We took a few deep breaths, got back down to business, and finally finished the 89$^{th}$ and final site.

Sadly, our editor made me redo all the pronunciations using consistent letter patterns, which I found dull and unimaginative. Our afternoon of hilarity wasn't wasted, though—it had been sheer joy.

Edda surprised me with a lavish meal of mushroom soup (tantalizing), shredded vegetable salad (scrumptious), olives, pickled beets, and fresh bread. When I was completely stuffed, she pulled out the main dish—a brightly-painted bowl of pilaf topped with a delicately seasoned vegetable and sausage goulash. Full as I was, I devoured every bit. As she served tea in flowered porcelain teacups, I felt like an actor in "Babette's Feast." It was better than the Thanksgiving dinner I was missing back home. I thanked my lucky stars for the meal and for my dear friend Edda.

Our last day of trekking together was a long one, which we finished at the Sair Han, climbing an outdoor stone stairway to a panoramic rooftop view of the Golden Horn and the Sea of Marmara. We were snapping photos of each other when a young man approached carrying a live chicken. He offered to show us the view from an even higher point, which Edda readily accepted. Seventy years old at the time, she was a youthful, sprightly woman game for adventure. He led us around the Tower of Eirene, a crumbling edifice on the corner of the han, and we clambered up ladders to the pinnacle for a spectacular panorama. Edda taught me to take advantage of every opportunity, which opened doors for me all over Turkey.

With an audible sigh of relief, I submitted our manuscript, maps, and photos to our publisher on schedule, oblivious of the months of revision and editing that lay ahead. I felt no pangs this time as I waved my favorite city goodbye—I'd be back in a few months to live at Robert College, one of the most picturesque spots in in Istanbul. Could it be that I was more at home in Istanbul than Minnesota? Was I happier there? Alone? It was something to consider, but I'd think about it later.

First I'd enjoy my first white Christmas in three years.

# 63 ALONE AT ROBERT

I returned to Istanbul two months later. The Robert College campus was magical even in February, tended like a botanical garden. Established in 1863 by American missionaries, Robert College is one of the oldest American schools outside the U.S. Most notably, though, it's revered as the finest prep school in Turkey. Families dream of having their children qualify to attend there.

My tiny apartment had wood parquet floors and deep marble sills beneath wide picture windows facing the woods. It was adequate space for Libby and me but offered little room for guests. I taped up calendar photos of Grand Marais and rearranged the furniture in hopes of warming things up. It was a little sad to display Minnesota scenes in my Istanbul home, but they were all I had. I popped on my rose-colored glasses and reminded myself that this was where I wanted to be, and I'd make the most of my new life. Heck, it was only a semester.

And I had the Bosphorus. Broad concrete walkways lined both shores of this wide waterway that was surely the main reason for Istanbul's location. Across the water I could see the historic Kuleli Military School, a castle-like edifice with high turrets, which I most loved at night when its lit profile reflected on the water. The Bosphorus divides Europe from Asia, and because it connects the Mediterranean with the Black Sea, it provides access to Bulgaria, Romania, Georgia, Russia, and the Ukraine. Hence, it's been a source of many battles. Aside from that, it's spellbinding. I vowed to walk it every day—just because I could. It took ten minutes to trek down to the water, an enchanting route of winding sidewalks, stone walls, and stairways (167 steps) lined in lush greenery, even in February.

On our first morning Libby and I strolled along the Bosphorus for an hour, passing fishermen who pulled in strings of *hamsi* (anchovies) on lines of up to ten tiny hooks. A number of stray dogs stopped to sniff Libby, who stood submissively with her tail down until they moved on.

Thankfully, she knew to act meek when she'd actually prefer to play. Private yachts and tour ferries lined the quay near the school entrance, a tall metal gate with security guards monitoring every visitor. In fact, the entire campus was surrounded by high masonry walls topped with coiled razor wire. I'd been told Robert College was a fabulous place to teach but that the teachers weren't particularly friendly or collaborative. I found that hard to believe. My friend Jamilah had moved to Robert, and I was eager to see her. It felt good to have a friend on campus.

I spent Saturday afternoon alone in my office reviewing notes from Elaine, the teacher I was replacing. I prepared a poetry lesson for my non-fiction classes and found materials for *Bless Me, Ultima* for my fiction class. Though I'd been too busy to miss teaching, I was excited to be back. Elaine had left numerous notes, an appreciated welcome. I hoped everyone would be as kind.

After a dicey sleep the second night, Libby and I trekked to the upper campus entrance—up 322 steps. I'd certainly get my exercise at Robert; it was work to get anywhere. Two snarling dogs met us outside the gate, so I snatched Libby up and we pretended to ignore them, hearts pounding. When we got home Libby settled on her marble window sill to watch for campus cats, intoxicated at each new sighting. The call to prayer resounded through the apartment, bringing a smile. It was good to be back.

I set my alarm for 5:30 for school, allowing ample time to walk Libby, shower, eat, and stop into the office before the 8:00 flag ceremony. I slept hard, and my eyes fluttered open to too much light. I squinted at the clock—7:45! Oh no!!! Heart pounding, I flew out of bed, shoved Libby out the door, threw on clothes, washed my face, let Libby in, and raced the two steep blocks to Gould Hall. As I sidled through the auditorium door, Mr. Chandler announced, "...and we'd like to welcome a new teacher, Ms. Ann Marie Mershon, who is replacing Mrs. Şeren." Applause. Blush. Nod.

My first day jitters worsened; I got locked out of the office (why lock it?) and couldn't find chalk for the chalkboard. Students came to retrieve me from the lunchroom when I didn't show up for my afternoon class—blush again. I'd have to read the schedule more carefully. I was presenting myself as a first-rate airhead.

My students were eager to please, though, and glad I was an older, experienced teacher. They were the crème-de-la-crème, the brightest students in Turkey, and I had the privilege of teaching these little geniuses. To get to know them, I decided to play Two Truths and a Lie. "Everyone take a notecard, write your name at the top, and number to three. Now think of two unique things about yourself that your classmates don't know, and invent a third one that's a lie. You can put the lie as number one, two, or three. I'll show you what I mean. I've already written two truths and a lie about myself. See which you think is the lie."

1. I am one of five children.
2. I have visited thirty countries.
3. I have gone canoeing and camping every summer for over 30 years.

After reading them through, I repeated each item separately so they could vote on which was the lie. They agreed the first one was untrue. "Sorry—I am one of five children and I've also canoed every summer for 33 years. Number two was the lie; I've only visited 20 countries, but I intend to improve on that." They were fooled because upper class families in Turkey tend to have just one or two children, and they assumed America was similar. "Once you finish, I'd like each of you to stand and read your statements to the class just as I did."

A slight girl with a ponytail and black-rimmed glasses rushed up to me. "I must go," she blurted, then ran from the room. When she didn't return, I asked, "Could someone go look for the girl who ran out? I'm concerned about her."

"It was İpek," her seat mate said. "She's probably at the counselor."

"She has a stutter and never talks in front of the class," another said. "I think she was scared."

After class I found the counselor, who confirmed that she'd been there. She explained that İpek lived in constant dread of stuttering before her classmates. In order to help her speak up in class, I had a meeting with İpek to devise a plan. I promised not to call on her unless she made eye contact with me, and she agreed to answer at least one question each week. Before long she was raising her hand almost daily. She still stuttered, but less. Her peers never laughed or teased her about it—Turkish kids are sympathetic. At the end of the semester she even stood in front of the class for a group presentation. Though she said little, it was a triumph for our sweet İpek. (Incidentally, İpek means silk, a fitting name.)

The real challenge for me at Robert was the teachers. They were generally kind, but more aloof than helpful. I shared an office with four other teachers, each with a desk, bookshelves, files, and a bulletin board. On my first afternoon a female office mate stormed in, slammed a pile of books onto her desk, and launched into a loud string of shocking expletives. Pull out the kid gloves, I told myself. I knew better than to comment. Was this what lay in store for office communication?

The second morning I entered the office with a cheerful "Good morning, everyone." The man near the door nodded without looking up, while the others stared at me like I'd pulled down my pants. How would I ever make friends with these people? Thank goodness for Philip, a wiry, gray-haired, energetic Brit in the desk beside mine. He had a wry sense of humor, and we gradually developed an easy camaraderie that was to be one of my few teacher friendships that semester.

Unlike at Koç, collaboration was rare, and level meetings often ended in heated debates over philosophy or expectations. Teachers seemed frazzled, always in a frenzy to keep ahead of their students. I knew that collaboration would have made everyone's jobs easier, but I was in no position to advise. A shocking example of the disjointed staff was when an administrator asked for someone to write a tribute to Elaine Şeren, the woman I was replacing. She'd taught at Robert for 29 years, yet none of her peers felt they really knew her. I thought that was a travesty and offered to have my students write short pieces about her. Their intimate, glowing tributes strengthened the article.

I wondered what accounted for the differences between the two schools. The Robert College English offices were spread across four stories of two buildings, while at Koç our offices were in the same corridor. Though it may not have been the major contributor, proximity certainly made collaboration easier at Koç.

After the first few days I called Jamilah to join me for dinner, but she was exhausted from travel and promised to call me later. I'd eat alone yet another night. My social world would be Libby and my Koç friends.

Winter descended on February 16th. Snow flurries began Saturday, and Sunday I woke to a wonderland—four inches of heavy, wet snow drifted by blasts of wind from the Bosphorus. As Libby and I walked that morning, she cavorted with the snow like a long-lost friend. School was cancelled for three days, time I would have loved to share with someone. Where were Annie and Susie when I needed them?

It wasn't easy. Most Robert College teachers had taught there many years and didn't need a new friend, and I'd missed out on the camaraderie that develops among new teachers each fall. Nonetheless, I managed. Jamilah joined me for dinner a few evenings, but she was devoted to her teaching and seldom socialized. I joined a Wednesday Turkish class, and my classmate Linda invited me to join her for Wednesday classical concerts at Bosphorus University. I enjoyed our Wednesdays together, but she spent weekends exploring the city with her husband. I was ecstatic when Sandra, another teacher, invited me to join her and a friend to see a play at Üsküdar Academy, across the Bosphorus. That was it for the whole semester. No one else reached out to me, and I was hesitant to push. Was it shyness?

I occasionally escaped my lonely apartment to explore the city with David and Dee. The bus to Sultanahmet took less than an hour, and it was a joy to connect with them. We often finished our day with beers on the Galata Bridge before they caught the service bus back to Koç. I should have planned more connections with them, but they were hours away. I met a few times with Aşkin and Söner, my young Turkish friends, but they were busy, too.

Because of my pitiful social life, I focused on my classes. With half of each day dedicated to preparation, I did some of the best teaching of my career. Of course, bright, motivated students certainly helped. One day as we discussed a scene in Bless Me, Ultima where Antonio was excited about learning to read, I shared a personal story. "I felt the same way. I was eager to start first grade, but I remember being heartbroken when I didn't learn to read the first day." I expected laughter—or at least a few polite giggles. Nothing.

"Did any of you feel that way?"

Kerem, a wiry, dark-eyed boy, raised his hand. "I'm sorry, Ms. Mershon, but I already knew how to read when I started school." I scanned the sympathetic faces in the classroom. The crème de la crème.

"How many of you could already read when you started school?" I asked.

Every single hand went up.

I was thankful that Robert College had a sensible grading system. Thanks to the Treaty of Lausanne, foreign schools were autonomous, exempt from the Turkish grading system. At Robert students earned percentage grades between one and a hundred, so there was less grade-grubbing and fewer tears. It made life much easier for all of us.

Sadly, though, finals at Robert were a horror. The floor of the school's massive gymnasium was covered with carpeting for long rows of desks—ten lines of 24 old-style wooden desks with side-arm tables. It felt medieval, like Harry Potter's Hogwarts School. Strictness ruled as teachers walked up and down the rows to prevent cheating. I couldn't imagine a more stressful test situation, but when I talked to Mr. Chandler about it, he responded, "This is how it's always been done."

For 150 years.

# 64 TULIPS, TULIPS, TULIPS

The March sun warmed my soul, and Libby and I headed down the hill, through the security gate, and off to the north along the glittering Bosphorus to find Emirgan Park, famous for its spectacular tulip displays. As usual, we encountered curious street dogs, quayside fishermen, *simit* sellers, a balloon man, and countless Sunday strollers. The traffic was *çok kalıbalık*—very congested; Istanbulites flock to the Bosphorus on  sunny spring days, and cars crawled along the coast road as we passed them by.

Two hours later we reached Emirgan, where a wide cobbled street led up from the Bosphorus, opening to a square crammed with tables of Turks enjoying the sunshine. I was the only *yabancı* (foreigner). As I nibbled on *töst*, a panini-like cheese sandwich, I chatted with a few older men at the next table. They were tickled that I could speak Turkish and described a short-cut to the park's back entrance—straight up the hill.

The park burst with elaborate displays of tulips, daffodils, hyacinths, and exotic blossoms. An arched wooden bridge spanned a "river" of blue hyacinths and tulips flowing beneath it in colored waves, and a brilliant multi-shaded rainbow of roses stretched across an entire hillside, infusing the air with their heady scent. There were thousands of tulips. No—millions, wrapping us in a cloak of springtime.

Tulips originally came from Turkey—not Holland. They were cultivated as early as 1000 A.D. and became a symbol for the Ottoman Empire in the 1500's. Bulbs were exported to Europe later that century, and in the 1700's tulips became a symbol of wealth and prestige, some bulbs worth their weight in gold. The Dutch began experimenting with tulips, though the Turks outpaced them in their love of the blossoms for years to come.

Families spread blankets and picnic feasts under trees, and children kicked soccer balls with their fathers and uncles while mothers and aunts relaxed in the sunshine. One woman clad in full black hijab played soccer with her husband and son, laughing each time she kicked the ball. Young lovers held hands as they meandered among the blossoms. Though an outsider, I was welcomed with smiles, and Libby patiently succumbed to the attentions of curious children. Turks either love dogs or are petrified of them; there's no middle ground.

A little girl with cropped dark hair followed us around over an hour, petting Libby whenever we stopped. When I handed her the leash, she gleefully let Libby lead her through the park. I knew enough Turkish to speak with her father, who explained that his wife wouldn't allow a pet in their house, though Elif often begged for one.

By four I was exhausted. Spurned by two bus drivers (no dogs), I hailed a taxi home. As we crawled back down the coast road, I was thankful for this enchanting day among the Turks. If only I'd had a friend to share it.

# 65  BILL, PLEASE

Visits from friends eased my loneliness at Robert. My niece Laura was studying in Lithuania and visited with a college friend, and Susie, Annie, and Annie's daughter Jess flew over for my spring break. We flew to Cappadocia, and after returning to Istanbul Susie wanted to go dancing.

"We could try the Reina," I suggested. "It's an exclusive night club down the road with outdoor dancing on the Bosphorus." We dressed to the nines, tucked money into our bras and headed out. We walked to the Reina, a star-studded world of beautiful people: men in 3-piece suits and women in sequins and jewels. We were underdressed, but nonetheless Susie forged on through the crowded room. Every table held plates of iced raw almonds and olives. The outdoor section was closed, but a waiter appeared bearing a tall table with hors d'oeuvres, a bottle of Smirnoff's, and cans of Red Bull.

I asked him in Turkish for cherry juice and a Sprite for Annie. "These are going to be expensive drinks," I warned. "Sip slowly."

"How much do you think?" Jess asked.

"Well, drinks in most night clubs are about 10 lira ($7), and they'll probably be at least twice that. We danced for over an hour, nursing our drinks. On my way back from the ladies' room I noticed people standing on the outside decks. "Hey, you guys, let's pay our tab and go dance outside. The doors are open, and we probably can't afford a second drink anyway." I signaled the waiter. *"Hesap alabilir miyim?"*

Instead of answering, he held up four fingers. Four. That would mean one of two things: it was either 40 lira total (about $32), a typical bar price, or it was 40 lira each, which was outrageous. I pulled out a 50 lira bill, but he shook his head. I was about to tell the others they'd have to cough up 40 lira when he held up his four fingers again. *"Dört YUZ,"* he said. Four hundred lira. Seventy dollars a drink!

I shook my head and said, *"Hayir. Çok pahalı."* Too expensive.

*"Dört YUZ!"* he insisted. Well, we didn't have it. All I had was fifty.

Before I knew it, the floor manager arrived, punching numbers into his cell phone and yelling at me in Turkish.

"Why don't you have money? Where is your credit card?"

"I don't have one. I'm an American. I'm a teacher."

"Where is your cell phone? Call your friends for money."

"My friends are in America. I don't have a cell phone here."

He continued to chastise me, but I'd exhausted my limited knowledge of Turkish and didn't understand. Suddenly a giant man in a black suit materialized, grabbing my right elbow. Jess had city smarts and sent Susie and Annie outside to wait for us. Jess and I remained to face the management's wrath with a mere 100 lira between us.

I envisioned the headlines: "Robert College Teacher Jailed for Nonpayment at Reina Club." I didn't know who was more in the wrong, but I knew this was one big fellow. He was careful not to make a scene, and I must admit, he looked friendlier than the floor manager. In my most assertive Turkish, I said, *"Müdür konuşmak istiyorum."* (I want to talk to the manager.) I wished I'd mastered the polite tense, but it was what it was.

*"Bir Dakka,"* He answered. One minute.

He led me to the lobby and entered an office. A small man in a thousand-dollar suit emerged. "Can I help you?" he asked in perfect English. Whew! Now we could work things out.

"We were just charged 400 lira for four drinks, and one was a soda!" I complained. "That's outrageous, and we don't have that much money with us."

"Well, what did you expect? This is the finest club in Istanbul. Did you think the drinks would be free?"

"No, but there's no indication anywhere of your prices. I expected it would be expensive, but not 100 lira a drink. I can get a nice hotel room for that."

"Well, how much do you have with you?" I looked at Jess, and we proffered our 50-lira notes.

"That will be fine," he said, taking our money. "But don't ever come back here again."

Monday morning I was relating our Reina adventure to my ninth graders when Susie and Annie stopped in. They embellished the tale with great mirth. After my students recovered from their hysterics, Kemal raised his hand. "Ms. Mershon, did you know the Reina is run by the Mafia? You should stay away from there. If you ever want to go out clubbing again, just call me. I can fix you up."

And I'm sure he could have.

# 66  ON A TUESDAY?

My friend Marnie had mysteriously alluded to an upcoming event at Koç. "Set aside May 27th on your calendar, Ann Marie. You won't regret it." I didn't realize until that week that the 27th was a Tuesday, and the three-hour trip each way was too much for a school night.

I e-mailed my regrets, and Marnie replied, "Oh, Ann Marie! It's live music—a private backyard concert. Maybe I can help with transportation. Please try to come!" Live music? Intimate setting? With Koç friends? That was different. I'd happily sacrifice a night's sleep.

I caught a student service bus to the Asian side (45 minutes),then hopped the train to Pendik (45 more with the wait). From there I walked four blocks to the mini-bus "station" for another 20 minute wait and a 40-minute ride to Koç. Two-and-a-half hours was record time for afternoon rush hour. The friendliness of Koç was wonderful, but was it worth being so isolated?

The guards welcomed me at the front gate with smiles and questions. I managed a short account in my limited Turkish before trekking across campus to the Paulus's. Only one of the Robert College guards had been friendly, his smiles manna in my solitary world. Oh, how missed the warmth of Koç. Nostalgia enveloped me as I strolled along familiar sidewalks and lawns and cut through the glass pyramid of the student commons.

Marnie and Tony hugged me and introduced their guest of honor. "This is Brooks Williams. We've known him for years," Tony explained. "He was named one of the top 100 guitarists in America." Brooks blushed. Tables were set with a vast selection of *mezes*, and a waiter approached me with a tray of wine glasses. I was home.

I basked in the warmth of my Koç friends, about twenty of us filling the house and spilling into the back yard. After an hour or so we congregated around the patio for the performance. A slant of early evening sun warmed our backs as we sat beneath shade trees, transfixed by Brooks' voice and guitar. He reminded me of Leo Kottke and John Fahey, two of my favorites. We were all mesmerized. The Turkish band teacher and his friend took center stage to share their Turkish-style guitar, and soon Brooks joined them, fascinated with the Turkish cadence and rhythms.

I caught a ride back to the Bosphorus with the band teacher and his wife, then a ferry and a taxi got me home before midnight—amazing! My hunger for live music and time with friends was sated, at least for the moment. Even on a Tuesday.

# 67 SEEKING LOGGERHEADS

Instead of twiddling my thumbs on campus after finals, I wheedled a spot chaperoning a biology trip to study sea turtles.

We flew to Dalyan Friday night, arriving to streets choked with people honking, chanting, singing, and waving flags—pandemonium. Turkey's soccer team had just beaten Croatia to win a spot in the European Cup semi-finals. More soccer mania.

Our first morning dawned bright and hot. After an introductory session, we walked to the wharf, the students carrying two massive wooden crates of scientific gear. We were met by a tall young man in Quicksilver Bermudas and a baseball cap, Captain Ramazan. He helped us into his wide, flat-bottomed boat. Cushioned seats surrounded an open floor, and a blue tarp canopy protected us from the mid-day sun. We chugged upriver, marveling at ornate tombs carved high into marble cliffs along the water. We moored near a group of sheep clustered in the shade, and teams got busy taking water samples, vegetation surveys, and river current measurements—a mammoth task.

At noon we motored down to the Mediterranean beach for lunch, the endless swath of sand busy with sunbathers and swimmers. Signs were posted against putting umbrellas in the sand, as sea turtles nest along the beach. We returned to the hotel to shower, nap, and analyze data. That evening Gaby, the lead teacher, taught us about sea turtles.

"Did you know that loggerheads can live up to 200 years? Their average life span is 30-60. The turtles reach sexual maturity at about 30, and females nest every three years, laying up to 35 pounds of eggs, often in three separate nests. Loggerheads migrate thousands of miles, and the females return to the beach of their birth to lay eggs. Recent satellite transmitter data has shown that Turkey's turtles migrate to Tunesia.

"A mature male can weigh up to 350 pounds. Another interesting fact is that loggerhead hatchlings increase their weight more than

6000 times from birth to adulthood. If we did that, we'd weigh about 42,000 pounds. The temperature of the nest determines the sex, too. Eggs on the top of the nest reach higher temperatures and become males. The rest are females. I think the dividing temperature is 29 degrees Celsius." I was absolutely fascinated, thankful to be included.

I adored my roommate Iffet. About my age, she'd graduated from Robert College, but her father had thwarted her plans to attend Bosphorus University by forcing her into an arranged marriage. It had broken her heart, but she'd accepted her fate. It infuriated me that this kind, brilliant woman was only a clerk in the school library. She'd been selected to chaperone this trip for the past three years, and she found it fascinating. I was sorry I hadn't met her earlier, but this long weekend had to do.

Sunday we crabbed. Captain Ramazan piloted the boat downstream as he tied chicken skin and a heavy weight (a bolt or a nut) onto each of eight large spools of heavy fish line. Once we were anchored in a choice location, students tossed their lines into the water around the boat. Within minutes, five of them were reeling in blue crabs, which Ramazan netted and brought on board.

Gaby explained how to determine the sex (yup—it was easy), whether the females were in berry (with eggs), and how to measure the carapaces (shells). Once finished gathering data, the students marked each crab's shell with a nail-polished X. Before long our bucket was a knot of inter-connected pincers and shells. "Only 14 crabs so far —it's a slow day," Ramazan said. "Maybe because of heat." As he dumped the crabs back into the river he added, "They'll burrow into the mud to cool off, and we'll come back this afternoon and try to re-catch them."

We chugged off to the beach again for lunch and a refreshing Mediterranean swim, then returned to our crabbing spot. We had disappointing results—only four crabs. One of the four was marked with a red X, so using the ratio of new catches to re-caught crabs, we computed the population of the 100 square meter area to be about 52, the same number as the previous year, when they'd caught 50.

That night half of us returned to the beach, where a team of university researchers studied loggerheads. "We take turns scouting the 3-kilometer beach every night, watching for turtles that come in to nest. We have to catch each turtle before she covers her nest, because they do an efficient job of throwing sand over the nest to hide it."

"We take measurements and mark the turtle, and once she's returned to the sea, we dig down about six inches and place a metal grid over the nest to protect the eggs from predators. The grid is spaced wide enough to allow the hatchlings to wriggle through. In 55 days we will watch the nest and try to protect the hatchlings as they head toward the sea. We then take any unhatched eggs for study."

The moon rose around midnight, barely lighting the beach as we waited. We got a radio report from one of the researchers and stealthily followed our guide along the dark beach. Our turtle laid her eggs quickly, so the researchers caught her for measurements on her way back to the water. They used red flashlights, invisible to the turtle. Our turtle was small, but the experience was huge.

Our last two days in Dalyan were adventures—white-water rafting and sea kayaking. Oh, heaven!

# 68 SHARING TURKEY – HOW?

Once back in Grand Marais, I began each day with a three-mile walk with neighbors—stimulating conversation, warm laughter, and farewell hugs, a welcome change from my solitary walks in Istanbul. I reunited with my woodland world, kayaking, canoeing, biking and hiking with friends. I allowed myself a summer of total freedom. Full moon bonfires, live music at local restaurants, dinners with friends, and blueberry picking up the Granite River...it doesn't get better. Istanbul was fascinating, but my Minnesota world abounded with close bonds and wilderness adventures. It made no sense to be torn between these two worlds, but I was.

I wanted to share the magic of Turkey with the world—well, as much of it as I could. I wanted people to know how warm and caring the Turks are and to understand that Islam is essentially a compassionate and moral faith.

I wanted to encourage educators to teach overseas, not only to expand their own horizons but to return and share that perspective with students. How could I best accomplish that? Articles? Speaking engagements? A book? Once the leaves had fallen, I settled on writing a memoir about my years in Turkey. As I planned, I pondered including Phil. He'd been important to me, and our relationship had eased my early struggles with loneliness, yet I was hesitant to share our intimacies without his permission. I hadn't heard from him in two years, so I decided to send him a birthday card and ask his permission to share our story. I didn't hear back for week and wondered if it would be enough to change his name in the book, as I hated to leave him out. Finally an e-mail arrived from that oh-so-familiar account:

> Hi Ann,
> My name is Becca. I was Phil's wife. We met at the hospital we both work at, I believe a few months after things ended between the two of you. I'm an Obstetrics nurse and we occasionally worked together. We had a wonderful first year together while dating. He was 15 years older than me and full of the qualities that I was looking for in a partner. I have 2 children (13 and 9) and he was a

*wonderful presence in their lives. We were married last July, a few weeks after Phil was diagnosed with stage 4 non-small cell lung cancer. I'm sorry to have to tell you that Phil passed away on August 26 after a year of chemotherapy and radiation. His illness and the way he dealt with it has touched so many lives. We had a year full of treatments and travel, taking life one day at a time. Definitely not a normal first year of marriage by any means. It was bittersweet knowing our time together was limited (the prognosis for this type of cancer is very poor). He was a man of grace and had peace about his situation. He died quickly and with dignity, at home. His memorial service was both beautiful and painful as we were married in the same church a year previous and most of the people there had celebrated our marriage with us.*

*He spoke fondly of you and his time with you. It sounds like you had affection for each other and enjoyed your time together. I'm glad that he had that opportunity in his life because it helped shape him into the man that I knew and loved. He loved Turkey and we had hoped to visit Istanbul together.*

*Your card would've meant a lot to him. Your line about "the woman of your dreams" brought tears to my eyes. We were each other's dream and were planning a life together. I feel honored to have been able to spend the last 2 years of his life with him, making him happy, loving him, supporting him through his nightmare of cancer. He was a good man, a breed few and far between. He impacted my life in so many ways. Truly the epitome of why we can't ask "why" - there is no answer, it just is.*

*I would like to give you my approval to include Phil in your memoir. I trust that you would honor his memory in your writing. I would like the opportunity to read what you wish to publish concerning Phil if that is okay.*

*Please feel free to contact me if there is anything I can help you with regarding Phil.*

*Sincerely,*
*Rebecca*

Tears blurred the words as I read, and I was sobbing by the time I reached the end—tears for Phil, for Becca, and even for my own loss. How could he be gone so quickly? It seemed just yesterday we'd been together. I was thankful he'd had a partner beside him as he navigated through his cancer. Becca was right. She was the woman of his dreams. I was too independent. Too tied up in my own world. Too far away.

Life is what it is—good or bad, joyous or painful.

# 69  TRAVEL BUDDIES

The following winter I returned to Koç for the second semester, an easy transition. Though some teachers had left, I knew most of the English staff and shared a small office with David, a comfortable arrangement. He'd broken up with Kerime, and I did my best to offer support. I weathered the archaic grading system and perilous grade moderation sessions, thankful for open and collaborative peers. There's a lot to be said for camaraderie, and we had it at Koç. I guess life is just a series of trade-offs, and social animal that I am, opting for connections wins out.

I also took advantage of having friends to travel with.

I wanted to see Mount Nemrut, famous for its huge carved heads, so I coaxed Stella, a new South African teacher, and Lorna, my British friend, to join me for the May First holiday weekend. We arrived in the eastern city of Malatya mid-day on Friday and checked into a paltry excuse for a four-star hotel. It was a warm spring day, and the streets were lined with blooming trees as we strolled to the city's famous street bazaar. We were immediately adopted by three young men, and sweet as they were, it took fifteen blocks and a few cups of coffee to shake them. Everywhere we turned, people chirped, "Hello!" "Hi!" "What is your name?" or "Where are you from?" We felt like celebrities as we were greeted by people of all ages, both male and female. The warnings about hostilities in eastern Turkey were clearly a myth. I'd never been welcomed so enthusiastically.

We finally found the bazaar, where copper workers pounded on pots bigger than themselves, knife crafters sharpened knives on foot-pedal grindstones, and welders worked beside them, eyes unprotected. The air was filled with an intoxicating cacophony of pounding and banging, drilling and sawing, different from anything I'd ever known.

Saturday morning as Stella and I explored the neighborhood behind our hotel, we encountered a woman scrubbing her carpet on the street. Dressed in the typical country scarf, plastic sandals, and *şalvar*, she looked up to greet us. After taking her photo I asked how to clean a carpet. She demonstrated hosing it down, sprinkling on laundry detergent and scrubbing it with a long-handled brush. Later she would hose it down and hang it over a fence to dry overnight. "*Çok kolay*," she said. (Very easy.) Right. I could just see myself scrubbing my rugs on the Devil Track Road. Maybe on my deck, though.

"She's invited us to have a cup of coffee," I told Stella. "It'll probably be Nescafe, but I think we should accept."

"Of course! Never pass up a free drink. We've choked down Nescafe before, and we can do it again," she said with a smile. A short blonde with bright eyes and a British accent, Stella was all enthusiasm.

The woman produced two low stools, set them on the street beside the carpet, then disappeared indoors. A group of neighbors joined us, all eager to chat. My weak Turkish was enough to communicate, at least a little. One woman beckoned us to a shed across the street where she proudly revealed a cache of newborn kittens. We oohed and ahhed, then returned to our stools for the most delicious Turkish coffee I'd ever tasted. We were enchanted with the warmth of our new friends. So Turkish.

At noon we met our tour to Nemrut, which included a night at the mountaintop Güneş (sunshine) Hotel, a concrete behemoth carved to look like stone. The inside was as frigid as the outdoors—winter jacket and mittens cold.

Once at the summit we trudged through hard-packed snow to a collection of stone heads and statue fragments dating back to the Kommagene dynasty of 80 B.C. to 72 A.D. Overlooking the Euphrates, they were once a shrine to the dynasty's gods and ancestors. Sadly, the conical heads had toppled from their seated bodies (once 32 feet tall). Now the multi-ton heads stood in a row protected by chains.

Though the area was nearly deserted, a group of ten school children in bright traditional costumes appeared from nowhere and performed an intricate folk dance accompanied by a flute and a drum. Their red shoes flashed as the sun set over the mountain. Dancing in honor of the May First Labor Day, the children hardly looked cold as we shivered in the sub-zero wind. They swarmed around us after finishing, thrilled that I spoke Turkish. Malatya and Nemrut, like nearly all the places I visited, had warmed my heart, more because of the people than the places.

Dee talked me into yet another weekend jaunt to eastern Turkey—this time to Mardin to see the unique architecture near the Syrian border. Well, why not? Eastern Turkey was the bomb as far as I was concerned.

On our flight to Diyarbakkir, Dee sat beside a Turkish physicist who helped us organize a taxi from the airport. Once she'd negotiated a fair price, she waited as we climbed in, then offered to help us at the bus station. In spite of our protests, she hopped into the cab. "I have nothing better to do, and it's been so interesting to talk with you. I can help you find the right bus, then head home from there." Only in Turkey.

At the bus station two ragged boys scurried up with a battered wheelbarrow and piled our luggage into it without a word. They led us to a line of white mini-busses, where our friend found the one to Mardin and made sure the driver understood where we were going. After a flurry of thank-you's, cheek-kisses, and goodbyes, she headed off. Would Americans be so kind?

We squeezed into a seat beside a woman and her little girl. She tried to chat with me, but I couldn't understand her dialect and smiled apologetically. She offered us chewing gum, which tasted suspiciously like a white eraser. We gnawed away, smiling and nodding amiably, unsure how long our jaws could bear the workout. The gum developed a hint of mint flavor after a half hour, but it never softened. I saw Dee surreptitiously spit hers into a Kleenex, and I swallowed mine.

The bus driver stopped near old Mardin, then waited with us until the city bus arrived. He told the new driver the name of our hotel, and we were on our way. We sat behind a paunchy fellow all in denim, who turned to greet us. "Hello. I am Yesür. Here is my card. I have a taxi service, and I would be happy to take you to a tour of the city." We'd been adopted at every turn by helpful Turks.

We called Yesür the next morning for a ride to the Deyrulzafaran Monastery (think saffron). He arrived with complimentary maps, guidebooks, and CD's on Mardin—all in Turkish. Inside the monastery we met a distinguished gentleman with impeccable English who guided us through, showing us the ancient Sun Temple, the larger Sun Church, and a small chapel on the roof of the monastery.

"Are you a monk?" Dee asked.

"Oh, no! I am an Iraqi Christian, and I fled my home because Christians are being persecuted in Iraq. Unfortunately, Christianity is associated with America, and many Christians are being executed. I am fortunate that I found refuge in this monastery. My wife was an English professor and my parents are retired teachers. They are here with us, as are my two children. They protect us here as refugees. As soon as I get the papers, we will emigrate to Australia. I could go to America and continue my career in engineering, but why would I want to live there? At one time most Iraqis loved America, but now it's different. Most hate the American government for what it has done to our country. How could I live in the country that has destroyed mine?"

"We hate the war, too," Dee said. "We can't apologize enough for the damage America has done. We're so very sorry!"

"We like to think Obama will change things," I said. "I worked hard on his campaign."

"Obama will not change anything. The damage is done," he said. I hoped he was wrong. Though Yesür had shown us only kindness, his hatred for our country felt toxic.

My last destination that semester was Gallipoli, pivotal in Turkish history. I recruited Lorna and David to join me for a tour I'd found online. As we stepped into the van, a vendor approached with hundreds of *simit* balanced on his head—a halo of bagel-like breads stacked 25 high on a wooden disc. How could we resist?

Sunshine, waves, and stunning vistas followed us along the sea as we drove down to the Dardanelles, a waterway leading from the Aegean to the Marmara. In a small village we were stopped by a circumcision procession of two little sultans mounted on horseback with family and friends following on foot.

At Gallipoli our sprightly guide Perihan walked us through numerous museums, graveyards, and monuments as she explained the campaign. "During World War I, the Allies wanted an ice-free sea route to Russia, and the only available option was through the Dardanelles, across the Marmara and up the Bosphorus to the Black Sea. At the time it was controlled by the Ottomans.

"The allies tried to seize the Dardenelles Strait, and after a thwarted naval attack early in 1915 they strategized to gain control of the Gallipoli Peninsula along the strait. The British enlisted the support of the Australian and New Zealand Corps (ANZAC) that were training in Egypt. So began a bloody 8½ months on the Gallipoli Peninsula beginning in April of 1915. As the British ships waited through the night to land, they drifted a few kilometers north of their goal. Instead of landing on a smooth beach with low, rolling terrain, they landed on a narrow strip below a high ridge. This one mistake cost them the entire campaign. The allies lost 43,000 men, and the Turks lost 87,000, with over 500 killed each day in hand-to-hand combat for nearly nine months." It was a devastating massacre on both sides.

In the end, the Allies retreated, pulling out their last soldiers on January 9, 1916, and leaving the Dardenelles Strait in the hands of the Ottomans. A young military commander, Mustafa Kemal (Ataturk), proved his genius in this battle and later became the first ruler of the Turkish Republic in 1923.

I was touched by the tales of kindness on both sides of the battle lines: soldiers tossing cigarettes, candy, and food across the narrow expanse between the trenches. There were stories of Johnnies (Allied forces) giving water to dying Mehmets (Turks), and Mehmets carrying wounded Johnnies back to the Allied trenches. We tried to imagine crouching in those narrow, muddy trenches hour after hour, day after day, week after week, starved and anticipating imminent death. Some regiments were completely wiped out, and many of the bodies were never identified.

I finally understood why this was such an important piece of history for Turks, Aussies and Kiwis alike. Time and again I was moved to tears, but never more than by Ataturk's words on a monument beside one of the many graveyards:

"THOSE HEROES THAT SHED THEIR BLOOD AND LOST THEIR
  LIVES...
YOU ARE NOW LYING IN THE SOIL OF A FRIENDLY COUNTRY.
  THEREFORE REST IN PEACE.
THERE IS NO DIFFERENCE BETWEEN THE JOHNNIES AND THE
  MEHMETS TO US WHERE THEY LIE SIDE BY SIDE HERE IN
  THIS COUNTRY OF OURS...
YOU, THE MOTHERS, WHO SENT THEIR SONS FROM FAR
  AWAY COUNTRIES WIPE AWAY YOUR TEARS; YOUR SONS
  ARE NOW LYING IN OUR BOSOM AND ARE IN PEACE.
AFTER HAVING LOST THEIR LIVES ON THIS LAND THEY HAVE
  BECOME OUR SONS AS WELL."
                                                 ~ATATÜRK 1934

I wept as I read this tribute to the depth of Turkish sympathy—the ultimate hospitality. What an incredible man Atatürk must have been. What incredible people these Turks.

"I've been offered a fall semester position at Robert College," I told David.

"So are you going to take it?"

"I really don't know. I love Turkey, but I'm supposed to be retired. I was looking forward to being home for the fall colors."

"Well, are you going to say no then?"

"I don't know." I needed to talk it through; snap decisions were hard for me, and I appreciated David's input. "If I teach next fall, that would mean a full year of teaching, which would make it all tax-free."

"Sounds like a no-brainer to me. Anyway, it would be nice to have you around next fall. Dee is leaving, and I'm going to be all alone with a bunch of young teachers."

"Oh, you poor thing. You'd have to hang out with all those beautiful young women. Terrible." No reply.

Taking the position meant good money, fabulous teaching, a tax exemption, and time with David, who had become my closest friend in Turkey. Retired or not, I could manage another semester. I e-mailed John Chandler with my acceptance.

A month later he sent me photos of a little off-campus apartment he'd found for me but added that that the teacher had negotiated a full-year leave. I loved the idea of living on my own in Arnavutköy, but a whole year was overwhelming. Tough decision. After a few days and more discussions with David, I agreed to teach the full year.

After finals I coaxed David to help me move my few belongings to Arnavutköy. My apartment was a bright little aerie with a view overlooking the Bosphorus, a short walk from campus.

After we'd piled my dishes, cleaning supplies, and linens amid the furniture in the apartment, I offered to treat David to coffee at Starbucks. It was a steep walk down to the Bosphorus, where we strolled in the sunshine as boats glided along the glittering water beside us. Bebek must have the most incredible Starbucks in the world, three stories on the Bosphorus. We sat on the shaded waterfront terrace sipping coffee as we talked about our summers. My mixed feelings about another full year in Istanbul were abating. I was absolutely and totally happy.

Dee, David, Annie and I shared a farewell barbecue outside the social center the night before we flew home. Annie, married to Koray, would of course stay on. Dee was moving back to the States, but David and I would return. It was a bitter-sweet evening, important to all of us.

Farewell friends.

Farewell Koç. Again.

Arnavutköy is Istanbul's San Francisco, with steep streets and Victorian-style Ottoman houses. Libby and I arrived in August, sunbeams brightening our new home—a hearty welcome. I loved the idea of living off campus. Though not luxurious, the apartment had granite countertops, heavily varnished wooden doors, and laminate wood-look floors. It was cozy and bright—exactly what I needed. I was pleased, too, with the mish-mash of furniture the school had provided, particularly a little semi-circular wood table that I settled by the living room window. And I had a second bedroom for company.

The entire apartment was coated with a layer of grit, so I unearthed my broom and a rag to tackle it before unpacking. I worked up a thirst, but—oh dear!—no drinking water. I needed to order a filtered water dispenser, but my cell phone needed a new sim card. I wouldn't risk drinking tap water, so Libby and I trekked down the steep hill to the grocery store and Turkcell, where I reactivated my phone. Libby was thrilled to be out, tail wagging as she sniffed her way down the long concrete stairway across from my apartment. The climb back up steep streets and the 203-step stairway with two heavy bags reminded me not to buy so much next time.

I put things away, guzzled a tall glass of water, and hopped into the shower—ARAUGHHH!!! No hot water! This was getting ridiculous! I gritted my teeth and scrubbed, reminding myself it wasn't as cold as the Lake Superior baths we took on our kayak trips. Once clean and settled, I put my feet up. Happy to be back, I still felt discomfited. I needed to let friends and family know I'd arrived safely, so I grabbed my laptop and headed for campus to try the internet. Luckily, I still had a Robert College ID from two years earlier so the guards let me in. The sunlight waned as I climbed the front steps of Gould Hall, where I sat beneath a massive pillar hoping to catch some wireless with my old password. Nothing. Things weren't going well.

Yawning as I trudged back down the darkening street, I spotted my elderly neighbor sitting on her tree-shaded terrace. *"Merhaba, Hediye!"* I said. *"Nasilsiniz?"* I'd met her the previous spring and remembered her name, which meant "gift." Her round wrinkled face broke into a broad grin and she hobbled over, inviting me for a cup of tea. I politely refused, requesting water instead.

Hediye hustled me to a chair at her patio table and introduced me to her near-deaf husband, Ömer, who sat in the shade beside their door. Soon she emerged from the kitchen with a tray of cheese, tomatoes, cucumbers, *dolma* (stuffed peppers) and, of course, tea. I feared the tea would keep me awake, but there was no refusing.

Still beaming, she shuffled around the corner to get her relatives. Tired as I was, it was a lovely welcome—a gift. My loneliness abated as they watched me eat and I tried to tell them about myself. Heidye insisted that I stop by every night for tea. Maybe daily visits would improve my Turkish. I finally tore myself away and dragged my tired body to bed, where I slept like the dead.

The next day I made a list of things I'd need help with. The refrigerator door opened the wrong way, the gas range had neither burners nor gas, the water heater needed attention, and there was no internet. I'd have to wait until Monday to contact Elvan, the housing coordinator. She agreed to manage everything but internet service. That was my job.

After a morning staff meeting I took a taxi to the nearby Bebek Telekom office to arrange for internet service, but of course it was the wrong office. OK, whatever. I hopped another taxi up the hill to the right one. I could barely explain my needs in Turkish, and when I scanned the complicated forms, I nearly cried.

"Can I help you with that?" asked a bright-eyed young Turk across the table. He took time to guide me through the forms with typical Turkish generosity. I'd soon have a working phone, internet, a functioning stove, and maybe even hot water.

For better or worse, I was back. And I was happy.

I settled into a comfortable routine as autumn enveloped Istanbul. I loved my sunny apartment, and my Lise Prep office mates were friendly. Imagine! Erica invited me to join her for yoga sessions, and Jake, a cutting-edge teacher with a wry sense of humor and a creative spirit, invited me to join his writing group. Our office was congenial as well as industrious, and we were constantly sharing materials and brainstorming new ideas. I hadn't taught on a team since early in my career, and I loved it. I made a point of having social plans every weekend, often with David. I refused to be lonely.

On weekend mornings I'd sit at my little half-round table with a hot cup of coffee and gaze out over the Bosphorus as ships both massive and minuscule navigated the busy waterway. Libby supervised the neighborhood cats from the bedroom window, perched on a suitcase I'd wedged beside the bed for her. The stairway below her had plenty of foot traffic, both two and four-legged, and I'm sure she imagined chasing every cat she saw. On our walks she was either scrabbling after a cat hidden under a parked car or  chasing another into the nearest tree. A few cats had computed the length of her retractable leash and would stop just beyond her reach to thumb their kitten noses at her.

A village-like community nestled in the city, Arnavutköy had once been the home of a Greek Orthodox church, a synagogue, and a mosque. The ancient synagogue was in ruins, but every Sunday I listened for the church bells, and of course the call to prayer resounded from the mosque five times each day. I loved it all.

One thing I didn't love that year was laundry. I had no washer, and Arnavutköy had no laundromat, so I washed everything by hand. I'd soak large items in the base of my shower, and I washed everything else in the kitchen sink. Soaking dirty clothes overnight in a bucket of soapy water made it easier to get them clean. The hardest part was rinsing and wringing. It took three rinses to get all the soap out, and my arthritis made it hard to wring the large items, especially the sheets. I rigged a few clotheslines from my window grates to railings across the outside stairway but the dripping clothes made the marble steps dangerously slippery. I grew accustomed to a home garlanded with laundry drying over racks, radiators, and doors.

I'd lost sleep over my new assignment at Robert—Lise Prep (LP), a prep year required of all incoming Robert College students, many of whom spoke no English. I'd never taught English as a second language, and I was petrified.

"You'll see, Ann Marie. It will take some months, but they'll pick it up on their own. Really!" Erica assured me with a smile. This tall sandy-haired young woman was invaluable as she helped me navigate the LP curriculum. She had the desk beside mine in the spacious attic office we shared with four other LP teachers.

"I use an interpreter for the first few weeks," she said. "Choose someone with high English scores to translate for you."

I selected an interpreter in each class to repeat my English instructions in Turkish. I asked everyone to write a short description of themselves and rate their level of English skill on a scale of 1-5. A few could barely write their names and a few English words, while others wrote extensive essays. Using that along with English proficiency scores, I seated them so that every student with low English skills sat between more proficient speakers. Before long students were translating instructions for their seat mates. It was a new adventure for all of us as we toiled in bright, high-ceilinged classrooms overlooking the Bosphorus.

Each day I faced confused and blank expressions, but everyone tried. The buzz in my classroom was a Working Buzz rather than a Goofing Around Buzz. My students were gentle guides for each other, and I was soon converted to total immersion for language acquisition. It works particularly well at Robert because of the combination of generosity and innate intelligence.

Not only were the students accommodating, but my office mates were the most collaborative group of teachers I'd ever worked with. Cyrus, our LP department head, had come from Koç. In fact, he was the man who'd met me at the airport. John Chandler had hired him from Koç, perhaps to promote a culture of cooperation at Robert. It was heavenly—well worth the damnable stairs I climbed to the office every day.

In addition to the trek to campus, I hiked 300 to 500 stairs up and down from my office each day. After a month of that brutal treatment, my knees began screaming at me. I tolerated the pain for a few weeks before calling Annie's husband Mike, a sports physician.

"Well," he said after some probing questions, "First of all, your knees need a rest. Stop climbing stairs and hills for the next few weeks." Right. When I shared his advice with my office mates, the walls reverberated with their guffaws.

I increased my daily ibuprofen and made an appointment at the American Hospital, where a doctor prescribed an involved series of exercises to strengthen my legs. Within weeks I was in less pain, though whether due to the exercises or to my legs acclimating to their grueling daily workout, I'll never know. I limited my Bosphorus visits to one a day. Libby would have to cope.

Time and again I was impressed at the warmth and dedication of my students. They were responsible, considerate, and kind, which made it sheer joy to teach them. I keep saying that, but it's true.

I was thrilled to learn that LP students don't take semester exams. The semester ended gently, and though we had class through exam week, it was business as usual—fun business.

LP students had three different English courses: Core English (ten periods a week), Oral English (5 periods a week), and Written English (5 periods). I taught one core class and two oral classes. I reveled in the oral curriculum, which incorporated my great loves of speech and drama.

All the LP students had been at the head of their classes throughout elementary, so those with poor English skills faced their first failures. Yağmur (Yah-MOOR), a shy doe-eyed girl, nearly broke my heart as I watched her struggle. A member of my core class, she refused to speak English for months. Yağmur had scored low on her English proficiency exam, though I suspected she knew more English than some of her peers. She'd obviously learned written English without oral practice and was afraid to speak. She spent most of the first weeks in tears, shaking her head whenever I spoke to her, often fleeing the room to cry in the counselor's office. (Yağmur means "rain.") Her pale face radiated sadness for weeks, and I'm sure it was a month before I saw her smile. A gift.

I seated her with Mehveş (May-VESH), a strong English speaker who took Yağmur under her wing and became her advocate throughout the year, tutoring and counseling her through countless English traumas. Clearly a perfectionist, Yağmur spent hours on the most minor assignments, often without help.

One day Yağmur's reading group (four novice English speakers) had a disagreement. She went ballistic, yelling at them in Turkish. As I approached her group she turned to me, tried to explain, and when she couldn't find the English words broke into tears and fled. Her group members explained that the rest of them wanted to quit reading their book because they felt it was childish and they were tired of fantasy. When they'd suggested changing books, she blew up. I sent Pelinsu to calm her down, and they returned after class, Yağmur's eyes swollen and red. Pelinsu explained that Yağmur had spent many hours reading ahead and preparing for the following week's discussion and was furious that her work had been in vain. Yağmur nodded, adding short phrases in English. I encouraged the girls to talk to their group members and come to an agreement together, then let me know later that day. Not surprisingly, they finished the book—for Yağmur. Of course, her confidence with English improved as the year wore on, and I'm sure she caught up with the others by her second year. But what a painful start.

The final assignment for my Oral English students was to evaluate the course in a final oral journal. As I listened to their recordings, tears blurred my online critiques. These kids had touched me deeply—I adored them.

Alara, in her halting accent, said, "This is the hardest journal ever because talking about the best lesson and the best teacher I've ever seen is very, very hard. Whenever your lesson started, I had a feeling inside me that I couldn't describe. We were all bored and tired in school, however the way you smile, make jokes and and distribute your positive energy filled us with joy." My heart nearly burst.

Ali, my tech pro, stooped to sweetness as well: "I think you were one of my favorite teachers since I started this school in my education life. I think you were a sweet teacher and to be honest I was really excited for the lessons all day. You never—I don't know the others—but you never gave me low grades, and that was one reason that I loved you so much. And second reason is that you were never angry with us and this is a difference that makes you different from the other teachers."

Can, who hated writing, said, "I am very sad today, because you were a friend, you were a teacher, you were a parent for me, and I will never forget you, Ms. Mershon." My goodness. How could I help but love them?

As a final farewell to my core class, I put together a little party in the Faculty parlor, a lavish lounge with antique furniture donated by the Borden family. It was the perfect venue for a farewell, and we all provided juice, cookies, and snacks. A few of the girls had been in tears for days over my departure, and Pelinsu's eyes were swollen and red, though she never abandoned her enduring smile. After we'd plowed through the food table, the kids guided me to the couch to present me with a farewell gift, gathering eagerly for me to open it. It looked like a liquor gift box, and I expected a bottle of Rakı. Better than that, though, it held an Oscar—a full-sized plastic reproduction with a plaque saying *"YILIN EN İYİ ÖĞRETMENİ."* THE BEST TEACHER OF THE YEAR

It's true what Uygar said about Turks. "You must only to love them." And they love back tenfold.

# 72  SWEET, SWEET ARNAVUTKÖY

Throughout the year I monitored the progress of Arnavutköy's street cobbling. A team of men had worked long days since the beginning of summer, ripping up and rebuilding the tangled maze of Arnavutköy's mountainous lanes—the reason for all the grit in my apartment that first day. The village was a maze of steep switchbacks and narrow side roads; the only direct uphill routes were long stairways.

Unfortunately, the heavy equipment and trucks for demolition barely fit through the streets, most of which could accommodate one lane of traffic and one of parked cars. When a big truck came through, workers had to knock on doors to find the owners of cars parked on the street to move them. Sometimes a car had to be towed, which held things up for hours.

After the old road was pulled up, the labor continued by hand. Heavy granite curbing and drainage pieces were hefted into place and secured with cement hand mixed in a wheelbarrow. Next workers clad in worn jeans and motley shirts shoveled gravel into one of three beat-up wheelbarrows and spread it on the road with spades, preparing for the granite cobblestones. Four men crouched on the street shoulder to shoulder, placing each 4-inch rough-cut stone into a wave-like pattern and tapping it into place, periodically adding a darker row for contrast. These four men placed about 100 feet of cobbles a day—back-breaking work.

One Friday I arrived home late to find the team pounding cobblestones by lamplight outside my door. I greeted them and brought out cold water. I'd already amassed a collection of cobbling photos, workers with sweat dripping from black curls as they crouched over their work. Some recognized and greeted me, and I took a group shot of them when they finished my street, Adalı Fettah Sokak.

Shortly after I posted my blog about the project, I received an e-mail from Yusuf, the backhoe driver. He'd been learning English online and wanted to practice by writing me. After exchanging a few e-mails, I offered to meet with him to chat in person. He was a sweet young fellow, arriving for our first "date" in a shiny leather jacket and pointy black shoes, hair slicked back. Though he looked a little hoody, he was polite and driven to learn. Originally from Eastern Turkey, Yusuf worked seven days a week, often ten hours a day. His dream was to wait tables in a resort community on the Aegean. I couldn't blame him, though I wondered if waiting tables would be any easier.

I loved visiting Arnavutköy's small shops. One day I noticed a butcher throwing bones into the street for stray dogs, so I started going to him for Libby's weekly chew bones. The local cobbler charged me only $10 to put Bjorn arch supports into my sandals. The bakery was another favorite stop. I loved their crunchy whole-wheat loaves and their delectable anise-flavored crackers. The scent of baking bread enhanced our morning jaunts.

The hardware stores were wonderful, too. I struggled with a knob on my kitchen cabinet, and after repeatedly screwing it in tighter only to have it fall off, I decided to look for a longer screw. Arnavutköy had a hardware store that spilled out onto the sidewalk under its red awning, and I started there, though with little hope. The proprietor nodded as I came in and proffered my knob. Try to imagine my pathetic Turkish, which was probably "I longer need for like this please?" The man nodded and walked back through cluttered, narrow aisles, pulling out a few drawers of assorted screws. He held my knob and screw in one hand as he rummaged through the drawers and compared them to one screw after another. He finally found one that matched mine in width, but it was too long.

I thanked him for his time, but he reassured me. "*Problem yok, Kesebilirim.*" No problem. I can cut it. He pulled out a mammoth pincers and worked that screw, turning and twisting it as he squeezed on the pincer. He ended up bending the screw, so I assumed we were done. "*Problem yok,*" he assured me as he grabbed a pliers to straighten it. He spend about fifteen minutes with me, and I was both amazed and relieved to have found a solution to my problem without a trip to the city.

I pulled out my embroidered Turkish money purse, and he waved me away. "*Hayir. Hayir. Çok küçük. Hediye,*" he said. No, no. It was small. A gift. I pressed him to take payment, and he refused a second time, then offered me a cup of tea.

How could you not love these people?

I had a similar experience with an electrician, proprietor of the cluttered Boğazıcı Elektrik. The owner's big German shepherd lazed contentedly outside the shop and didn't even muster a growl at Libby as we stepped by.

The young electrician, clad in a black stocking cap, jacket and polar plus shirt, sat behind a desk in the back of his tiny shop, which was crammed with sundry electronic devices and accoutrements. He stood as I walked in, and when I showed him my broken hair dryer, he gestured me to a seat. Would it be that quick? He plucked a screwdriver from the mountain of wires, tools, drills, cables, and newspapers covering his worktable and dove into the task on his lap (no space on the table).

As he worked we chatted about life in Arnavutköy, the Black Sea area he came from, our parents, and Libby, who had warmed to him. My Turkish had improved in Arnavutköy, and although an intelligent conversation was still beyond me, I could chat. A few men came into the shop, greeted us, then showed him a bulb or electrical connector. He'd give them a code number and explain how to navigate their way through the hundreds of boxes of electronic paraphernalia piled on shelves and floor. They helped themselves, pocketed their purchases, told him what they'd taken, then headed off. He never wrote anything down, though at least fifteen items walked out the door while I was there. I wondered how they'd ever sort out the money, but I didn't have the vocabulary to ask.

The electrician spent a half hour fixing my hair dryer, soldering wires with an iron he heated against his electric floor heater. He, too, refused payment but offered me tea. I promised I'd be back for it later and left a ten-lira note on the table ($6). Precious little for a half hour of his time.

I enjoyed meeting my neighbors in Arnavutköy. No one but Hediye ever invited me for tea, but I became quite friendly with a neighbor who walked his massive bulldog, Pablo, at the same time I walked Libby. Candan was a retired military envoy and spoke excellent English.

One morning as Libby and I turned the corner to start up the hill, I saw Pablo pulling Candan up towards us on their morning constitutional.

"Good morning, Ann Marie!"

"And good morning to you. I haven't seen you for a while. Have you been gone?" Instead of responding, Candan glared past me up the hill.

"*GIT!!! HAYIR!!!*" he screamed. I turned to see a huge kangal watchdog from a mansion up the street, hackles raised as he stalked toward us. Somehow he'd gotten loose. I grabbed Libby as Candan screamed at the kangal and tried to pull Pablo home. "They are both males," he yelled. "It's a big problem."

"*HAYIR!!! GIT!!!*" He screamed again as he strained against Pablo, who was eager to attack. Within seconds, the dogs were at each other, snarling and growling. Candan dove into the middle of the fray, trying to pull Pablo away. I tied Libby to a post up the road and raced back. "How can I help?"

"Can you get Pablo?" Candan cried over the ferocious din. I was petrified that Candan would be mauled as he tried to protect his dog. He was older than me, no match for the two massive beasts.

I grabbed Pablo's leash and pulled with more strength than I thought I had. The kangal had Pablo's jowls in his teeth. Candan put his arms around the kangal's neck, and both of us strained to pull them apart. I finally got Pablo loose, his jowls dripping blood and saliva. I tried to drag him down to Candan's house (another mansion), but there was no way he'd leave his master. I managed to pull him to a lightpost, where I tied him and hurried back to Candan, still struggling to hold the kangal. It was still snarling at Pablo, who barked frantically as he strained at his leash.

"Go to that gate and call the people on the intercom. I know them," Candan said. "They speak English."

I buzzed at the gate, but the person who answered spoke only

Turkish. I didn't know the word for fight, but I knew "dog" and "hate" and no doubt sounded upset. Candan was calming the kangal in spite of Pablo's worried barks.

"It's going to be OK, Ann Marie. Thank you so much," Candan said as the automatic gates finally opened and he pulled the dog inside. I untied Libby and headed off, relieved to leave the drama behind, yet amazed that Candan had been as concerned for the kangal as for his own dog. So Turkish.

Arnavutköy was a diverse community. Like Candan, many of my neighbors lived in fabulous homes. Just below my apartment was a mansion larger than our classroom building at Robert. I couldn't see much of it behind its high walls and iron gates, but it filled an entire city block and was probably 20,000 square feet, if not more. There was another social strata in my neighborhood, as well—that of the gececondus. These were houses thrown together supposedly overnight, and Turkish law allowed people to legally inhabit them if they moved in before dawn. (Turkish gece means "night" and kondu means "put," so it means "put up overnight.") Many of these structures were molded of concrete and brick and couldn't have been built in a day, but they seemed cozy enough, though probably dark. I think my apartment building might have been classified as a gecekondu, though the owners had brought it up to code.

On a late November walk with Libby, I was shocked to see that one of these homes had been demolished. Not built overnight—destroyed overnight. It had been torn down with heavy equipment, the rubble revealing a kitchen sink and living room window. Where had that sweet lady and her daughter gone? Why had their home been destroyed? The next time I saw Candan, I asked.

"That land belongs to the Greek Orthodox Church, and I imagine they ordered the demolition. The little place next to it will be destroyed as well," he said. "It's a terrible time to do this, in the middle of winter, but these houses are illegal."

"Why do you think they destroyed it?" I asked.

"Who knows? Maybe the owners did something to anger the church, or perhaps to anger public officials. The church can't benefit from destroying these homes. Even though religious minorities are protected under the Treaty of Lausanne, they are not allowed to build anything new in Turkey. I'm sure they're forbidden to either sell or develop their property."

"Do you think some of the wealthier neighbors could have had them destroyed so they'd have a better view?" The torn-down home had a commanding view of the Bosphorus.

"I doubt that, but you never know. Sometimes Turkish politics are difficult to understand."

I brought up the topic with my office mates that morning. Cyrus told me about a new school in Istanbul, the Kemer School, that had been bulldozed two weeks before it opened that fall. Apparently the school had been built illegally, which was the case with many buildings. (The Koç school had been built illegally and the government required the Koç Foundation to build schools across Turkey.) The real problem was that the chair of Kemer's board of directors owned a liberal newspaper that had criticized the current government, most likely resulting in the demolition of the school. Frightening—nothing like transparency in politics.

That demolished apartment sat in ruins all year, perhaps a reminder to those who might cross the "powers that be." I was haunted by that dark side of Arnavutköy, Istanbul, and Turkey.

## 73 FREE RIDE TO STUTTGART

One bright morning Cem, a junior with intense dark eyes and inimitable charm, climbed to my attic office. After the usual preliminary politeness, he asked, "Do you have any experience with debate?

"Well, I used to be a speech coach, but I've never coached debate. Why?"

"I'm president of the debate team, and we need a chaperone for the European Debate Championship in Stuttgart."

I was flattered that he thought of me. He'd been my student a few years earlier, and I'd enjoyed his spunk. Chaperoning would mean a free trip to Germany, and I was tempted. "When is the tournament?"

"That's the hard part. It's at the end of November break, and both our advisors will be gone on trips. Could you please help us? I thought of you right away." Cem's St. Bernard eyes pleaded, his voice warm.

"Well, I don't have any plans yet, Cem. Let me think about it. I'll talk with your advisor and let you know." He knew he had me.

Once in Stuttgart, our hosts took us by train to our respective homes —the five debaters with host families and me in the Romantica Central Hotel. I checked into my shared accommodations, a lush corner room with antique furniture and—one bed. What?

"Can I help you?" the attendant said as he hurried from the back office.

"I think there's been a mistake. I'm sharing a room with another debate advisor, but there's only one bed."

"Is that a problem?"

"Is that a problem? It certainly is! I won't share a bed with a total stranger. We'll need a room with two beds."

"I'm sorry, but we have no such rooms available. This arrangement was made by the organizer." I hadn't been impressed with anything about this event so far. Cem had struggled to get information about the tournament, and I'd received no acknowledgement of my own e-mails—and now this! They put me in staff housing, a sterile dorm-like accommodation, but I had a bed to myself.

Our first morning was a wet walking tour of Stuttgart's city center. The drizzle dampened everyone's spirits, though mine lifted at the State Theater when I realized it was the home of the Stuttgart Ballet. As I waited to inquire at the box office, a lithe, silk-haired Slovenian debater asked if I planned to attend the ballet. Jiva was a dancer and desperately wanted to go, so we purchased tickets for the following evening. I couldn't believe my good fortune: the Stuttgart Ballet!

After a few more sites, we stopped to imbibe in Christmas Market crepes and sausages—anything warm. I was shocked to see my five Muslim debaters pose for a photo as they bit into pork sausages. What would their parents say? Oh well, not my problem.

Our fledgling team was only in its second year and worked diligently for each debate, so we were excited that they won more than they lost.

After the second evening's debates, Jiva and I raced off to catch the train into the city. Spirits soaring, we hurried to the theater and were struck with the sumptuous décor of the lobby's marble columns, plush carpeting, classical friezes, and dazzling chandeliers. Cocktail tables set with hors d'oeuvres and champagne anticipated intermission.

The coat check clerk examined our tickets and immediately directed us to the next level, considerably less extravagant. When we showed our tickets there, we were dispatched up yet another flight of uncarpeted stairs to a barren lobby. We swallowed our pride and waited for the endless pre-intermission applause to abate.

When we finally got in, we were again met with lavish décor: dazzling chandeliers, tasteful classical trim, and a recessed ceiling painted with mythological figures in a night sky that we could almost touch from our nosebleed seats. Once the lights went down, the real magic began with a dance to a choral requiem by Gabriel Fauré. Black-robed singers filled the orchestra pit beside a small orchestra, and the heavy velvet curtains parted to reveal a stark white stage with a mass of dancers in variously decorated white leotards. The dancers shuffled onstage as one, swaying torsos and arms in repetitive sweeps to the music. Soon they divided to mesmerize us with intricate ensemble and solo dances, a marriage of modern dance and ballet. Never in my life had I experienced a more spellbinding dance performance; the fusion of voice and dance was perfection.

Thunderous applause filled the theater as dancers and soloists took bow after bow. They'd choreographed numerous bowing sequences, each of which must have been repeated three or four times during the ten minute applause. Jiva and I were spellbound.

The next day's debate topic was "There is no rush to applaud Obama." I was astounded that Europe was so focused on our American president. My debaters paced the school courtyard as they planned and practiced their points. Koret, our only female debater, practiced her introduction for me, her long, wiry curls bouncing on her shoulders as she spoke. "I'd like to thank you for your applause right now," she began. "Though it may seem premature, of course I'm going to win this debate, and I want you to feel free to show your appreciation before I speak. We all know what the outcome will be. I'm waiting—your applause? ...Nothing? ...Of course it's too early to applaud me. I haven't had a chance to perform yet, and neither has President Obama." Sadly, they lost the debate on a split decision. Our young team had won five of their eight preliminary debates, two of their losses split decisions. Seventh place gave them a spot in the semi-finals—truly impressive for a rookie team that had won just one debate in their only previous tournament.

They had an hour to prepare for "This House Believes that David Beckham and Tiger Woods are more relevant than Shakespeare," a challenging topic. They were out-classed by a Shakespeare-quoting team from Korea, but they handled their loss graciously. The debaters had all become friends over the week, and I was pleased to see my team genuinely congratulatedtheir opponents.

Of course, they're Turks.

Our return flight was delayed, and I was exhausted by the time we got back. Maybe that's why it happened. I caught a taxi to pick up Libby and return to my apartment, but when I got to my front door—

no backpack. No key! ARAUGHH!!!!!! I screamed for the taxi, and he stopped, but no pack. I must have left it in the bus from the airport.

Libby had a sore paw, so I carried her the dark half-mile to campus to retrieve a spare key I'd hidden outside Erica's apartment, and on the way back I tripped on a speed bump and fell flat on my face. Once into my apartment, I took stock. The pack had my computer, my camera, my cell phone (as well as the school's), gifts for people who had subbed for me, student projects, and about 800 Euros (school money). I tried to convince myself that these were only material things, but the reality was that if it wasn't found, I'd be out about $4000.

I couldn't sleep, so I made myself a hot cup of *salep*, my favorite Turkish drink made from ground orchid root, milk, and sugar sprinkled with nutmeg. I crawled into bed hoping it would soothe me then spilled it all over the quilt and the bedroom floor. Not my day. Cleaning up the mess woke me up even more.

The next morning I hurried to the Gursel service bus office at school, where Murat kindly searched out the phone number of our driver, called him, and learned that he had checked the bus and found nothing. Oh, my GOD! I turned next to the headmaster's secretary, who contacted the guards, local taxis, and began her own investigation while I climbed up to my office and tried to focus on schoolwork. Right. By then I was a basket case, consumed by anxieties. Everyone was being incredibly helpful, but I couldn't stop shaking.

"This is Turkey," Cyrus assured me. "If you lost it in Turkey, you'll get it back. Really." I wasn't so sure.

At 10:00 I got a call from Murat. They had located my pack. "I'm sorry, but I can't pick it up until tomorrow. You will have it at the end of the day. I hope that is O.K."

My goodness! Any time would be perfect! The next afternoon I found my pack sitting beside Murat's desk. He had me check to see that everything was there, which it was, down to the last euro. Cyrus had been right. Only in Turkey.

"Is there someone I can reward for this?" I asked.

"Of course not," he replied. "What we always say is that Gürsel is your home. We are happy to help you." How very Turkish. Their kindness was beyond anything I could ever hope for. Stuttgart had been fascinating, but my memories would be about the kindness of the Turks.

I understood the fasting of Turkey's *Ramazan* holiday and sympathized with the gorging of sweets at the end with *Şeker Bayram*, but the slaughter of *Kurban Bayram* was beyond me. I was usually traveling during that long holiday, but I'd heard tales of sheep being slaughtered on roadsides. It mystified me.

One morning during *Kurban Bayram* Cyrus commented about several people dying because of the slaughter. A man was sacrificing a cow when his platform collapsed, crushing him under the animal, and two more had suffered heart attacks while trying to control animals they planned to sacrifice. Apparently 1000 people across the country were injured in the first two days of the *bayram*, certainly the darker side of this celebration intended to focus on giving.

My friend Sandra had e-mailed a flyer from Migros, a Turkish grocery chain. It featured photos of the heads of sheep and cows, advertising the prices for each. "You can choose Irma or Edna or Eunice, or perhaps you'd prefer Bossy," she wrote. Silly, I know, but *Kurban Bayram* was unusual for us Westerners.

My Turkish office mate İrem opened my eyes to the generosity of this holiday, sharing her family's traditions. I also discussed it with Özdemir, our school newspaper editor.

İrem and Özdemir both came from small cities with strong traditions. In fact, İrem invited me to spend *Kurban Bayram* with her family, which made me sorry I'd made travel plans. When I polled my students I learned that only a third of their families followed the traditions of this holiday, most of them from rural communities. Of course, no one complained about the time off school.

According to İrem, *Kurban Bayram* is the most important Islamic religious festival of the year. Celebrating Abraham's near-sacrifice of his son, the head of each Turkish household sacrifices a sheep on the first morning of the four-day holiday. Early that morning everyone goes to the mosque for *bayramnamazı*, a short prayer. Then they gather to chat in the courtyard before heading home to prepare for the *kurban*—the sacrifice.

Wealthier families hire someone to do the *kurban*. He recites verses from the Koran, then slits the sheep's throat. I noticed that neither Özdemir nor İrem chose to speak in those terms; they seemed sensitive about the slaughter, but it is what it is. İrem's family has a butcher perform the *kurban*, which might be done on a sheep, a goat, or a cow (often purchased together by a few families).

Özdemir explained that a hired man would cut up the meat into large pieces and place them on huge flat trays, which the family men carried into the house. There the women would divide the meat into smaller pieces and package it. In İrem's family, her job was to make labels for each package based on a long list they'd compiled of people they felt needed help. Each sheep was divided into fifteen to twenty packets, a good deal of meat. Once packaged, the portions were piled into the trunk of a car and delivered to the homes of the needy, with some meat kept behind to serve guests.

The rest of the holiday was spent visiting family, friends, and business associates. The women of the household had devoted weeks to baking and cooking for all the visitors. "We make a list of everyone we want to visit," İrem explained. "It includes all the relatives and also friends and business associates. We usually have a list of about 100 people to visit in the three or four days of *Kurban Bayram*. You just have about fifteen minutes to eat a little and have some tea. We usually have sweets at people's houses, and you get sick of eating all the sweets, but you know Turkish hospitality. There's no way you can say no, so you just eat some more," she said with a smile.

İrem went on to explain that when people weren't home, they left a note letting them know they'd stopped. She said her father cleverly hurries to the home of anyone he sees out visiting because then he can get by with just leaving  a note. With 100 people to visit, I'd do the same.

Özdemir's grandfather was a community and political leader, so his family often slaughtered two or three sheep. Until his grandfather died at 101, they stayed at home and let other people visit them. "I'm not exaggerating when I tell you 100 people visited my grandfather every day. We had to have a lot of food ready. I sometimes went out to visit my relatives, but there was always someone home with my grandparents."

This holiday both horrified and impressed me, but İrem and Özdemir helped me understand its significance. I'd always been impressed with the generosity of Turks, and I was shocked to learn that although they have socialized medicine for everyone, Turkey has no welfare system. It's because people take care of those in need. Once on a trip through the mountains of northeastern Turkey, our hippie host sat with us after a dinner of grilled fish he'd caught that day. As we chatted, a number of men stopped by to say hello and hand him money. It occurred to me that it might be for drugs, so I asked about it.

"After men pray at the mosque they bring me money for the poor; I am trusted to distribute it to those in need. This is how we take care of each other."

Amazing. *Kurban Bayram* was just another example of this Turkish generosity.

My most bizarre adventure was orchestrated by David. He had attended the annual camel wrestling tournament in Selçuk a few times, and I was jealous. Finally in Turkey at the right time, I worked with David to recruit teachers from both Robert and Koç to attend this ludicrous event.

We stayed at the Nişanyan House, an elegant pension high in the whitewashed mountaintop village of Şirince (Sheer-EEN-jay). I'd been there with Jana and again with Laura and Ross, but I'd never stayed in that sweet village. Our home for the weekend was the Kerevetli Ev (Wooden Platform Bed House), built entirely of stone. The ancient residence was named for its harem, the room where women had lived and slept during Ottoman times (pre-1930). The largest room in the house, it was surrounded by a cushioned bench along two walls of casement windows. A low table sat in the center of a deep red Turkish rug, but the crowning glory was the bed. A few wooden steps led up through a set of posts and railings with curtains hiding a massive bed that could have comfortably slept five women.

After lingering over coffee the first morning, we headed down to catch a mini-bus to Selçuk, where the camels would be on display before the Sunday wrestling match. The air reverberated with the distant beat of drums and horns as we meandered through the bustling street market. We followed the sounds to discover...

Ta-da!

Drummers and horn players.

No camels.

We did find some rain, though. The smell of grilling camel meat and sausages made my mouth water, and I suggested we find a restaurant out of the rain.

After *mezes*, meats, and sufficient beers, we headed back out to the street. It had finally stopped raining, and in the square we discovered ornately-costumed camels that paced and pawed the ground as drummers and horn players riled them with vibrant and haunting rhythms. The camels wore intricately decorated felt halters embellished with mirrors, cowrie shells, bobbles, tassels and embroidery in bright colors. Their tall wooden saddles perched on equally ornate cushions, reds predominating, with more bells, bobbles, tassels, and bright straps and scarves. Some had *Maşallah* embroidered on them (May Allah protect...).

As the camels became aroused, they frothed at the mouth, looking like someone had slathered them with shaving cream. Froth bubbled from their wide, loose lips, and they occasionally shook their heads and spewed it over the crowd. The camels were ready for action, though their drovers (handlers) kept them under control, walking them in circles to calm them. Even then, the camels would roll their heads back and forth to the beat, almost like dancing. The air smelled of wet fur, like eau de goat.

We finally returned to our mountaintop villa, where we dined on pistachios and *çiğ köfte* (spiced bulgar and tomato wrapped in lettuce leaves) and played word games by a crackling fire until the wine was gone and we could no longer keep our eyes open.

Sunday we woke to a downpour. "If it's raining the camels just mope and won't wrestle. If it doesn't stop, they'll probably cancel the whole event," David warned.

He was right.

Poor camels. They never did get to wrestle. Poor us.

David explained that when the camels wrestle, they're all dressed up like we'd seen them, and they basically just push each other over. The main attraction of camel wrestling was the crowd—a rowdy group grilling, drinking, jeering, and cheering on the camels. In past years he'd been offered food and drink by everyone. Oh, so Turkish.

English teachers all, we curled up by the fire to read away the rainy Sunday. It wasn't so bad.

The next week I received an invitation from my young Turkish friend Uygar ("You must only to love them" Uygar) who was visiting his parents near Bursa, across the Marmara from Istanbul. I'd never stayed in a Turkish home and was excited to see Uygar. They picked me up at the bus station, quite late. At the door I removed my shoes and was offered a pair of high-heeled slippers that I could barely squeeze my toes into. I hobbled through the apartment to discover a table set for dinner, even at 10 o'clock. Though I'd eaten earlier, I joined them for a sumptuous meal of çorba (soup), dolma (stuffed vegetables), fried artichoke hearts, salad, bread, and dessert. Neziye had been cooking all day, so I couldn't refuse. I was as stuffed as the dolma I'd just devoured.

Their apartment was lavishly decorated with ruffled white curtains, an antique velour couch, and carved antique tables—all more ornate than I was accustomed to, "modern Turkish." Uygar showed me their view overlooking the Marmara then beamed as he pointed out his mother's paintings. He coaxed her to sing a few traditional Turkish tunes with her oud, a rounded 10-stringed instrument. It was lovely, but so late! Bleary-eyed, I dragged myself to bed.

I woke late, was greeted with kisses from Uygar and his mother, then enjoyed a breakfast of gözleme (like a potato quesadilla), olives, tomatoes, and cucumbers. As we ate, Uygar translated. "My mother says you should let your hair grow long and dye it black." Neziye was a fashion queen—in her way.

"Natural," I answered, indicating my white-blonde hair, a color some call platinum. She nodded and smiled back, then patted her long, attractively coiffed black hair that actually did make her look younger. It wasn't until that moment that I realized only elderly women leave their hair gray in Turkey. Future research affirmed my theory—all the gray-hairs on the street were tourists or ex-pats.

Uygar and his parents, both retired teachers, proudly guided me through their community and the nearby city of Bursa, but my favorite part was getting to know them. I was a little jealous to learn that they'd retired from teaching at 45, typical in Turkey.

Before Sunday dinner with relatives, Uygar's father, Hakki, suggested we check the bus schedule for my ride home. It turned out all the busses were full. "Unbelievable!" he said. "You never have to reserve for a bus. We'll just go at 5:00 and try to get you a seat." I was petrified that I might miss school on Monday.

As we prepared dinner, Uygar's aunt stepped into the next room and placed a linen on the arm of the couch. I assumed she needed a nap and focused my attention on kitchen tasks. The next time I glanced over, she was kneeling in quiet prayer, an unobtrusive ritual. I was touched.

Thanks to Hakki's fast talking, I got a seat on the bus in spite of a waiting crowd. Perhaps he said I was a teacher, or maybe he used the "Robert College" card. Whatever he did, I was thankful for the ride home. I felt a pang of guilt, though, as we drove away from the dejected Turks still standing at the bus stop.

# 76 AGONY!

That week changed everything. I woke Saturday morning with a kink in my back and hoped to work it out walking down the hill to buy *börek* (a baked filo and cheese specialty) for my Grand Marais guests, Dominique and her daughter Sophie. My back seemed better, so we headed off to Termal as planned. Our Turkish coffee sloshed in its tiny cups as the seas tossed the ferry on our crossing, and poor Sophie struggled to keep down her breakfast. As I stood up the twinges hit again, and when we learned that the ferries had been cancelled for the rest of the day I nearly cried. It meant taking a bus back around the Marmara, hours longer than the ferry. By the time we got to the hot springs, I couldn't stand up straight. Stabs of pain shot down my thigh with each step. I melted in the hamam hot tub for an hour, a soothing balm, then collapsed onto the massage table for a heavenly pummeling treatment. Then I stood up.

The pain was now so intense I had to walk stooped over, an old crone. The three-hour bus ride home was agonizing. No matter how I squirmed and contorted, the pain eased only intermittently between excruciating spasms. I hobbled off the bus in Istanbul, hugged Dominique and Sophie farewell, and caught a taxi home. I needed an emergency room, but what would I do with Libby? I called my friend Amy, Libby's second mother at Robert. "Of course we'll take her. She can stay with Mustafa and I'll come with you to the hospital."

"You don't need to do that," I said. "I'll be fine." The lie of a woman who hates to impose. Actually, I was petrified. I was an ocean away from home, family, and close friends, and this might be serious. Amy's offer was gold.

"I can translate for you, and you'll need support. Can you walk Libby up here?"

"There's no way I could even walk a block."

"I'll call a taxi to pick you up. He'll drive you here to drop Libby off then take us to the hospital."

We waited only minutes in the American Hospital's sparkling white emergency room. The doctor spoke halting English as he examined me. "I'm not sure what is causing pain, but maybe herniated disc. I'm giving you intravenous pain killer. Lie still for half hour to see if it helps." A half hour later the pain was still intolerable, so he tried an opiate, which barely eased the intense pain in my thigh.

"Could it be sciatica?" I asked, shaking as I recalled my mother-in-law bedridden with it for weeks.

"I do not think it is," he said. "The sciatic nerve runs down the back of the leg, and this is the front. You must stay in bed for three days with medicine. If it is not better, you will return here on Wednesday." He gave me pain pills and four prescriptions and, still stooped over, I paid my $40 bill at a marble-topped counter.

I thrashed through a sleepless night, each relief-seeking movement initiating throes of agony. This was worse than childbirth. The next morning I called school, and Cyrus reassured me. "We'll cover everything, Ann Marie. What can I do to help?"

"I'll need someone to fill my prescriptions for me. I really can't walk anywhere."

"Done. Take care, Ann Marie. It will work out."

Minutes later Jenny stopped by to pick up my prescriptions and get them filled, returning with meds and mood-improving pastries. The pain was horrific in spite of the pills, but a fetal position helped. "If I had to live with this pain," I thought as I hobbled to the bathroom, "I'd have my leg amputated at the hip." I was in too much pain to be frightened. I just wanted it over.

I felt guilty dumping my classes on other teachers, but I couldn't even manage lesson plans. Erika and Cyrus, both saints, filled in for me and compiled plans for other subs when they couldn't.

Wednesday morning I took a taxi to the hospital. Alone. After an excruciating exam, Dr. Onur ordered a series of MRI's on my back and neck. The hospital MRI machine was scheduled solid, so I hobbled across the street to another lab—agony. An hour later my heart pounded as Dr. Onur perused the lab report and scanned my films. As I waited, I noticed that Onur was his first name. Interesting.

"I can't say for certain," he said, "but it looks like you will need surgery. You can see here that there is a problem with the cartilage between the L2 and L3 vertebrae. I want you to see a neurosurgeon. I'll make an appointment with Dr. Tunç."

Tears welled. Please, no. "Can you make it for today?"

"Of course," he said. "I'm calling him right now." After a flurry of Turkish, he smiled kindly. "He'll see you right away. I'll get you a wheelchair." I was still trying to wrap my brain around the idea of surgery. In Turkey? I couldn't imagine. Be assertive, I told myself. Insist on the Mayo Clinic. My parents believed in the magic of Mayo, and I needed my family—Laura, Dad, Dustin and Ross. I just couldn't do this in Turkey.

Deep breathing stilled my anxieties as Dr. Tunç studied my information. A small, stocky man with a round face and warm eyes, he explained, "You have a herniated disc, which often doesn't require surgery, but there are three indicators for surgery. One is intense pain, one is loss of strength, and one is when the disc herniates into an enclosed spinal cavity. You have all three, and you must have surgery before you lose more strength. I can schedule you for tomorrow."

"Oh, no!" I moaned, tears welling. "I want to have it at the Mayo Clinic. Could you arrange that?"

"We'll see if it is possible, but do you think you could make the trip?"

"I don't know," I answered, almost in a whine. My throat was constricting, and I couldn't help it. "Can you please see if it can be arranged?"

"We'll do what we can. I'll put you on my schedule for tomorrow, and if we can get you to Mayo, we will. You go home and call in the morning to see what we have been able to arrange."

I caught a taxi home, feeling desperately alone. Back surgery in Turkey? My heart pounded, my head ached, and I began to shiver. Anxieties almost superseded the agony, but there was no escaping the searing pain in my thigh.

Struggling up the stairs to my apartment proved to me that there was no way I could manage a flight home. I called Dad and Laura, hoping they'd insist I come to Mayo. Neither did, but they both expressed concern. Laura offered to fly over to be with me, but I knew her life was more than full with her two children and executive position, and she hadn't exactly loved Turkey. My anxieties calmed as I looked at things more logically. Maybe Laura's caring gesture was all I'd needed.

I e-mailed a Koç friend who'd had back surgery, and he responded promptly with laudatory praise. "My American Hospital surgeon used techniques which weren't yet available in the States. I haven't had as much as a twinge of discomfort since the operation. I feel rejuvenated by it, in fact." John Chandler called to tell me he'd had back surgery at the American Hospital, and he had every confidence in the system.

I was convinced.

Dr. Tunç had suggested micro-discectomy, a non-invasive procedure that would remove the herniated tissue compressing my nerve. The recuperation time would be only a few weeks, and the pain would be alleviated immediately. I called his office and arranged surgery for Friday. I needed Thursday to prepare lesson plans. In retrospect that seems foolish, but at the time my guilt overrode the agony of one more day.

Early Friday morning I checked into the hospital, where they immediately settled me into a private room. I crawled on the bed and adopted the fetal position. Aside from the high-tech hospital bed, it was like a hotel room. The walls were a warm taupe, and it was furnished with a brown corduroy couch, a wide-screen TV, and an antique cherry chair with a matching table. I had a small refrigerator, built-ins for my clothing, and a cavernous bathroom supplied with hotel-type toiletries. My picture window overlooked the rooftops of Nişantişi, an elite community. I also had free wireless. All that for $300 a night, including an extra bed (in the couch) and meals for another person.

My minimal Turkish was enough to banter with orderlies who wheeled me to various pre-surgery tests. I was too miserable to read, so I listened to an audio book: Dan Brown's *The Lost Symbol*, not exactly a cheering tale, but I'd downloaded it after attending his talk at Bosphorus University. My greatest fear was that they'd make me lie flat for the surgery, but by the time I was wheeled into the operating room I was feeling no pain.

"Ann Marie! Ann Marie! Ann Marie!" Hazy smiles welcomed me back to reality. A nurse removed my oxygen mask. "I'm so cold!" I said, shivering uncontrollably. Warm air enveloped my body, calming me as it blew beneath my blankets. I drifted off for a few moments, then realized they were wheeling me back to my room. NO PAIN!!!! I was groggy, but elated. My legs were stretched straight for the first time in days. No pain at all. My new nurse, Nurgül, offered a sip of water as she took my stats. "When can I eat?"

"Only small sips of water, and no food until 10:00 because of the drugs. They will make you sick." I hadn't eaten in 24 hours, and I was famished. Nurgül, dear heart, brought my tray an hour early. Two ceramic bowls—one with weak chicken broth and the other with chilled pear juice. Manna. A few hours later an orderly brought in a late-night *kahvaltı*, a Turkish breakfast of cucumbers, white cheese, and bread. Solids. Yum.

I slept through the night except for the usual nursely interruptions, then woke at 7:00, energized and ready to go home. Well, not really, but gleefully pain free. I wanted to call my sister, but it was midnight in Minnesota; Laura would be sound asleep. I'd revel in my joy alone.

A vested and bow-tied caterer entered with two breakfasts. "*Arkadaşım yok*," I informed him. (I don't have a friend.) Turkish hospitals assume that you will have a *refakatçi*, a friend or family member who stays in the hospital with you. Each evening an orderly offered to make up the couch bed for my non-existent *refakatçi*. I learned later that the Turks had the highest survival rate of all injured European soldiers during wartime, possibly because of this system—no surprise when I considered their compassionate culture. I'm an independent woman, yet I yearned to have Laura or Annie beside me. I was the only patient on the entire floor who stayed alone, and it was hard. Walking the halls, I saw that some rooms had huge living rooms attached, filled with relatives. Amazing.

"Buck up," I told myself. "You chose to live overseas, and this comes with the package." I refused to dive into a pity pool, so I dove instead back into my audio book and Kindle. I'm not big on television, especially in Turkish.

My energy held through the day, which was fortunate because I had visitors. A student arrived with his mother and sister, handing me a certificate for a bouquet that sat in the hospital flower shop; flowers weren't allowed in the rooms. Dangerous microbe-laden carnations? Strep dahlias? Oh, well.

Erika and her husband stopped by with a latte from Starbucks. Heaven. Later that Day Amy and Mustafa brought me another one along with a report on Miss Libby. More students arrived with another flower certificate and a three-layer box of chocolates, which I shared with visitors, nurses, and staff.

Sunday I woke weak and exhausted. What was this? "You are tired because your liver is working hard to clear the drugs out of your system," Dr. Tunç explained. "You were taking some very strong drugs for the pain, and they are toxins in your system. You are doing well."

"What about the tingling in my leg? There was none yesterday, but it's starting to bother me."

"You may have these sensations for some time. Your nerves are rejuvenating, but it will not last more than a few months," he said.

It was nothing compared to the pain I'd had. I'd manage. I was released on Tuesday, and my friend Sandra accompanied me home after an eye appointment at the hospital. We headed down the elevator and found the flower prison, a glass enclosure with shelves of floral arrangements in various stages of decay. Sandra laughed as the attendant placed two huge bouquets on the counter, both wilting. "I think I can make something from the combined survivors," I said with a smile as we each took a vase. I picked up my four prescriptions, which cost $1.90 (the Turkish government subsidizes prescription drugs).

It was an uncomfortable, jostling ride home, and Sandra hauled my bag and wilting flowers up the stairs to my apartment. When I took final stock, I realized that I did have a friendship base in Istanbul, and

I was thankful for everyone's help. It was nothing like the depth of my relationships at home, but people had been there for me—Cyrus, Jenny, Erica, Amy, and Sandra. I also learned another important lesson: The U.S. doesn't have a corner on quality health care. The American hospital was incredible, and my surgery, doctors and surgeons fees totalled under $13,000, a third of what it would have cost in the States.

I had a few weeks off school to recuperate, and little by little I ventured out into the burgeoning spring along the Bosphorus. The school relocated my office and classes down to the main floor, as I'd never have managed my daily 300 stairs. At first I'd slog through the day, drag myself home and collapse on the couch, but within a week I was nearly normal again. Thank goodness.

My spring was busy with school, a weekend at Sandra's new apartment on the Princes' Islands, and visits from Mayu, Jana, and finally my niece Laura, who was touring the world with her partner Yvette. It was a busy, joyous time for me.

That year I'd experienced two medical issues: sore knees and back surgery, and they say bad fortune comes in threes. I had one more week of workshop before heading to Germany to visit my friend Deidre and attend Jana's wedding. Monday morning dawned cool and bright, and as Libby pulled me down the cobbled street above our apartment, our least favorite kangal lunged ferociously on his chain. I always stepped into the road at that point just in case the chain broke (which had happened). As I stepped back up onto the sidewalk, something grabbed my foot. POW! I crashed to the ground face first. I'd fallen before, but never so hard. I shook my head and took stock: scraped elbow, skinned knee, coffee cup intact. I'd be fine. A car slowed to check on me, but I waved them off, embarrassed at my clumsiness. As I struggled to my feet a sharp pain screamed through my left foot, nearly toppling me again. Not good. I hobbled around the corner, trying different approaches with each step to ease the pain, fearful that a neighbor might step out and see me. It was a slow process, but if I put weight on my heel and kept my toe up, I could manage. I crawled up the steps to my apartment, Libby licking my face. She had an uncanny ability to sense injury.

I e-mailed John Chandler. "I won't be at the meetings this morning. I think I may have broken my foot, but I'll ice it to see if it gets better. If it doesn't, I'll go to the hospital this afternoon." Everything would be fine, I assured myself as I lay on the couch with an ice pack. I might not be able to tango with Aşkin and Söner Wednesday night, but I'd get to the school party and Duygu's wedding on Saturday.

The phone rang. "Ann Marie? John Chandler. We're sending a driver to bring you to the hospital. There's no point in waiting if your foot is that bad. You might as well get x-rays as soon as possible." The X-rays revealed a double fracture in the two smallest bones of my left foot, and I returned home with a hard cast, a "walking boot," and a sparkling new set of crutches. No dancing, no parties, no nothing. But I'd go to Germany, no matter what.

Every cloud has a silver lining. People were wonderful. I was excused from meetings, and once word was out, received condolences and support at every turn. Then my niece Laura called from Olympus on the Mediterranean.

"I got your e-mail. How are you?"

"Pretty miserable. I'm missing out on all the last-week events, but I'll be fine."

"We're coming back to help you. We don't really like it here, and we miss Istanbul." Laura and Yvette arrived on Wednesday, bless their hearts. I'm not sure how I would have managed laundry and Libby and packing without them. I'd only been able to get Libby to the bottom of the apartment steps for her daily you-know-what, and the first time they took her for a walk she pooped three times (much to their glee). The girls took over packing, errands, cooking, and cleaning. Godsends.

My cloud had other silver linings, too. David trekked over from Koç Thursday night to join us for dinner and a tearful farewell hug. He picked up the gold coins I'd purchased for Duygu's wedding, which I'd miss. Istanbul is far from being handicap accessible, and I was still in pain.

Friday night Aşkin and Söner drove three hours from the far side of Istanbul for their goodbyes. "You can't say goodbye on internet!" Aşkin explained. Gosh, I loved those guys. My closest friends may have been in the States, but I'd found some darned fine ones in Istanbul.

The last night I called Güler, our principal, to join us for a farewell dinner at the Takanık fish restaurant by the water. She insisted that instead we come to her lavish campus home and have our meal delivered. "You can bring Libby. My little dogs will love to see her." Her table was set for a feast, a lovely farewell dinner.

As my father would say, "I'm so blessed!"

# 78 ONE MORE YEAR?

After seven years and nine semesters in Turkey, it was time to take stock. Had my experience changed me? How could I be so torn between these two places? Was I happier in the U.S. or in Turkey? Where did I belong?

I thought back to a day when I'd sat outdoors with my morning coffee, marveling at the Bosphorus view. A butterfly flitted over waving grasses, sun glinted off the water, music wafted from a nearby stereo, and the sun warmed my back. Libby lay quietly under my chair, waiting for a cat to pass by.

I'd come to love all the things that made Istanbul unique, and it felt like home. Libby was at home here, too—language no issue, loving to be outdoors. She never purported to any religion other than an appreciation of the natural world. The only real difference for her was that Istanbul had neither chipmunks nor deer, so her focus was cats. Mine was my students, typical teens—eager to be accepted, full of life, concerned about relationships, parents, clothing, sports, and plans for the summer. And such workers they were. It was a joy to teach them.

Istanbul was wonderful, and the Bosphorus was stunning. But as usual, I sat alone. Thankful for my time in Turkey, I still yearned for friends and family.

Before I left, John Chandler asked me to consider another year at Robert. I'd refused earlier, but one of the new hires had been denied a work visa, and the position had re-opened. "We'd love you to stay," he said. Cyrus coaxed me as well. "You fit in so well here, Ann Marie, and you're a positive influence. The kids love you, and so do we. Are you sure you won't stay on?" Erica and İrem added their encouragement, along with Margaret (dean of students) and Güler (principal). Maybe I should.

I considered. Carefully.
Turkey had a secure hold on my heart.

The Bosporous enchanted me.

My students were sheer joy.

My Lise Prep peers were collaborative, supportive, and fun.

I taught half as many students as in the States.

I had plenty of time to prepare.

The money was great—and tax-free.

I could afford extensive travel.

Friends visited from home.

I'd built relationships both in and outside of school.

I was finally getting the hang of Turkish.

I loved Istanbul.

Yet...

I still spent most of my time alone.

I hated getting up at 5:30.

I missed my sons.

I missed my sister Laura.

I'd missed seven years of Erin and Matthew's growing up.

I yearned for my Grand Marais buddies—lifelong friends.

Dad and Eileen were getting older, and I needed their hugs.

I missed winters of deep snow, skiing and snowshoeing.

I missed morning walks with my neighbors.

I wanted time to write.

I needed outdoor adventures.

I'd hardly lived in my new northwoods home.

I missed being loved.

The decision haunted me. What kept luring me back to Istanbul? What drew me home? It was a tough call.

As I hobbled onto the airplane (thank goodness for wheelchair service), I remembered facing back surgery alone. I tucked Libby's case under the seat and thought back over the past years. They'd been a grand adventure, and I'd made many friends—good friends. David had become a bosom buddy, but he was even more independent than I was. I knew I'd see more of Sandra whether I stayed or not.

I closed my eyes as the other passengers boarded and tried to visualize myself at Robert another year.

I couldn't do it.

I belonged in Minnesota—at least for now.

# AFTERWORD

Though 2012 marked the end of my teaching in Istanbul, I've returned a few times. I organized a tour for friends in the spring of 2013 (they were all entranced), and the following spring I went with a friend to update my Istanbul guidebook (and visit friends and favorite places).

My love life finally sorted itself out. I dated a number of men I met online and finally found one who seemed perfect—until he dumped me for a younger woman. Go figure. We kept in touch (why?), and while I was volunteering at an orphanage in Ethiopia, he contacted me and suggested I might want to connect with his recently-divorced buddy. Well, why not?

Jerry, also a retired teacher, turned out to be a wonderful partner—skier, biker, kayaker, carpenter and all-around good guy. We even share the same Miers-Briggs profile: ENFP. We bounce between his home in Wisconsin and our new one on Devil Track Lake near Grand Marais. Jerry's been to Turkey with me twice, and I know we'll be back.

Wonder of wonders, in spite of my resolution never to marry again, we tied the knot in a tiny riverside ceremony in Wisconsin.

I'm pretty darned happy.

- - - - - - - - - - - - - - - - - - - - - - - - - - - - - - - -

**If you enjoyed this book, I'd appreciate a review.**

**Please go to Amazon.com, pull up** *You must only to love them,* **and at the bottom of the page after the reviews, click on WRITE A CUSTOMER REVIEW.**
**Many thanks.**
**Ann Marie**

# ABOUT THE AUTHOR

A retired English teacher, Ann Marie Mershon lives on a woodland lake with her husband Jerry and their two dogs.

She grew up in a wooded suburb of Minneapolis, and in her mid-twenties she and her husband moved north to the wilderness they'd always loved. She has two grown sons who live in California and Puerto Rico. After 30 years of teaching English in Minnesota, she moved overseas to complete her teaching career in Istanbul, writing weekly e-mail missives and posting blogs about her experiences there.

Ann Marie discovered her passion to write in the late 1990's. She penned a weekly newspaper column for five years, wrote numerous articles for newspapers and magazines, and published two books. Her first was a middle-grade historical novel, *Britta's Journey~An Emigration Saga,* about the emigration of a family that settled near her home. Her second book, *Istanbul's Bazaar Quarter, Backstreet Walking Tours,* was a collaboration with Edda Renker Weissenbacher, a Turkish woman who guided small groups on walking tours through Istanbul.

Ann Marie writes every day but always finds time for hiking, biking, swimming, kayaking, canoeing, skiing, or snowshoeing with her friends in the wilderness she calls home.

# ACKNOWLEDGEMENTS

I have many people to thank for helping me write and edit this memoir. My writing buddy, Joan Crosby, has diligently edited portions of the book over the past years; I treasure our 20-year Mutual Admiration Society.

I thank the members of my writing group who have guided me through parts of the process, providing emotional support as well: Beryl Singleton Bissell, Betsy Bowen, Rose Arrowsmith DeCoux, Kelly Dupre, Marcia Hyatt, Jean Marie Modl, Nina Simonowicz, Bonnie Swanson, and Kari Vick.

My friend Sue Robinson spent many hours encouraging and advising me in the process, convincing me to stick with my ungrammatical title—for its charm.

I appreciate, too, the time and effort of my many readers who made suggestions for improving the book: Shelley Alvin, Shelley Berg, Annie DeBevec, Bonnie Gay Hedstrom, Gail Hedstrom, Howard Hedstrom, Madonna King, Ann Lindstrom, Karen Neal, Sue Nordman, Judy Renkiewicz, Sue Robinson, Nina Simonovich, Bonnie Swanson, Laura Soderlind, Sally Wagner, and others. (My memory is about as bad as my record-keeping, so I hope I haven't left anyone out.)

A special thanks goes to my son Dustin, who worked with me on the cover. His skills as a graphic designer far surpass mine, and his encouragement has energized me.

And of course I appreciate my husband Jerry, who has supported my work in countless ways, from leaving me space to write and listening as I shared my frustrations to bringing me steaming mugs of coffee as I worked.

Lucky me, huh?

Made in the USA
Middletown, DE
13 August 2016